Guitar Electronics for Musicians

by Donald Brosnac.

&

Amsco Publications
New York/London/Sydney/Cologne

THIS BOOK IS PUBLISHED THROUGH THE PERMISSION OF BOLD STRUMMER, I WEBB ROAD, WESTPORT, CONNECTICUT 06880.
THE ORIGINAL ISBN NO. IS 0-942760-00-X.

Cover photograph by George Taylor.
Cover styling by Ben Sutton.
Cover design and art direction by Pearce Marchbank.

© 1983 Wise Publications
A division of Music Sales Limited, London

Order Number: OP 42324
ISBN: 0.7119.0232.1

Exclusive Distributors:
Music Sales Corporation, 257 Park Avenue South, New York, NY 10010 USA.
Music Sales Limited, 8/9 Frith Street, London W1V 5TZ England.
Music Sales Pty. Limited, 120 Rothschild Street, Rosebery, Sydney, NSW 2018, Australia.

Printed in the United States of America by
Vicks Lithograph and Printing Corporation

A catalogue record for this title
is available from The British Library.

Contents

CONTENTS

Section III: Schematics

Introduction

All musicians, guitar repairmen, instrument retailers, as well as anyone else who wants to increase their knowledge of guitar construction and function, will benefit from reading this book.

Musicians: will find that a better understanding of their instrument will enable them to wield their guitar as a skilful tool to create musical moods and emotion provoking sounds unique only to themselves.

Repairmen: will find explanations of the design and function of many electric guitar components as well as a comprehensive section of schematics showing the wiring of over 50 electric guitars and basses.

Retailers: will find this book to be a valuable aid in understanding the operation of the equipment they sell and therefore, better satisfy the needs of their customers.

This book divides guitar electronics into sections so that each facet can be clearly understood. There are over 350 photos and drawings to facilitate the understanding of each of the subjects covered. The following is a description of the sections covered:

Pickups: from vintage to state-of-the-art . . . pickups for acoustics and electrics . . . what a pickup is, how it works, and how to select the one **you** need . . . all about the many types of alnico and ceramic magnets . . the why and how of coil winding, shielding, and multi-lead wiring for more power and a multitude of tones.

Wiring: the how and why of guitar circuits . . . an explanation of all the components that make up volume and tone circuits . . . the function of pots, capacitors, switches, jacks, grounding plates, chokes . . . new wiring circuits being devised . . . and more.

Schematics: pages and pages showing how to wire instruments and pickups made by Gibson, Fender, Gretsch, Schecter, DiMarzio, Ovation, Lawrence, Hi-A, Duncan, and information covering stereo, phasing, splitting, series/parallel . . . and many other wiring configurations.

This book concludes with a glossary that is as extensive as a chapter; and the index gives a fast reference for solving problems such as hum, feedback, or no sound.

This book has been three years in the writing and has received the personal attention and assistance of the following individuals:

Alembic – Susan Wickersham
Armstrong Guitars – Dan Armstrong
Bartolini/Hi-A – William & Pat Bartolini
Barcus Berry – Jack Henzie
DiMarzio – Larry DiMarzio
       Steve Kaufman
       Steve Blucher
Duncan Pickups – Seymour Duncan
Fender – Leo Fender
       Gregg Wilson
       Fred Tavares
       Mike Fleming
       Jim Murphy

       Ken Young
       Vince Basse
Gibson – Gary Aumaugher
       Seth Lover
       Walter Fuller
       Dave Sutton
       Terry Green
Guild of American Luthiers – Tim Olsen
Lawrence – Bill Lawrence
Mighty Mite – Neil Henderson
Power Pots – Mark McKee
Rickenbacker – F.C. Hall
       John Hall
Rowe-DeArmond – Horace Rowe
       Stephen Tosh
Schecter – David Schecter
       Herschel Blankenship
       Tom Anderson
       Tom Stinson
       Tom Keckler
       Shel Horlick
       Gene Rushall
Stars – Ron Armstrong

This book is for everyone associated with electric guitars. People familiar with guitars are likely to approach this book casually and find it simple to follow. However, persons unfamiliar with guitars and uninformed about the innermost workings of them, may approach this book with trepidation. There is no need for any apprehension because electric guitars are basically very simple. They may come in many styles, colors, and sizes, but their hearts are nearly always the same. This book is written to give an understanding of what parts an electric guitar is composed of and how these parts operate and interrelate.

This book is arranged in operational order. It starts with the origin of a guitar's sound (a pickup), and follows that sound signal on its path through a guitar and then to an amplifier. After this, information dealing with hot-rodding and repair are explored.

Many different models of guitars share the same components, e.g., several Gibson electric guitars share the same pickups and controls. For this reason, individual instruments are not the focal point of this book; rather, the individual components, i.e., pickups and controls are emphasized.

Many persons may not know what kind of pickups their guitar has, and they may not want to spend the time reading every page of this book trying to find what section is relevant to their guitar. The following chart groups common instruments into classifications. A person can then look in the table of contents and index for information that would be apropo.

Single coil pickups generally have the inside wire of the coil as the ground lead of a pickup because this wire lays against a bare bar magnet or cylindrical slugs.

Humbuckers generally use one inside coil wire for the hot lead and the other inside coil wire for the

INTRODUCTION

ground lead. Humbuckers pose a problem because the ground and hot leads need to come from the same location of each coil. It is felt that using the outside lead is not the best choice.

BRAND NAME USAGE

There are several guitar companies that make equipment that fits onto the instruments made by other companies. In situations like this, names of one company are mentioned in the promotional material of another. This has created an awkward situation of possible brand name infringement. Please take note that FENDER, STRATOCASTER, STRAT, TELECASTER, TELE, PRECISION BASS, P-BASS,

JAZZ BASS, and J-BASS are some of the registered trademarks of C.B.S. Inc. LES PAUL, ES-335, and GIBSON are some of the registered trademarks of NORLIN Inc. DUAL SOUND, SUPER DISTORTION, PAF, and SDS-I are some of the registered trademarks of DIMARZIO Inc. SUPEROCK, and Z+ are registered trademarks or SCHECTER GUITAR RESEARCH.

There are many other company names that are registered trademarks. These names are used only when they are vital in clarifying a subject being described. It is hoped that this book will assist an understanding as to which companies created which products.

Guitars with Humbucking Pickups
B.C. RICH: SEAGULL, EAGLE, BICH
FENDER: STARCASTER, TELECASTER CUSTOM, AND PRECISION BASS (NEW)
GIBSON: EB-3, ES-335, L-6S, LES PAUL STANDARD/CUSTOM/AND THE PAUL, SG STANDARD
GRETSCH: COUNTRY GENTLEMEN, SUPER CHET
GUILD: STARFIRE

Guitars with Single Coil Pickups
FENDER: TELECASTER, JAZZ MASTER, STRATOCASTER, MUSIC MASTER, MUSTANG, PRECISION BASS (ORIGINAL), JAZZ BASS
GIBSON: ES-125, MELODY MAKER, SG (ORIGINAL), LES PAUL (ORIGINAL)/SPECIAL, AND PRO
RICKENBACKER: 360 GUITAR (ORIGINAL), 4001 BASS

Section 1

1. Types of Pickups

TYPES OF PICKUPS

The word "pickup" refers to a device that "picks up" the sound of a musical instrument and converts it to an electrical signal. In this sense, pickup is a self-explanatory term. A pickup is sometimes called a transducer which is just a technical name for a device that can change one type of energy into another. Since this is what all pickups do, all pickups are transducers. They convert string or guitar body vibrations into electrical energy.

Not all pickups made are covered in this book. Some are omitted because their function is similar to a pickup already described. It would take a great deal of space to describe each and every pickup made; also, it is common for pickup companies to change product lines.

Pickups used on musical instruments are of two types: Contact devices or Electromagnetic devices. These two types can be divided into several subcategories. For example, contact pickups can be:

condenser, dynamic, or piezo. Electromagnetic pickups can be: single coil, double coil, or triple coil. A further subdivision of electromagnetic pickups involves impedance and the subcategories here would be: high-impedance, mid-impedance, and low-impedance.

Contact pickups use a vibration energy sensing element which is "in contact" with a vibrating area. This is where the name contact pickup originated. These pickups can be built into a part of an instrument or stuck on the outside surface of an instrument. The sound from a contact pickup is very much like the natural acoustic sound of an instrument.

Electromagnetic transducers, i.e., magnetic pickups, are usually affixed to the top of an instrument below the strings. Sometimes a magnetic pickup is suspended between the strings and the top of an instrument so that it will not touch the vibrating top. A large heavy pickup can certainly reduce the sound of a delicately vibrating soundboard. Magnetic pickups produce an "electric guitar" type of sound.

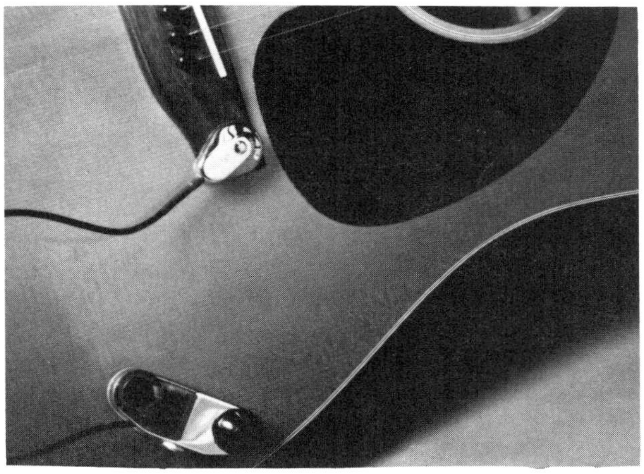

Fig. 1 Contact pickup with volume and tone controls – made by Rowe.

Fig. 2 Electromagnetic pickups on a guitar.

2. Contact Pickups

CONTACT PICKUPS: THEIR ORIGIN, DESIGN AND USE

The first method used to amplify the sound of an instrument was to use a microphone in front of it, and this method is still used today. In fact, many people feel it is the best way to increase volume. However, there are several problems associated with playing into a microphone. For example, you have to remain in one location because any slight turn from the mic will reduce the volume. Also, a sensitive mic can pick up

unwanted sounds that are within its proximity. It would seem that an obvious solution to this problem would be to put a mic directly into an instrument so it would have a sheltered reception. Unfortunately, this is not effective because the sound within an instrument differs from the sound that comes out of a soundhole.

It's the sound **outside** an instrument with which we are most familiar. Attempts to amplify this outside sound resulted in the first real pickup device. In the early twenties, people took microphones apart and

CONTACT PICKUPS

Fig. 3 Playing into a mic.

mounted the microphone's air vibration sensing element on the outside vibrating surface of an instrument. When used in this manner, the instrument's body vibration was amplified. These makeshift pickups were not too successful because microphone design was not perfected at that time. To better understand the function of contemporary pickups, it is helpful to clarify the basic operation of these first innovative devices. Normally, a microphone's sensing element is sensitive to air pressure and this sensing element is moved back and forth by the waves of air pressure striking it. The element is coupled to an electronic device that changes this motion into a corresponding electrical signal. This is the basic function of a pickup. Ideally, this signal produced by the pickup, moves a loudspeaker's cone back and forth in direct relationship to the air pressure waves that the microphone (pickup) originally sensed.

Instrument pickups have been, and still are, being made from two types of microphones. The two main types of mics are: condenser and dynamic.

Since dynamic or condenser elements are used in some pickups, let's take a look at how they work.

CONDENSER MICS AND PICKUPS

The word condenser refers to the electrical phenomenon of two separated surfaces holding an electrical charge. Condenser mics use two thin conductive plates separated by a small gap. When vibrations strike this structure, the plate(s) vibrate and this causes a change in the distance between them. When the gap closes, the current can jump (or flow) more easily from one plate to the other. When the gap increases, the resistance to current flow is increased. Therefore, this pulsing of current is related to the pulsing of the sound waves striking the element. The pulsed current is conducted by wires to an amplifier for amplification. This is a general explanation, but in actual practice there are many small details. Most are only important to engineers and of little importance to a performer.

Note that current flow is controlled by the plates, but to be accurate it is necessary to clarify that no current is actually produced by the plates. They simply

regulate the back and forth flow of a charge of a current. When the gap is reduced, the current flows one direction, and when it is increased, the current flows the other direction. The current charge of the plates is constantly supplied by a power source, or the current charge may be permanently induced in the plates. An induced charge, which is retained by the plates, is called an electret charge. This charge remains on the plates and is just bounced back and forth when the plates vibrate and this produces the alternating current of sound waves.

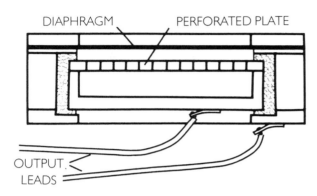

Fig. 4 Condenser mic elements.

Some of the first pickups were condenser types. In fact, the condenser pickups built by Lloyd Loar for Gibson, are the earliest substantiated pickups which means that Lloyd possibly made the first electric guitar circa 1924. The vibration sensing elements of these pickups were half dollar sized copper disks in a bakelite case. Unfortunately, these devices were prone to absorbing moisture and picking up static electricity which caused the devices to behave erratically. Since the development of other types of sturdy, stable, high fidelity pickups, condenser pickups have not been extensively used. Recently, condenser pickups have been redesigned and will likely be more widely used in the near future.

DYNAMIC MICS AND PICKUPS

Whereby condenser elements function by regulating a flow of current, dynamic elements actually **create** a current. Dynamic microphones are based on a

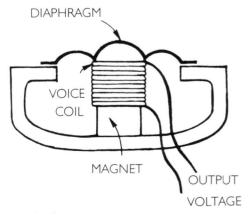

Fig. 5 Dynamic mic elements.
REPRODUCED COURTESY OF AUDIO-TECHNICA

very old electric principle: that of electric generators. Faraday demonstrated that if a wire was quickly passed through a field of alternating magnetic currents, the wire would react by displaying a flow of electricity through it. This is the basic principle of dynamic microphones.

The dynamic microphone element functions as follows: The air sensing diaphragm is connected to a cylindrical sleeve and this sleeve is wound with fine copper wire. This wound sleeve fits around a cylindrical magnet, and when air vibrations hit the diaphragm, the sleeve is moved up and down over the magnet. This motion causes a current to be created in the wire winding, and each end of the wire winding is directed to an output jack where it is then directed to an amp and finally a speaker. The speaker recreates the pulses into air waves or sound. Interestingly enough, a speaker is built on the same principle as a dynamic microphone. There is a coil winding around a tube (called a voice coil) that fits over a magnet. The waves of current flowing to a voice coil create a reverse effect of a mic and the changing current waves create an attraction and repulsion to the magnet. This results in the voice coil being pulled in, and being pushed out. Because the voice coil is connected to a paper speaker cone, this paper cone is also moved. The movement of the speaker cone creates sound waves in direct relationship to a current flowing to the voice coil. Since a speaker functions the same as a dynamic mic, a speaker can be used as a source of a signal, it can be a mic. Many walkie-talkies use a single device as a speaker **and** a microphone. However, the poor sound

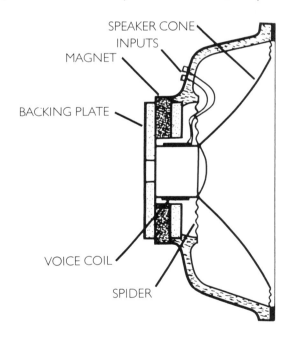

Fig. 6 Elements of a speaker.

quality of these units reveals a handicap. It's very difficult to make a device that is excellent at being both a microphone and a speaker. A mic must be very delicate to be sensitive to all pitches, a loudspeaker must be robust to produce a loud sound. To do each

job as well as it can be done, each has to be made differently. A dynamic instrument's pickup can dispense with the air sensing diaphragm because the wire coil can be fitted to a plate that fastens directly against the surface of an instrument.

Ribbon Mics

Ribbon mics are a dynamic type mic because they have the ability to create their own output current. Inside a ribbon mic, there is a thin metallic ribbon suspended between the poles of a magnetic circuit. This ribbon serves both as the voice coil and the diaphragm. Ribbon mics are capable of very fine performance, but are fragile to both high acoustic pressure or wind, and vibration. For this reason, they are generally only used in stationary locations.

PIEZOELECTRIC PICKUPS

Piezo pickups derive their name from piezoelectricity which is the charge of electricity induced in a crystalline substance by the application of pressure. Piezo is pronounced pi-e"zo, and is derived from the Greek word "piezein", meaning "to press."

There are electrical charges evenly distributed and balanced on a crystal's surfaces. When many crystals (e.g., table sugar) are pressed, a remarkable thing happens; the electric charges move from one surface to another. The charge is displaced by pressure. Now the crystal has a greater amount of positive charges on one side, but if we squeeze the other way, the charge reverses.

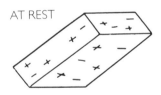

Fig. 7 Piezo crystal at rest.

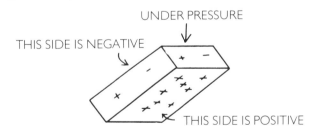

Fig. 8 Piezo crystal under pressure.

A piezo crystal can be used as a vibration sensor and each vibration pulse will cause a change in current. This produces a current pulse that is an exact duplicate of the vibration. This duplication makes a piezo a good pickup element since all that is necessary is to connect a wire to each of the two surfaces of the crystal.

One small problem with a piezo pickup is that the current output is very small, and a pre-amplifier is virtually always necessary to achieve high volume. A single amplifier cannot always boost the signal by itself.

A piezo pickup works most efficiently when placed

in an area of great changes of pressure and stress. The Ovation company is using a pickup that is located in the best possible location: the saddle in the guitar's bridge. The pressure of the guitar strings presses on the·saddle which in turn presses on the piezo crystals. When these strings vibrate, the pressure on the pickup varies in relationship to the vibrations of the strings.

Barcus Berry also makes several piezo pickups. Their piezo "Hot Dot" is an encased crystal in the shape of a cylinder smaller than one eighth of an inch in diameter and is connected with a wire lead. This pickup is generally inserted in a hole drilled in an instrument bridge.

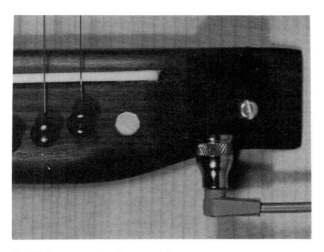

Fig. 10 Prototype Les Barcus pickup.

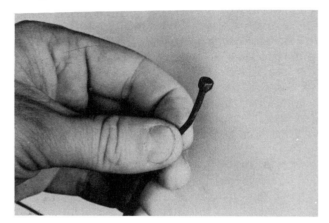

Fig. 9 Barcus Berry Hot Dot.

Fig. 11 Barcus Berry pickup 1335.

BARCUS BERRY

After a Hot Dot is installed, it is one of the most trouble free pickups and probably the most easily installed permanent contact pickup. This pickup is installed in a hole drilled in the bridge of a guitar, and a wire goes from the little Hot Dot unit to an output jack. In order to simplify the system, Barcus Berry has developed a combination output jack end pin to which a guitar strap can be fastened. A Hot Dot can be installed so that there is no visible sign of a pick-up except the special end-pin. Barcus Berry makes a mini volume pot which can be wired between the pickup and the output for a volume control. This pickup and its wiring is very susceptible to picking up hum; therefore, if a volume pot is used, it is suggested that it be shielded. A satisfactory shield is made from the casing of a shielded Switchcraft output jack. A hole for the pot shaft needs to be drilled in the backing cap and the prongs of the jack must be removed from the canister.

All the pickups that Barcus Berry makes for guitars, mandolins, banjos and fiddles, are similar. In fact, a Barcus Berry pickup for a guitar could be used on a banjo and vice versa. However, each of the Barcus Berry pickups is specifically made to the size, shape, and tonal demands of the instrument it was designed for. All of these pickups have single piezo elements. The exception to this is the Les Barcus pickup which has a BI-MORPH two element crystal.

Most Barcus Berry pickups consist of a piezo sensing element within a little box connected to a cord

Fig. 12 Barcus Berry preamps.

which terminates in an output jack. The Barcus Berry Jr. is an example of this construction. The one Barcus Berry pickup not in a box is the Hot Dot. This tiny pickup is inserted in a hole drilled in a guitar bridge.

The new Les Barcus Signature pickup is a special design that gives five times the output of a Hot Dot and it can be used without a preamp. The standard guitar pickup No 1335 is very similar to the Hot Dot. It is stuck on with mastic or silicone rubber. Barcus Berry has found that a 100% rigid mount actually reduces output.

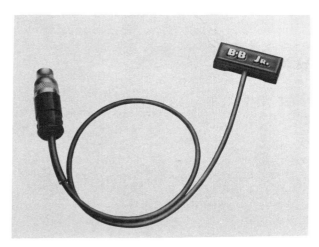

Fig. 13. Barcus Berry Jr.

DIMARZIO
Acoustic Model

This pickup is an inexpensive and easy to use contact device. It doesn't require a preamp, but the use of one doesn't hurt. The problem with feedback and string scratch sound is less than with many other pickups. This is in part due to the frequency response, the highs are rolled off. It is a very durable, simple pickup which can be mounted anywhere on the instrument. It is a high impedance unit and is compatible with standard amplifiers.

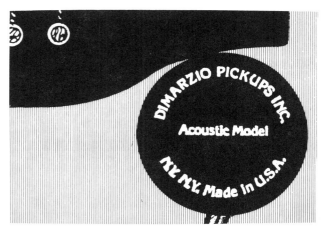

Fig. 14 DiMarzio acoustic pickup.

FRAP

Frap is a pickup company that derived its name from: **F**lat **R**esponse **A**udio **P**ickup. A bit of confusion can develop because the name is also used for one of the pickup systems made by this company.

The Frap

The Frap is a sophisticated system that uses a very fine preamplifier and a three element piezo contact pickup. The pickup unit is a small rectangular box that can be stuck to the surface of an instrument with wax (which is supplied with the pickup). A greater output can be obtained if the pickup is attached with silicone rubber. However, wax can be used to try several possible locations for mounting because the sound, volume and color will be different at different areas. If a Frap is installed inside a guitar, it would make a discreet

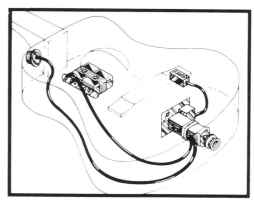

Fig. 15 Frap Git system.

electric guitar since it is hidden within the instrument.

The Frap has a clear, trouble free sound. When playing bass notes, the annoying trebles of string fingering sounds are reduced, but when playing high treble notes, the high, clear sounds of those tones are heard. Also, the response has been shaped so that feedback is reduced as much as possible without sacrificing tonal quality.

The "IT"

This is an economy version of the Frap System that resembles the larger unit. The little contact pickup mounts with wax or it can be glued. However, this pickup is attached to a preamp by a 12ft. cord, too short to leave the preamp behind you on an amp, but too long to clip the preamp to your belt. The Frap Git has an unpluggable cord which solves all the cord problems of the "IT".

OVATION ACOUSTIC/ELECTRIC PIEZO PICKUPS

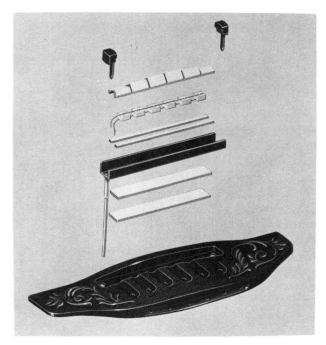

Fig. 16 Elements of Ovation piezo pickup.

Because of its full tone, clarity, and hassle free operation, the Ovation pickup was very impressive when first introduced in 1969. Ten years later it

CONTACT PICKUPS

remains on the forefront of the most popular acoustic pickups. The unique construction of the Ovation acoustic electric pickup is that it is built into the bridge saddles of selected Ovation models. This position allows for the utmost in clarity and volume because each string is individually sensed. The pickup uses six piezo wafer crystals, one under each string (or "course" on the 12 string). The crystals are gold plated for a firm electrical contact, and then the crystals are wired together in parallel so that the sound of each string is combined for a full tone. The output of the preamp is high impedance so it is compatible with all guitar amps. The basic Ovation preamp has a single volume control, whereas the more advanced model has a dual stereo tone and volume control. This advanced preamp is used with Ovation's most advanced piezo pickup.

Fig. 17 Ovation preamps.

Ovation offers its basic piezo pickup on 6 and 12 steel string guitars as well as a nylon six string model. The most advanced Ovation pickup is a stereo model which has string positions 1, 3, and 5 as one channel and string positions 2, 4, and 6 as the second channel. This results in sounds bouncing between the two channels when a melody is being played on several strings.

The Ovation piezo pickups are not simple contact pickups stuck onto instruments, they are complete, sophisticated pickup systems requiring virtually no maintenance. The reason for limited maintenance is due to the fact that the pickup, the preamp, the the wiring, the on/off switch and the jack are all built into the instrument at the factory. The built-in amp allows for high volume with minimum sound distortion. Therefore, Ovation guitars have a high signal-to-noise ratio. The built-in jack acts as an automatic on/off

switch connecting the battery to the preamp. When a cord is inserted into a guitar jack, the battery is connected to the preamp, but when the cord is unplugged, power is shut off. This extends battery life because a switch cannot be accidentally left on.

PICKUP ADHESIVES

Contact pickups are held onto instruments with soft adhesives, or they are permanently attached with epoxy or silicone rubber. The most common soft adhesive is beeswax. It remains soft at cool temperatures and it's fairly sticky. The disadvantage is that on cold days it gets hard and won't stick, and on hot days it can melt, making a runny mess. Sometimes a wax-stuck pickup just pops off.

To mount pickups, some people use a sticky goo that can best be described as a white tar, it will remain sticky at times when wax doesn't, but it is prone to slowly sliding; therefore, the pickup can fall off.

The following drawing shows how to mount a pickup. You must be careful not to press so hard that you break the instrument.

If you remove a contact pickup that is adhered with sticky adhesive, some of the adhesive may remain on the instrument. To clean off the sticky residue, use instrument cleaner polish. If it's very thick, use mineral spirits on a soft cloth. Be delicate – stop if any of the instrument's finish comes off on the cloth.

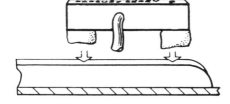

Fig. 18 Mounting a contact pickup.

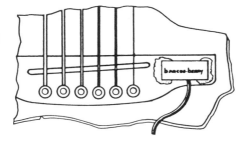

Fig. 19 Contact pickup on bridge.

Where a contact pickup is mounted can determine the sound quality. Try several locations, one may be preferable over another.

Fig. 20 External contact pickup and jack.

3. Magnetic Pickups

Fig. 21 Early Rickenbacker pickup, top view.

Fig. 23 Early Rickenbacker pickup, side view.

The first documented magnetic electric guitar pickup was made in 1931 by the Rickenbacker Company. This pickup was on Rickenbacker's solid aluminum guitar, both the guitar and pickup were the creation of George Beauchamp and Paul Barth. The patent number (2,089,171) was not obtained until 1937. This pickup had tungsten steel magnets, but today's cost for tungsten steel would make the pickup unbelievably expensive. This is the reason Rickenbacker no longer makes this pickup.

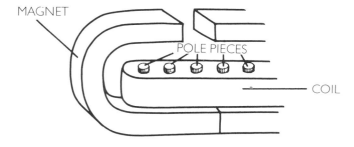

Fig. 22 Elements of early Rickenbacker pickups.

In 1932 the Dopyera brothers, founders of Dobro Co., made a few of their resonator guitars with electric pickups built into them. This project was done as a joint effort between Dobro and guitarist, Art Simpson. This guitar's pickup consisted of a bar magnet wound with copper wire, and just like the Rickenbacker pickup, it was a high impedance device. The high impedance enabled these pickups to mate with a fair degree of efficiency when plugged into a tube amplifier. This Dobro instrument is thought to be the first commercially made electric Spanish guitar. Later in 1932, Dobro began making one-piece cast aluminum electric Hawaiian guitars.

A later Dobro related venture was Valco. This company claimed it made the world's first modern electric guitar. It was based in Chicago and was founded by Victor Smith, Al Frost, and Louie Dopyera. It was the successor to the National and Dobro companies.

In 1934 or '35, the Gibson Company began to make electric Hawaiian guitars and electric banjos. The drawing shown is of an early Gibson pickup believed to be a prototype made in about 1932. In 1935, Gibson electric Hawaiian guitars started to become popular, but it wasn't until 1937 when Gibson introduced electric Spanish guitars that electric guitars started to become popular. The Gibson ES 150 guitar with the Charlie Christian pickup was the electric guitar that won the respect of musicians and the admiration of audiences.

Paul Bigsby, was an independent musician/inventor, and made the first modern solid body electric guitar in 1947. By the word 'modern', it is meant that this was the first solid body electric Spanish guitar rather than a Hawaiian slide-type guitar. Paul made his own pickups and most of these pickups used a bar magnet wound with copper wire. It was this instrument that ushered in the era of the modern electric guitar and

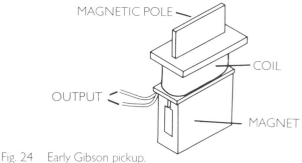

Fig. 24 Early Gibson pickup.

subsequently contributed greatly to the birth of rock-n-roll.

In 1948, the Fender Company produced the world's first mass produced solid body electric Spanish guitar. This guitar, the Broadcaster, had pickups consisting of six alnico cylindrical magnets wound with copper wire. Because of legal complications surrounding the name, Fender soon changed the name to Telecaster, perhaps the most famous guitar name in the whole world. Now, over thirty years later, this guitar is still a popular seller.

MAGNETIC PICKUPS

In 1952, Gibson unveiled their Les Paul electric guitar. Les Paul, a renowned guitarist, was the designer of this instrument. The first Les Paul guitars had single coil pickups which were nicknamed soap-bar pickups, the name is derived from the shape of the pickup. Around 1956, Les Pauls began to be made with humbucking pickups, these pickups are the world's most famous. They are the esteemed P.A.F., "Patent-Applied-For" humbucking pickups.[1]

Magnetic Pickups: Design

In principle, magnetic pickups are related to dynamic microphones. That is, both use electromagnetic forces; but in a magnetic pickup there is no physical coupling of a vibration and the pickup.

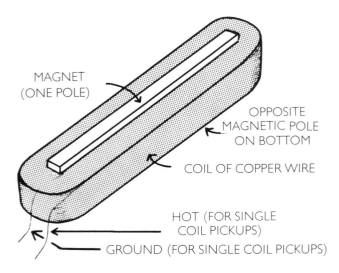

MAGNET
(ONE POLE)

OPPOSITE
MAGNETIC POLE
ON BOTTOM

COIL OF COPPER WIRE

HOT (FOR SINGLE
COIL PICKUPS)

GROUND (FOR SINGLE COIL PICKUPS)

Fig. 25   The most basic form of a pickup.

A dynamic microphone is coupled to a sound source through vibrating air and the moving air actually causes the microphone element to move. A magnetic pickup picks up magnetic motion, not air motion. It is a changing magnetic situation that results in an output of changing electricity. This is how it works: If an iron string vibrates over a coil of wire that is wound around a magnet, strange things happen! All of a sudden the coil of wire is being coursed with a flow of electricity. When the strings move down to the coil/magnet, the current moves one direction; and when the string moves the other direction, the current reverses. This alternating current can be directed into an amp which will reproduce all the vibrations of the string. In other words, the vibrating string pulls and pushes against the invisible magnetic force of the magnet. This causes the magnetic lines of force to move. A way to see these magnetic 'lines' is to place a magnet under a piece of heavy paper and sprinkle iron filings/powder on the paper. Now gently shake the paper and watch the iron filings form a pattern. If a nail is then moved under the paper near the magnet, the pattern will change. A string can effect a magnetic pickup the same way. It moves the magnetic force. If you recall the dynamic microphone operation, you will remember that if you quickly move a wire through a changing magnetic force,

1. SEE PAGE 125

the wire will respond with a flow of current. What does this have to do with a string vibrating over a pickup? Well, if a string is moved and the magnet remains still, the wire coil around a magnet in a pickup will also become filled with a flow of current.

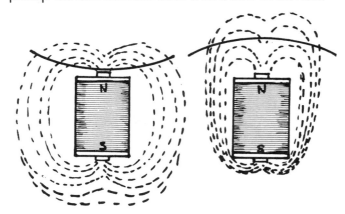

Fig. 26   How a string effects the flux field of a pickup.

Magnetic pickups are very simple in theory and they can also be very simple in practical usage. For this reason, many people have made and are making, magnetic pickups. One of the first discoveries about magnets was that they can be made out of a lot of materials. Magnets made? Yes, they are. Naturally magnetic lode-stones do exist, but virtually all magnets used today are man-made.

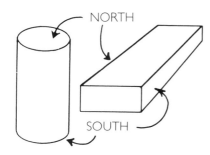

NORTH

SOUTH

Fig. 27   Cylindrical and bar magnets.

A magnet is made by subjecting suitable material to a strong current which pulls all the magnetizing forces in one direction. Ordinary iron has its magnetic forces evenly mixed, and therefore nullifying each other's forces. Applied current can change this evenly mixed condition so that the "north" forces are at one end, and the "south" forces are at the other end. The forces of a magnet are measured in gauss and oerstads. Gauss is a unit used in measuring magnetic intensity; whereas an oerstad is a unit used to measure magnetic reluctance, or in terms applicable to pickups, a magnet's ability to resist demagnetization.

Pure iron doesn't make the most powerful magnets because the mixed forces in iron cannot retain the alignment as effectively as other metals. One very useful mixture in magnets contains: Aluminum, Nickle, and Cobalt. Notice the underlined letters, Al Ni Co – Alnico; a most important magnetic material because its properties are more conducive to magnetization than

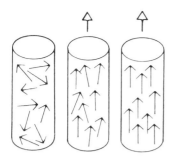

Fig. 28 Forces inside a magnet: Unmagnetized, partially magnetized, and fully magnetized.

any other material.[2] The formula of alnico 5 is the most famous. There are many alnico formulas and each formula produces different gauss and oerstad figures. Many people can hear the different sound resulting from the use of different magnets. The replacement of a full strength alnico 5 magnet by a full strength 8, will create a noticeable increase in treble response. A ceramic magnet increases treble response even more than an alnico 8 magnet. Therefore, the difference in sound may be more detectable when magnets of ceramic materials are used because ceramic magnet pickups are generally more sensitive than simple alnico. This results in getting greater output and more trebles. Ceramic magnets are becoming the most popular due to low cost of the materials. The rare earth magnets, such as samarium cobalt, are very strong – that is, they have a very high oerstad figure. Unfortunately, these magnets are very expensive.

Ceramic magnets can also be obtained in many formulas.

Pole Pieces

A pole piece derives its name from "pole" of a magnet. A pole piece is a device that acts like a pole of a magnet and it serves as an emanating point of a magnet's flux. A pole piece acts to concentrate and direct the magnetic field so it is in an optimum shape and direction to sense (be affected by) the vibration of the strings. When speaking of magnetic pickups, a pole piece is any structure on the tope of the pickup that "aims" the force of a magnet(s) at the strings. Pole pieces can be of many shapes and sizes.

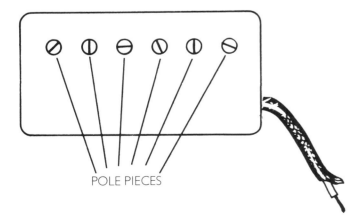

POLE PIECES

Fig. 29 Pole pieces.

2. SEE PAGE 125

A pickup may have a single metal bar as a pole piece (the ES 150 Charlie Christian pickup), or six individual adjustable height, slotted-screw pole pieces (the Gibson "Laid Back" pickup), or twelve adjustable height, allen screws (the DiMarzio "Super Distortion" pickup), or more than twelve (the Carvin and John Birch pickups). Even if a pickup does not have visible pole pieces (the Schecter Superock), it will still have unseen internal pole pieces.

Wire Coils

The windings of wire around a magnet are often spoken of in semi-mystical terms. When trying to determine how many coil turns to use on a pickup, you can always wind to 6,500 turns which is a magic number for some pickup manufacturers. Although some people may speak of arcane creations, many facts are known and have been proven. For example, the more coil windings around a magnet, the more the magnetic pulsations will be sensed, i.e., more windings increase amps, and so the more powerful a pickup will be. Keep in mind that the closer the wire is to the magnet, the more sensitive the coil will be. This is because the magnet's field of effect doesn't extend too far out from it. If a coil of large sized wire were used, the resulting bulging coil would have many wire turns a good distance away from the magnet. For this reason, small diameter wire is used which allows for a small coil to be tightly wrapped around a magnet.

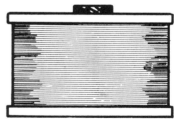

TALL = CLARITY
SQUAT = BASSY SOUND

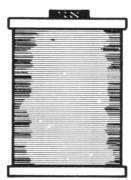

Fig. 30 Pickups can be thin and tall or short and wide.

The diameter of the wire most commonly used is 42 gauge.[3] However, pickups are made with wire anywhere from 36 to 54 gauge. The finer the gauge, the more sensitive a pickup will be. Unfortunately, as the gauge gets smaller the price of the wire starts to skyrocket. Rickenbacker once used 54 gauge, but the cost made the price of the guitars so expensive that they were not competitive in the market. Many guitar players didn't appreciate all the work that Rickenbacker put into it. Wire for pickups is finer than the hair growing on your head and it breaks **very** easily.

The wire used is solid copper which is rather weak material. It's coated with a poly-synthetic or some other insulating substance to prevent windings from shorting out. For years the standard coating on magnet wire was lacquer, but lacquer tends to chip and crack; therefore, newer synthetic coatings are now used.

3. SEE PAGE 125

MAGNETIC PICKUPS

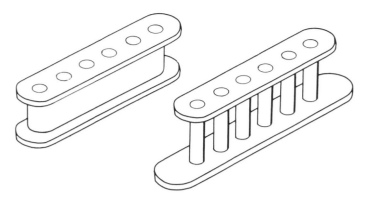

Fig. 31 Bobbins

Bare wire cannot be used because the coil windings would short-out causing a reduction in induction and therefore, output. The wire must conduct like one very long wire.

G	R	G	R	G	R
22	16.2	35	331	48	6750
23	20.3	36	415	49	8420
24	25.7	37	512	50	10600
25	32.4	38	648	51	13400
26	41.0	39	847	52	17000
27	51.4	40	1080	53	21200
28	65.3	41	1320	54	27000
29	81.2	42	1660	55	34300
30	104.0	43	2140	56	43200
31	131	44	2590	57	54100
32	162	45	3350	58	68000
33	206	46	4210	59	85900
34	261	47	5290	60	108400

G=AMERICAN WIRE GAUGE #
R=RESISTANCE IN OHMS "per 1000 ft."

Fig. 32 Resistances of copper magnet wire.

Resistance

How much wire to wrap around a bobbin is a difficult question to answer. The exact amount has to do with what kind of sound you are after and what kind of amp you are going to use. The skinnier a wire is, the harder it is for electricity to flow through it because of less surface area. In addition, the longer a wire is, the harder it is for electricity to flow all the way along it. These restrictions to flow are called **resistance**. Notice on the gauge chart that as the gauge number gets bigger, the wire is getting smaller, and the resistance increases.[4] Although some people measure the amount of wire in a coil by counting wire turns, many pickup manufacturers rely on using d.c. resistance as a means of judging how much wire to put into a coil. Generally, more windings give more output. When you get past a d.c. resistance of approximately 16K ohms, additional windings (wire turns) begin to strangle a pickup's output through the extremely high impedance of the coil. There are some fairly well accepted amounts of windings on a coil for a pickup:

4. SEE PAGE 125

16

Single Coil Pickups:
Clear tone = 3 to 6K ohms
Medium tone = 6 to 9K ohms
Loud heavy tone = 9 to 14K ohms*
Humbuckers (both coils):
Clear tone = 4 to 7.5K ohms
Medium tone = 7.5 to 9K ohms
Loud heavy tone = 9 to 14K ohms*
*These pickups would be high-output distortion models.

These preceding assigned tonal qualities are generalizations applicable to most pickups, but there are exceptions such as clear sounding high d.c. resistance Lawrence pickups.

Fender Stratocaster = 6K
Fender Starcaster = 12K
Lawrence AT-170 = 14K
Bartolini Acoustic = 2K
Gibson "Original" = 7.8K
Gibson S-1 = 5.38K
Schecter Z+ = 10K
Schecter F500T = 7.5K & 14K
DiMarzio X2 N = 14K

Fig. 33 D.C. resistances of some popular pickups.

When to use #43 wire and when to use #42, can be a very important decision. For example, if #43 is substituted for #42 (and the pickup is wound to the same d.c. resistance) a pickup is liable to have a thinner, more treble sound with less power. This occurs because the higher resistance of #43 will mean that the pickup coil would have less windings to equal the same d.c. resistance, and therefore it would be smaller than if #42 were used. It is interesting to note that the first Telecaster lead pickups had a wire gauge of #43, later this was changed to #42 wire.

High frequencies have a harder time flowing than low frequencies because high frequencies use up a lot of energy with their fast wave fluctuations. What all this means is that if you make a big coil winding of small size copper wire, you could have a powerful loud pickup, but the trebles won't all get through. Remember this: high output pickups have many windings and a fat loud sound, but some trebles will be lost. If a minimum of winding is used, the pickup's output will be lower, but the sound will be quite clear with increased treble. Some companies use high induction magnets to reach out for trebles, but this doesn't completely solve the problem of treble loss. Bill Lawrence, founder of Lawrence pickups, recommends using low magnetic induction with a high Q coil for a more balanced tone.

Impedance

Impedance is the resistance to alternating currents and the output of a pickup is an alternating current. The measurement of a pickup's impedance is important because it reveals the tonal quality of a pickup.

Impedance is determined by the constraining influence of a magnet's field on a coil. If the magnet is put in sideways instead of vertical, the magnetic field will form around a coil differently, and this will affect impedance. One problem with impedance is that as frequencies rise, trebles are impaired. This impedance/ resistance problem is most evident in humbucking pickups since they use two coil bobbins. Humbucking pickups have more windings than single coil pickups and the added windings increase the impedance and resistance.

Generally, the minimum amount of windings are those windings which produce a needed impedance figure that is compatible with an amp being used. Since d.c. resistance figures of pickups are fairly well correlated to the impedance (alternating current [a.c.] resistance) of most pickups, we can use resistance as an informative guide to a pickup's behavior. It certainly doesn't hurt that d.c. resistance is a lot easier to measure. Few people have the necessary equipment to measure a.c. resistance. Pickups with a resistance of 6,000 to 12,000 ohms are generally considered high impedance, whereas 1,500 to 4,000 ohms is generally referred to as mid-impedance. Pickups around 2,000 ohms could be plugged into a low impedance or a high impedance amp, but they are not quite at home in either because they are neither high nor low. Below 1,000 ohms is generally low impedance. For information about the impedance of a particular amp, check with the manufacturer.

Hand Winding

The term "hand-wound" is rather misleading because a person is not employed to hand wrap magnet wire, turn by turn, around a bobbin. Rather, a person is engaged in hand guiding a wrapping machine. Due to poor operator training, it is common for simple winding machines to wind coils which are flared. In order to produce coils of a desired shape, some manufacturers use hand guided winders, whereas other companies use new sophisticated machines which follow pre-set parameters.

Resonance Peaks

Virtually all electronic devices have one frequency that will cause them to oscillate more easily than any other frequency. This would be the natural resonant frequency of a device. The center of the resonant band is called a resonance peak.

Coils used in pickups have resonant peaks. If a pickup has a peak of 6,000Hz, the sound of the device will be more treble than if the device had a peak of 1,000Hz.

Some people feel that resonance peaks are the best indicator of the sound of a pickup. DiMarzio has said: "We feel the resonant peak may have more relevance than impedance or d.c. resistance because it will definitely give an indication of frequency response. It will provide a good idea of the type of timbre a pickup will create. The voltage may then determine how pronounced the effect will be."

For more information on the factors which raise or lower resonant peaks, read the sections on Bartolini, Lawrence, and Armstrong. Basically, more windings

and lower gauss lowers the frequency of the resonance peak; less windings and higher gauss raises the peak.

Humbucking Pickups

A single bobbin of wire around a magnet will make a pickup. This device will pick up the motion of a metal string vibrating above it. Unfortunately, it can also act as an antenna and pick up nearby stray electrical waves: the hum of fluorescent lights, 60 cycle hum, radio stations, automobile spark plug systems, etc.

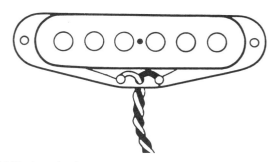

Fig. 34 Single coil pickup.

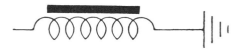

Fig. 35 Schematic diagram of a single coil pickup.

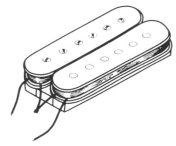

Fig. 36 Dual coil humbucking pickup.

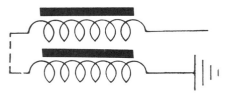

Fig. 37 Schematic diagram of a humbucking pickup.

Until 1956, hum was just something that had to be accepted with electric guitars. At that time, Seth Lover, who worked for Gibson, devised an anti-hum pickup called the humbucking pickup which cancelled out hum. Imagine it in this way: Ocean waves are high spots between low spots. If you could evenly combine these high and low spots, you would have a flat, quiet ocean, i.e., the waves combined out-of-phase. A hum-bucking pickup combines two waves of interference and puts them together out-of-phase.

There is an opposite magnetic polarity field in each coil, and nearby and inside the coils are magnetic

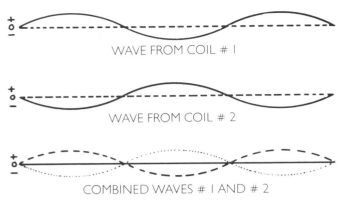

Fig. 38 How a humbucking pickup combines wave forms.

conductors. This means that the top of one coil is magnetically north and the top of the other coil is magnetically south. If you look at the series and the parallel diagrams, you can see that the positive connects to the negative. You would expect that this would cancel the signal, but your expectations are only half right. Half of the pickup's signal is cancelled – the hum half. The coils of a humbucking pickup are wired out-of-phase so that any signal received by them is cancelled, but the opposite magnetic polarity of the coils puts any signal magnetically sensed, back into an in-phase signal .

In summary: A humbucking pickup acts in the following manner – **any signal (i.e. hum) "seen" by the coils is cancelled, and any signal (i.e. string vibrations) "seen" by the magnetic poles is accepted.**

THE LINKING OF COILS IN A HUMBUCKING PICKUP

Traditionally, the two coils of a humbucking pickup are linked together in a series circuit; however, the coils can also be linked in a parallel circuit. When describing series or parallel wiring within a pickup, the only concern is with the paths of resistance and not the actual electronic positive to negative connections. This is because these positive and negative points become inverted when passing through opposite magnetic polarities in the humbucking pickup's two coils. The following diagrams show (1) the linking of two coils in a series humbucking mode, and (2) in a parallel humbucking mode.

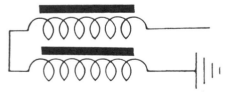

Fig. 39 Schematic diagram of a humbucking pickup (series linked)

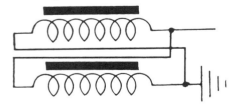

Fig. 40 Schematic diagram of a humbucking pickup (parallel linked).

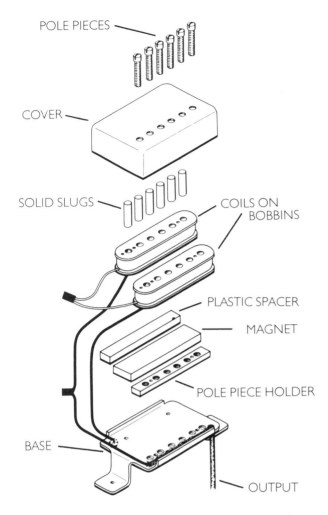

Fig. 41 Exploded view, a new Gibson Humbucker (series linked).

Series Linking

Notice that a series humbucker has the white insulated outer coil leads from both coils joined together. The leads coming from the inner portion of both coils have black colored insulated wire, and the black wire from the coil with the solid slugs becomes the hot output lead. The black wire from the coil that has the adjustable screw pole pieces is soldered to the base plate of the pickup. The braided shield of the coaxial pickup output wire is also soldered to the base plate. The base plate is used as a connection between the grounded shield and the black wire. This base plate connection effectively and efficiently forms a ground connection to the black wire and the entire metal case surrounding the pickup. Having the case of the pickup included in the ground circuit, helps to shield the pickup from receiving electro-static hum. Humbucking pickups can cancel 60 cycle per second hum, but not electro-static hum which is manifested at 120 cycles. Therefore, a pickup needs a metal shield to cancel electro-static hum.

Note: Either of the black wires from the coils could be grounded, or either could be hot. The diagram and the description given is the choice made by Gibson.

Parallel Linking

Parallel linking of a humbucking pickup is as follows:

The inside lead of the first coil is soldered to the outside lead of the second coil, and then an output wire is soldered to this junction. Then the outside from the first coil is soldered to the inside lead of the second coil. Another lead is then soldered to this junction. This results in two output leads, either could be hot or ground, the choice is arbitrary. A parallel linked humbucking pickup is not mechanically linked as two series configurations. As previously mentioned, parallel linkage is not concerned with the actual electrical connection, but rather, the parallel **relationship** of the paths of resistance.

There are some drawbacks to both series and parallel linkages. In series linkage, there is a loss of high frequencies, and it is almost impossible to achieve an overall sound that is clear and delicate. In parallel linkage, the output level is reduced considerably, and it is virtually impossible to create a solid, beefy sound. A common double-pole/double-throw switch can be connected to most humbucking pickups to enable the player to achieve both of these sounds on one guitar by flipping the switch. See the wiring section for instructions on installing a series/parallel selector.

The Electronic Function of Series & Parallel Pickup Circuits

When two equal resistances are linked in parallel, the resultant resistance is one quarter of the sum total. When two resistances are linked in series, the resultant resistance is the sum of the two individual resistances. For example, if one 4,000 ohm coil is wired in series with another 4,000 ohm coil, the total resistance of this device will be 8,000 ohms. In parallel linkage, if one 4,000 ohm coil is wired in parallel to another 4,000 ohm coil, the overall resistance of this device will be 2,000 ohms. Impedance measurements of these devices will react in a similar way to the resistance measurements. At this point, it is helpful to recall that high impedance and resistance tends to impair trebles and cause intermodulation distortion (lack of sound clarity). Also keep in mind that an increase in impedance often relates to an increase in induction, and this induction increase correlates very well with an increase in output.

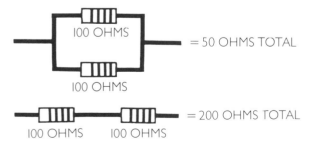

Fig. 42 Parallel and series resistances.

Series vs Parallel Linkage

Series and parallel each have their own distinctive sound. The series sound is characterized by high volume with a good degree of bass and a favorable signal-to-noise ratio. A parallel sound is characterized by less volume, very bright and clear trebles, and a less favorable signal-to-noise ratio.

Placement of Pickups

The location of a pickup will affect the tone as well as the overall volume. When a pickup is very close to a bridge, bass tones are greatly reduced. Pickups that are closer to the end of the fretboard than the bridge will give a fuller, less treble sound and vice-versa. The bridge pickups on Telecasters and Stratocasters are angled so that the treble side of the pickup is closer to the bridge than the bass side. If the bass side were as close to the bridge as the treble side, the bass would be very thin and weak.

A pickup near the end of a fretboard is referred to as a **rhythm pickup,** i.e., the pickup is suitable for playing full-sounding chords and rhythm patterns. A pickup near a bridge is referred to as a **lead pickup,** i.e., it's suitable for playing sharp, clear single notes that stand out. When closer to the bridge, lead pickup positions yield less output because the energy level of a string is lower. If two identical humbuckers are used on a guitar, the lead position pickup will have less volume than a rhythm position pickup. In order to equalize the difference in volume, guitars with two humbuckers often use rhythm and lead pickups which are different in tone and output. If there is a pickup in-between the rhythm and lead positions, it's referred to as a **middle pickup.**

Three humbucking pickups on a guitar are superfluous to many players because it can be difficult to find a place to pick the strings without having a pickup in the way because they fill the entire area from the bridge to the end of the fretboard. In addition, three simple humbuckers will give less tonal variations than a single tapped humbucker. One tapped humbucker could give ten distinct sounds.

When two magnetically identical humbuckers are used, it's common to turn the lead pickup around. This is done so that the magnetic poles of one pickup don't interfere with the poles of the second. If pickups were both installed so that the south pole coil of one pickup was contiguous to the north pole coil of another pickup, the volume and full tone of the pickups would be impaired.

Fig. 43 Orientation of pickups on a Les Paul.

MAGNETIC PICKUPS

Output Levels Of Some Popular Pickups
Courtesy of William Bartolini

Bartolini Acoustic Pickup	
Lawrence L200	= ½ of a Fender Strat
Fender Telecaster	
Rhythm	= ¾ of a Fender Strat
Fender Stratocaster	= ⁴/₇ of a Gibson "Original"
Gibson "Original"	
Humbucker	= 70 millivolts (third string hit by medium pick)
Schecter F500* ⟩ DiMarzio Fat Strat	= 1.25 X a Gibson "Original"
Bartolini Beastie II ⟩ Gibson L6S	= 1.5 X a Gibson "Original"
DiMarzio Super II ⟩ Bartolini Beast	= 2 X a Gibson "Original"
DiMarzio Super Distortion	= 3 X a Gibson "Original"
DiMarzio X2 N	= 4 X a Gibson "Original"
Bartolini ESI+	= 12 X a Gibson "Original"

*Schecter tapped F500 has two output levels, one is about the same as a regular Fender Strat pickup, the other is about the same as a Gibson "Original".

+ this pickup is battery powered.

MAJOR PICKUP AND GUITAR ACCESSORY MANUFACTURERS

DAN ARMSTRONG

Dan Armstrong is somewhat of a mystery figure. Most people that are into electric guitars have heard of him, but few know him. Dan has traveled a lot and has worked on electric guitar/pickup projects both in the U.S. and England.

In 1967, he was trying to remedy a short in a pickup and ended up making his own custom made pickup. In 1969, he met Bill Lawrence, and after they had a few talks together, Dan became more interested in working with pickups.

Many people think Dan Armstrong created the Danelectro guitars, but Dan states that they were created by Nathaniel Daniel. He did revamp them however, and eventually owned the company. The Danelectros were made out of Masonite and 2 x 4's. For the double cut-away model in copper and black, the supplier paid $30. The dealer paid $46 and the instrument was sold to customers for $55 at such places as Manny's in New York. Today these same instruments sell for $200 to $300 or more. The pickup on Danelectro instruments is incredibly simple. It consists of handwound wire around a bar magnet and there is no bobbin. The loose scatter wound wire-turns produce higher peaks than those of tight even coils. This pickup is held together by wrapping of black electrician's tape and it is stuffed into a short chrome plated cigar shaped container.

When Ampeg bought Gramer Guitars, they weren't in the guitar business and had to consult guitar experts as to "how to improve" the guitar. It was natural for Ampeg to come to Dan's guitar shop in New York and ask for advice, and after some discussion, it was realized that the smart move for Ampeg (a manufacturer of amps) was to make an electric, not acoustic, guitar. Because of Dan's relationship with Ampeg, he became the designer, and he was assisted by Bill Lawrence. (Together, both men developed the sliding placement pickup.) Instead of having a separate rhythm and lead pickup, the guitars had modular pickups. The clear plastic body of the guitar came about through the suggestion of Mike Gurian. A few guitars were made of black plastic, but Dan feels that this material was too much like rubber. However, some people really love these black beauties and have a lot of respect for them.

Fig. 44 Danelectro pickup.

Dan also designed an amp for Ampeg, but disagreements finally resulted in Dan's leaving the company, and in 1971 he went to England. While in England, Dan designed several experimental electric guitars. One of these designs used the strings as a very low impedance coil with only a magnet under them to complete the pickup. Nowadays with the availability of low impedance solid state electronics, this concept could be revived. He also talked with a man from Orange Amps about co-manufacturing a guitar, but Dan ended up producing the instrument himself and had an owner of a furniture company in England do the actual woodworking. When the instrument gained popularity, the woodworker demanded a much greater sum for making them; therefore, the project was terminated. After this, Dan designed an array of effects boxes called Dan Armstrong Sound Modifiers which came in a myriad of colors and names. One of these designs was called the Orange Squeezer, a compressor type of design that raised gain as input voltage dropped, or conversely, did not boost gain when the input was strong.

Dan has come to some definite conclusions about winding pickups. He said that once he unraveled a hot old Strat pickup and a hot old Gibson P.A.F. humbucker, and he was surprised to discover that both pickups had the same number of turns. Today he winds to that "magic" number. Now, this may cause many people to try to unravel and count the many thousand turns of a coil, but if 'Ol Dan is pulling our legs on this one, we'll be awfully embarrassed to be caught counting the turns. Anyway, Dan states that it's the turns and the length of wire used that matters, not the d.c. resistance.

As for other pickup details, Dan feels that single coat PVC insulation is the best because a too-thick insulation can make the coil too bulky. As for magnets, ceramic has an advantage in that it doesn't have the proximity effect that alnico has; that is, as a string moves closer to the ceramic magnet, it doesn't accentuate the bass over the treble. As for exotic, rare earth magnets such as samarium cobalt, they are very expensive and they are too strong – "Darn near weld the strings to them." As for resonant peaks, more wire lowers them and so does using a smaller magnet.

Dan has known David Schecter for some time; and again, it was only natural for Dan to do design work for Schecter Guitar Research. The pickup system he has worked on is called the Z+. The Z+ is a patent-pending method of using a magnet between bobbinless coils. The total d.c. resistance (both coils) is about 10K. The impedance is higher than most other pickups, and it also has more treble; therefore, a .01 micro farad capacitor is used on the tone control.

BARTOLINI GUITARS

William Bartolini began making Hi-A (high asymmetry) pickups in 1974 and in 1980 he was producing over thirty models of patented single coil and humbucking pickups.

Bill has a strong background in electronics and this background shows in his pickups which offer features found in few other pickups. Some of these are: four coil humbuckers, hexaphonic guitar pickups, and pickups with built-in preamps. Bill has several concerns about pickup construction and operation:

1. Magnet or core material doesn't make much difference in arriving at a certain type of sound; the interactions of a pickup's components play the major role.

2. Capacitance effects are important in coil design. Capacitance results from turn-to-turn coil windings.

3. Flux linkage/leakage influences output. The strings above a pickup cause flux leakage. The motion of a string modulates this action, and any change in flux is monitored by the coil.

4. Pickups should sense vibrating strings in an asymmetrical fashion. Only the vertical motion of strings, not the side-to-side motion, should be sensed. If this is done, a more natural sound will result.

5. How a pickup interfaces with a guitar's controls heavily influences a guitar's final sound.

Some of the most unique Hi-A pickups are described in the following text.

Model 3-A Acoustic Guitar Pickup

This single coil pickup for round hole guitars is nearly as hum-free as a humbucker. Although its output is not tremendously high, the sound it has is very clear and clean. There is string-to-string volume balance built into the pickup.

Fig. 45 Acoustic pickup.

Model 1B – The Beast II

This humbucker has four coils delivering the possibility of several tonal possibilities through the use of multiple resonances (each coil has its own resonant peak, and therefore its own distinct tone). There are two output pins connected to each of the four coils. This eight pin output configuration gives a possibility of at least seven different tonal voices, some of which are; high output, high clarity, one-third out-of-phase, and two-thirds out-of-phase.

Fig. 46 Mini size Beast II.

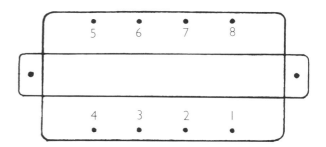

Fig. 47 Bottom of Bartolini Beast.

Model 36L – Hexaphonic

This Stratocaster size pickup has six sets of leads which result in a separate output of each string. Bartolini also makes humbucking hexaphonic pickups as well as quadraphonic bass pickups.

MAGNETIC PICKUPS

Fig. 48 Hexaphonic pickup.

Model EVQ – Variable "Q" Electronic Pickup

This pickup has one active coil and one non-active, hum-canceling coil which together help create a narrow aperture (string sensing) system. The built-in preamp allows the tone control to vary the band-width Q factor from .5 to 15. This allows a wide latitude of possible tones.

Fig. 49 EVQ pickup.

JOHN BIRCH

John is an Englishman who developed the concept of double screw pole pieces which are designed to reduce dead spots between the pole pieces when bending the strings. John has made many pickups of this configuration of both humbucking and single coil models.

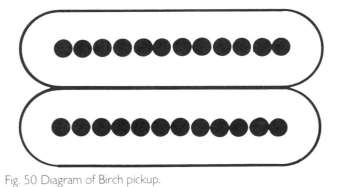

Fig. 50 Diagram of Birch pickup.

PETER COOK

Cook makes finely crafted electrics. One feature

Cook has worked with is to install a parametric equalizer as a tone control. When turned quickly this

Fig. 51 Peter Cook guitar.

control sounds like a wah-wah device because it is a band-pass filter. The guitar has one knob that raises or lowers the band, and another knob that controls the volume. Anyone could take apart a wah-wah pedal and put one in a guitar; however, many wah-wah pedals have a poor signal-to-noise ratio as well as being fairly expensive.

DIMARZIO

In a very short time DiMarzio pickups have gone from being an unknown to being the most known.

Larry DiMarzio's interest in pickups began one day when his electric guitar burned out. Larry said, "I didn't have money to build a new one (so) I decided to make my own." That first DiMarzio pickup took Larry thirty-six hours to build. However, he wasn't satisfied with it, and he continued experimenting. Being both a professional musician and a repairman put him in a unique position. Playing with a band offered him an unparalleled opportunity to test out the creations he made in his shop. As he says: "The only way to really test a pickup is to take it on stage and use it."

Larry got very intrigued with the fact that pickups could be so individualistic. Also, he became aware of all that a pickup could do. As he has said: "I heard a lot of guitarists complain about their pickups. It's not that the pickups they were using were bad pickups, but rather they just weren't suited to the music that people were playing. Some of the major guitar manufacturers hadn't done anything to update the pickups they designed in 1955, and the sound back then just wasn't what the guitarist wanted (today)."

Larry had designed many pickups years before DiMarzio Inc. was formed. The company really got going when Steve Kaufman joined forces with Larry. Steve was the principal agent in S. Hawk Company which specialized in sound modification/signal processing devices. Together, Larry, Steve, and later Steve Blucher, made DiMarzio Inc. what it is today.

As for why people play DiMarzio pickups, Steve Kaufman has stated: "The only reason anybody plays DiMarzio pickups is for the sound. It's not that there is any single DiMarzio sound, it's just that DiMarzio pickups are versatile enough to allow the guitarist to achieve the special sound he wants . . . Endorsements have helped us gain recognition, but they also make for some serious credibility problems. For example, Al DiMeola endorses DiMarzio pickups, but he doesn't use them exclusively. So, if a kid goes to a concert after reading that DiMeola uses our stuff and sees him playing something else, his credibility is sometimes shaken." Professional musicians may use several brands of pickups in the course of their work, but still feel they would like to endorse just one.

Many companies offer their instruments with DiMarzio pickups as an "optional extra". Such is the status of these pickups. When a DiMarzio pickup is seen on a guitar that sells for about $200, it can be a bit baffling because two of these pickups can equal half of the price of the guitar itself. The reason that Hondo and other makers of economy instruments can keep their prices so low is that these are specially made units.

All DiMarzio pickups are made in the U.S.A. The DiMarzio pickups on economy imported instruments are very similar to the more expensive standard DiMarzio pickups. These economy pickups are simple in design but there is nothing of lower quality in them.

DiMarzio's expertise in pickup making is reflected in three subjects which don't receive much publicity. These items may be subtle details, but they are important to overall pickup quality:

1. Larry's special skill is making pickups with a pre-determined sound. Tension on coil winding is a major factor in this regard. His company's winders are not simple friction control tension machines because these can cause a breakdown of the insulation on the magnet wire.

2. Single coil pickups were heated and then dipped in a hot wax bath to help insure that the wax penetrates deep. Recently DiMarzio switched to a non-wax process of coil solidification.

3. Lead wires used on all DiMarzio pickups are Teflon coated for maximum durability and heat resistance.

PICKUPS MADE BY DIMARZIO

The DiMarzio Company now manufactures a wide range of magnetic pickups plus one contact model. Other companies have copied his designs, but since

DiMarzio got the ball rolling, his designs have served as the basis for many other designs.

DiMarzio X2-N

This very high impedance pickup has solid pole pieces and uses three ceramic magnets. The four wire leads allow full wiring options: phasing, splitting, parallel and series. This pickup has a very high output.

Fig. 52 DiMarzio X2-N

Super Distortion Humbucker

This ceramic magnet pickup is a replacement for large Gibson style humbuckers, and its design is based on that "hot" classic pickup's design. The higher output is achieved by more windings and greater magnetism. Care has been taken so that high frequency response still comes through. Note that the d.c. resistance is 13.68K ohms, whereas a Gibson "Original" is 7.8K ohms.

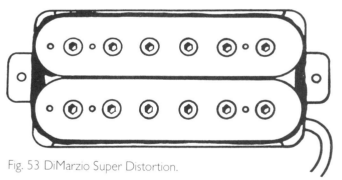

Fig. 53 DiMarzio Super Distortion.

Dual Sound Humbucker

This is basically the same pickup as the Super Distortion but there is an added feature: the coils are switchable so that the pickup is linked in series or parallel. This gives different resistances and impedances, and therefore – two sounds. The two d.c. resistances are 13.68K ohms and 3.42K ohms. Note that the parallel mode has ¼ the resistance of the series mode. It's better than split pickups because when it's switched to its lower resistance – bright mode – it's still humbucking.

DiMarzio PAF

This pickup is modeled after the first Gibson humbucker and its "old" sound is achieved as a result of several construction features. The two most important are a special winding of the coil and the use of an alnico 5 bar magnet. The tight coil winding is calibrated to the magnet used. The early DiMarzio pickups were rather unrefined, but now their pickups are a joy to take apart and examine. Everything is purposeful and nothing looks shoddy. The most obvious DiMarzio change from the Gibson design is the molding of little plastic feet into the bottom of #2 coil bobbin so that the bobbin sits in a level position. Note that in the photo of the PAF pickup that the ground does not connect with the coils. Both coils are wound in the same direction. The outside leads are used as the series link, and both inner leads are drawn out inside a two lead coaxial wire. One wire is black and the other is white. Either could be ground or live which means that it's easy to wire a phase switch. Also, it's easy to link the pickup in parallel or series with another pickup. Refer to the section on wiring for further details.

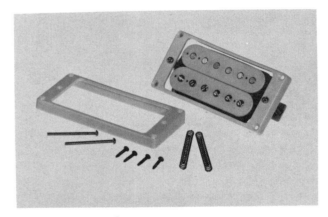

Fig. 54 DiMarzio PAF.

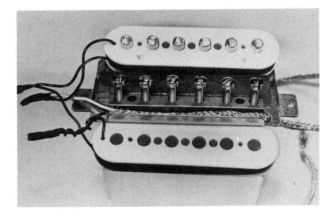

Fig. 55 PAF disassembled to show leads.

SDS-I

These super distortion Strat type pickups offer several laudable features. First, they have fully adjustable pole pieces. Second, output is higher than common Strat pickups. The d.c. resistance is 8.68K ohms, whereas Fender Strat pickups are about 6K. Third, the combined design features of this pickup make for a more even frequency response. The magnetic string pull which causes uneven sound is 50% less in this pickup.

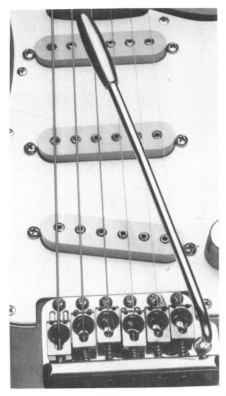

Fig. 56 DiMarzio SDS-I, note adjustable pole pieces.

Acoustic Model II

This pickup is for acoustic steel string guitars and it mounts in the soundhole. Very thoughtfully, the mounting flanges are of non-scratching nylon. The tone of this pickup is more acoustic than most other magnetic pickups. This clear sound is the result of a lower impedance. The d.c. resistance is 5.83K ohms. This pickup slides on a track so you can adjust what portion of the strings you want it to sense.

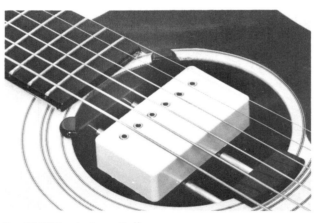

Fig. 57 DiMarzio Acoustic II.

Seymour Duncan

Duncan possibly makes the most diverse line of pickups: high/output distortion, single coil and dual coil pickups, staggered-height (pole piece) single coil pickups for both right and left handed guitars. These staggered-height pickups resemble the first Strat pickups. Duncan also offers replicas of the '59 Gibson, Patent-Applied-For humbucker which are the most accurate copies of these pickups made to date. They

Fig. 58 P.A.F. style Duncan pickups.

Fig. 59 Broadcaster and Old Strat style (reverse coil) Duncan pickups.

are available with double cream, double black, and zebra bobbins. Duncan offers a line-up of pickups for all common instruments plus Duo-Sonics, Mustangs, and Musicmasters. Many Duncan pickups are available in a tapped configuration.

Seymour Duncan is involved with pickup rewinding and making new pickups as well as doing design work. He feels that rewinding has given him insights missed by many other people and that the years he spent dissecting a multitude of pickups, along with creating a vast array of "copies", have been a good teacher. His customers may want a pickup that sounds like a P.A.F. humbucker, an old Rickenbacker, or a hot vintage

Telecaster, etc., and he has learned to track down the features which produce the distinctive tone for each model.

The oldest pickup that he has re-created is the 1930's Gibson ES-150 mid-impedance pickup. This pickup uses 36 gauge wire which is very unusual in this day and age because most pickups today use 42 gauge wire. His next oldest re-creation is his P-90 style model which is next of kin to the "real rock and roll" soap bar (single coil) pickup. If you have any other type of pickup in mind, he could most likely make it.

Some of Seymour's observations are:

1. Magnets: Ceramic magnets are too strong to give a pickup a mellow "vintage" sound; alnico 5 is best for producing this type of sound. Alnico 8 gives higher trebles, but it pulls the strings more and causes distortion.

2. Coils: Unless it is potted properly, winding too fast produces a spongy coil that squeals. When other people make Gibson copies, they always seem to use the same wire winding direction as Gibson, whereas Fender pickup winding direction varies. Sometimes Fender has a coil with the top coming and the bottom going, or sometimes it's the reverse. This means that if you mix Fender pickups from different years, you may create phasing problems.

3. Variances: It's very difficult to make pickups that are 100% identical. There can be a variance of +or - .005 in cylindrical magnet slugs and this variance affects the strength of each. Bobbins can vary in dimensions, and wire is not always uniform in diameter. All of these aforementioned variances affect resistance, impedance and capacitance. Variances continue to occur even after a pickup is made. While it rests, the magnets lose their power; just two years can weaken a Fender pickup and three years can weaken a Gibson pickup. This weakening can produce an audible change in a pickup. Heat, shock, and alternating current fields can also play havoc with magnets. For example, an alternating current field of an amplifier's transformer can age magnets.

4. Tension: The tension in winding can stretch wire and change the diameter and length which in turn affects the d.c. resistances. Seymour took readings on the resistance of five coils wound to an exact number of turns and found the following d.c. resistances: 13.79K, 13.58K, 13.72K, 13.69K, 13.65K. Yes, pickups are individual!

5. Layering: When wire is wound on a coil, it can be wound evenly in layers or it can be put on helter skelter.

6. Encapsulation: The encapsulation of coils and pickups can be hit or miss. Seymour took apart a Fender pickup to show me that the wax often doesn't penetrate the inside of a coil. On this particular coil, the inner windings were unwaxed and loose. To prevent this problem, Seymour uses a vacuum saturation technique to insure a solid pickup.

7. Vintage Sound: It is the aging of pickups which causes confusion. When someone wants an "old" Tele sound, does he want the sound of an old Telecaster

when it was new, or the sound of a 1950 Tele today with its weak magnets? Seymour provides both with his "new" old-style pickups, and "aged" old-style pickups.

The following is quoted from Seymour who explains "new sound" vs "old sound":

"For perhaps the last five years, a certain phobia has been developing among guitarists and bassists throughout the land, 'They just don't make 'em like they used to', especially pickups. Both of the major manufacturers of electric guitars in this country, Gibson and Fender, have fallen victim to the scrutiny of the pickiest bunch of ears in the west – us, 'them guitar pickers'.

"So why the difference? (between old and new). Well truth is, the big '2' aren't out to destroy your (vintage) sound, and your '57 Strat or '55 Les Paul sound that way (vintage as compared to modern) because of the changes in the way the pickups are manufactured (now, as compared to 1955-60).

"A long time ago, the pickup coils were wound on the equipment which seems antique, and stone age crudeness by comparison with today's pickup winder. Some of the reason for the advanced equipment is all the money spent on guitars in the early '60's helped the big manufacturers to afford good technical gear. Occasionally, coils wound in the old days were sloppy in their wrapping. Today, even though they are wound more consistently and the same gauge wire is used, the new pickups tend to have a thinner insulation resulting in a physically thinner coil and thinner sound. Old coils have wraps which go across each other, up and down indiscriminately due to hand winding, while new coils are neatly parallel around the coil bobbin.(because of advanced string winding machinery), and are stair-stepped together from one layer of winding to the next. What this means is that older coils have slightly higher voltage output, and are distorting due to uneven space in the wrapping. They are more inconsistent from one pickup to the next in the same model, making it much easier to get a lemon. New coils are much more consistently wound and have a little less voltage output, but a little more frequency response (a cleaner top end in your sound especially). They don't distort within the pickup as the spacing of wraps is quite uniform.

"If you measure the d.c. resistance of the old coil and a new one, they will be quite similar. Real close is the best that the 'Big 2' can do even today because the coils are wound to a certain number of mechanical turns and wire is chopped. However, for truly balanced coils, the wire should be wound a little more than necessary (20 turns too much) and then electronically metered and trimmed to balance exactly when cut. This difference in mechanically alike coils is due to inconsistency in the wire used to wind pickups which is either 42, 44 or 46 (or about the size of a human hair). The wire is usually stretched when it's being wound, producing this inconsistency.

"So, if you like that old nasty sound of 'X-150 Jetstar Dumptruck' or whatever other kind of guitar, most often it is the sloppy coil that turns you on. Any pickup

winder can be made to be sloppy, most aren't in the first place because it's considered to be undesirable among engineering and technical types. So if you need to sound like '1957 Dogbreath' go find an old pickup and pay through the nose, or go get yours wound that way, or realize that other replacement gear will do the job."

SPECIFICATIONS ON THE 42 AWG MAGNET WIRE:
(SINGLE BUILD INSULATION)

Diameter/inches (minimal)	.0024"
(nominal)	.0025"
(maximum)	.0026"
Nominal area in circular mils	6.25
Minimal increase in film	.0002"
(overall diameter in inches)	
(minimal)	.0026"
(nominal)	.0028"
(maximum)	.0030"
Nominal ohms at 1000' (feet) 20°cent.	1,659 ohms
Nominal ohms per pound. 20°cent.	84,510 ohms
Pounds per 1000' (feet)	.0196 lbs
Feet per pound	50,940 (feet)

(HEAVY BUILD INSULATION)

Minimal increase in film insulation	.0004"
Overall diameter in inches	
(minimal)	.0028"
(nominal)	.0030"
(maximum)	.0032"
Nominal ohms per 1000' (feet)/20°cent.	1,659 ohms
Nominal ohms per pound/20°cent.	82,290 ohms
Feet per pound	49,600' (feet)

PLAIN ENAMEL – (OLEO-RESINOUS) normally a dark maroon color (used on the newer Strats)
POLYURETHANE – comes in a variety of colors, RED, GREEN, CLEAR, BLUE ETC.
FORMVAR (POLYVINYL FORMVAR) used on the older STRATOCASTERS
BONDABLE POLYURETHANE (HAS A FILM OF THERMOPLASTIC ADHESIVE) reacts to heat or alcohol.
BONDABLE FORMVAR (HAS A THERMOPLASTIC FILM ADHESIVE)

OLD VS NEW

See the old and new information for comparing Strat pickups. Although Strat pickups have not undergone a great deal of change, there are subtle differences.

The "Formvar" insulation on the magnet wire was thicker than what is used today. If two coils are wound with the same gauge wire, and to the same number of turns, the one with thicker insulation will produce a fatter coil. The outer windings of this coil will be further from the magnets.

The amount of windings on Strat pickups has varied,

as the comparisons show. Seymour says: "Many people think that it's the number of turns alone that can make this pickup have its unique sound, but it is mostly the varying lengths of the magnetic rod pole pieces which give it its sound. Due to the magnets being of varying lengths, there is an inner phasing of the pole pieces which gives it that sound."

SEYMOUR DUNCAN RESEARCH LABORATORY

A Comparison Of Old And New Stratocasters

Features	1954 Stratocaster	1978 Stratocaster
OHMS	6.05 K Ohms	5.66 K Ohms
FLATWORK MATERIAL		
Top	vulcanized fibre (black)	vulcanized fibre (black)
Bottom	vulcanized fibre (black)	vulcanized fibre (black)
FLATWORK THICKNESS		
Top	.064" (inch) 1/16 inch	.064" (inch) 1/16 inch
Bottom	.097" (inch) 3/32 inch	.097" (inch) 3/32 inch
MAGNET DIAMETER	.192" (inch)	.187" (inch)
MAGNET LENGTHS E 6th	.684"	.656"
A 5th	.687"	.656"
D 4th	.717"	.656"
G 3rd	.718"	.656"
B 2nd	.636"	.656"
E 1st	.657"	.656"
MAGNET FEATURES	rough sandcast markings ground end	slightly tumbled
BOBBINS LACQUERED	yes	yes
COIL DIRECTION	start/left (wound clockwise)	start/left (wound clockwise)
MAGNETIC POLARITY	north (first few years of production; changed to south)	south
MAGNET WIRE GAUGE	42 heavy Formvar	42 plain enamel
INSULATION	above	above
TURNS	8,350	7,600
BLACK LEAD WIRE	ground/beginning of coil	ground/beginning of coil
WHITE LEAD WIRE	hot/finish of coil	hot/finish of coil
POLE SPACING	.407" center to center each pole	.407" center to center each pole
WINDING LENGTH (Outside of E 6th to E 1st)	2.225" outside E 6th to E 1st	same as 1954 Stratocaster
TOP LENGTH OF FLATWORK	2.616" – ends are filed	approx. same as 1954 (all below not filed)

MAGNETIC PICKUPS

Features	1954 Stratocaster	1978 Stratocaster
BOTTOM LENGTH OF FLATWORK	3.312"	approx. same as 1954
TOP WIDTH OF FLATWORK	.60", inside ends are filed	approx. same as 1954
BOTTOM WIDTH OF FLATWORK	.905", inside ends are filed	approx. same as 1954
TOTAL DEPTH OF PICKUP	.718" top to bottom	.656" top to bottom
EXPOSED COIL UNDER COVER	yes	yes
LEAD WIRE MATERIAL	cloth braid (push back) 22 gauge	plastic coating

Typical Properties Of Cast Alnico V Magnets Used In Stratocaster Pickups

Typical Residual Induction (Br)	12,400
Typical Coercive (H)	640
(Bd Hd) max Megagauss Oersteds	5.50
Average Density – Pounds per cubic inch	.264
Coefficient of Thermal Expansion	11.6
Tensile Strength – pounds per sq. inch	5,450
Transverse Modulus of Rupture – pounds per sq. inch	10,500
Hardness – Rockwell	50
Resistivity – Micro Ohms per cm per cm² at 25 degrees C.	47

Average Ohms Of Stratocaster Pickups

YEAR	FRONT	MIDDLE	BACK
1954	5.91K	5.38K	5.85K
1955	6.02K	5.96K	6.01K
1956	6.13K	6.34K	6.28K
1958	6.41K	6.39K	6.65K
1960	5.96K	5.85K	6.31K
1963	5.62K	5.58K	6.11K
1963	5.97K	5.41K	6.19K
1965	6.27K	5.48K	5.76K
1966	5.80K	5.91K	5.78K
1970	5.60K	5.50K	5.31K
1973	5.57K	5.52K	5.58K
1974	5.11K	5.45K	5.52K
1979	5.65K	5.71K	5.66K
1980	5.91K	5.80K	7.32K

NOTE – New Model Stratocasters are using a hotter pickup in the back position.

BACK POSITION CAN BE CALLED:
Bridge position pickup
Lead pickup
Treble pickup

FRONT POSITION PICKUP CAN BE CALLED:
Rhythm pickup
Neck pickup
Bass pickup

USING THE FOLLOWING COMBINATIONS OF COIL AND MAGNET POLARITY WITH SINGLE COIL PICKUPS, WILL GIVE YOU THE FOLLOWING RESULTS.

	CW-N	CW-S	CCW-N	CCW-S
CW-N	In (phase)	Out (phase)	Out (phase)	In (hum)
CW-S	Out (phase)	In (phase)	In (hum)	Out (phase)
CCW-N	Out (phase)	In (hum)	In (phase)	Out (phase)
CCW-S	In (hum)	Out (phase)	Out (phase)	In (phase)

In (phase) means the two pickups are in phase when used together

Out (phase) means the two pickups are out of phase when used together

In (hum) means the two pickups are in phase and work as a humbucker reducing hum.

CCW-S Counter clockwise coil and south magnetic polarity.

CW-N Clockwise coil and north magnetic polarity.

CCW-N Counter clockwise coil and north magnetic polarity.

CW-S Clockwise coil and south magnetic polarity.

THE STANDARD RECOMMENDED TENSIONS OF STANDARD MAGNET WIRES USED IN GUITAR PICKUPS.

AWG	TENSION GRAMS	TENSION OUNCES
40	53 grams	1.9 oz.
41	42 grams	1.5oz.
42	33 grams	1.2 oz.
43	26 grams	.9 oz.
44	21 grams	.74 oz.
45	17 grams	.6 oz.
46	13 grams	.46 oz.

USING STRAT PICKUPS

Duncan gives the following info so that Strat owners can get more from their instruments:

"There is a factor which determines the sound and output of a pickup. – 'Strat-itis' is often heard when playing high on the fingerboard on the lower strings. It is hard to distinguish the notes and impossible to get it in perfect pitch around the 12th fret. What I do to help cure this, is done in a couple of ways. First, I raise the back pickup quite close to the strings without hitting the pickup when pressing the string at the last fret. Then lowering the bass at the last fret, and then lowering the bass side of the middle and front pickups, keeping the treble side still up. The larger mass of the bottom strings becomes more magnetized because the pickups have the same magnetic polarity, the string then becomes magnetized at three points with the same field. Because like magnetic poles repel and unlike poles attract, there is a repelling of the magnetic field on the strings which causes the pickups to produce a very unattractive sound. Lowering the pickups on the bass side will help considerably. Another solution that helps, is to wind the middle pickup in the opposite direction and reverse the magnetic polarity. This does two things: (1) reduces 'Stratitis' and allows humbucking linkage if coils 1 and 2 or 2 and 3 are used together.

"Strats have always had a noise problem. When Strats were first made, guitarists used a heavier gauge of string than is used today. The result of this is that signal-to-noise ratio has worsened with the use of lighter gauge strings. The players today use such light gauge strings that a very hot signal is not generated. This means amps are turned up louder and hum is therefore, louder."

FENDER

In some ways, Fender can be thought of as the founder of rock 'n' roll. Although Gibson made electrics more than ten years before Fender, Fenders were unique in that they weren't hollow like a normal guitar. In 1948, Fender introduced the "Broadcaster" guitar which had an ash body with two single coil pickups and a bolt-on, one piece maple neck. The rhythm pickup had a d.c. resistance of around 6.5K, whereas the lead pickup had a figure higher than this, and wire gauge numbers 42 and 43 were used. Many of these pickups vary in d.c. resistance, some as high as 11K. Since Gretsch had the name Broadcaster in use, Fender's guitar became the Telecaster. Teles made today are nearly the same as those made thirty years ago.

Fender – Research and Development

Fender has a Research and Development Department that's continually working on checking the quality of production, developing new ideas and evaluating new products on the market. One avenue of exploration is studying the science of hearing. One part of Fender's studies of hearing involves placebo and Hawthorn effects. For example, when a listening audience is told that one Strat has a normal pickup, and another Strat has a "special" new pickup, the group will definitely hear the difference, but if they are told that both models are the same, there is a tendency for the group to not detect any tonal difference. This "expectation" is very influential in marketing the aura of "vintage" instruments. Many people buy "hot" pickups and then convince themselves that the sound is unique.

The subject of replacement parts has had Fender somewhat perplexed. Persons familiar with the guitar scene will note that many companies make hot rod parts advertised to fit on Fender guitars. Fender was greatly amazed because these companies took advantage of the Fender name, and Fender couldn't figure out why these parts gained such popularity. It appears that the popularity is related to a person's desire to individualize and hot rod their possessions.

As for pickup design, Fender is continually experimenting. The single coil pickup is best known as a "Fender creation" and therefore, it receives a lot of attention. One problem with a Fender single coil pickup is that it's not humbucking. A simple way to achieve humbucking would be to wind a coil around three north polarity slugs and then wind a coil around three south polarity slugs. The two sections could then be linked to form a humbucker, but it could look like a single coil pickup if put in one case. If the idea of these 3 and 3 pickups is given a little thought, it makes a lot of sense; however, further thinking will reveal that when two coils are series linked, the resistance doubles, and the tone is greatly altered. If they are linked in parallel, the resistance halves, and the tone is also altered. It's difficult to make a humbucker that behaves and sounds like a single coil pickup without hum.

The Fender electric 12 string used split pickups with each half mounted separately. The Precision Bass still uses this layout. The old Dutch electric, the Egmond, used split 3 and 3 pickups. On this instrument, each half of the pickup was put in a full width case. The cases extended under all six strings. There were three dummy pole pieces in each case.

Fender uses a simple procedure for R & D testing of the response of new pickup designs. A pink noise signal from a signal generator is fed into an amp, and a loop of 12 gauge insulated wire is hooked up to the speaker wires of the amp. This loop is then placed around a single coil pickup, and the output of the pickup is then directed to a Hewlett Packard Analyzer with print-out capabilities. If a dual coil pickup is used, then half the loop (a length of straight wire) is laid on the pickup between the two coils. Since this method of testing does not use strings, it is not subject to their individuality, and this makes the test results more uniform. Heath Co. makes an inexpensive signal generator that could be used by amateurs.

Fender Tele and Strat Pickups

These single coil, non-humbucking pickups use six alnico magnetic slugs surrounded by a wire winding. The company has alternated in using staggered height magnets and same height magnets. The staggered height units give a better string-to-string volume balance. Nowadays, however, many people don't feel staggered height is needed because the extra-light gauge strings being used by musicians today function very well with same height pickups. Even so, staggered height pickups are worshipped by some musicians and although these pickups are nearly thirty years old, they are still in demand.

The first Telecaster pickups were those on the 1948 Broadcaster. The lead pickup had three-sixteenths of an inch flat pole magnets in the lacquered bobbin which was wound with 43 gauge magnet wire and a black waxed string wrapping. In 1954, Tele lead pickups began to receive slightly raised pole pieces.

The switching tone control circuit of older Teles is different from newer models. Telecasters before 1953 had the following switch positions: Pickup (p.u.) #2, p.u. #1, or p.u. #1 routed through a large value capacitor. This third selection gives a very bassy sound because the capacitor has diminished the trebles.

The plate on the bottom of a Tele lead pickup is composed of magnetically conductive metal, and it is used to reshape the magnetic field of the pickup and thereby boost the output. This plate also has a second function, that of being a shield/ground conductor. The shield function is the action of the plate shielding the bottom of the pickup and contacting the magnets. The ground conductor function of the plate operates in the following manner: A ground wire connects the plate to the ground output of the pickup, then three metal screws pass through holes in the bridge and are threaded into three holes in the plate. The screws continue the ground circuit from the plate to the bridge and on to the strings. The Telecaster offers one of the most clever string ground paths available However, there is one penalty to this system. The plate can contribute to unwanted feedback and noise by acting like an unwanted antenna. With a pickup cavity painted with conductive paint (and connected to

ground) this feedback can be substantially reduced. Fender is now painting the cavities of their instruments with just such a paint.

Fig. 61 Old Tele lead pickup, top view.

Fig. 62 Bottom of old Tele pickup mounted on bridge.

Stratocaster

Hendrix made the sound of his Strat **the** sound of rock 'n' roll. Stratocasters haven't changed much since they were first made in 1956. The only noteworthy change is that the coils are evenly wound – gone are the tulip or blimp shaped coil windings.

Fig. 60 Fender Telecaster.

Fig. 63 Fender Stratocaster.

BASIC PARTS OF A STRATOCASTER PICKUP

1. Magnets: A Stratocaster pickup has six cylindrical magnets, the centers of which are .407 of an inch apart. These magnets are flush with the bottom of the bobbin and protrude through the top fiber piece. These magnets are alnico five which is composed of the following parts: 8 parts aluminum, 14 parts nickel, 20 parts cobalt, 3 parts copper, and the remainder iron.

These six magnet/pole pieces were arranged in a staggered height configuration on the first Stratocasters. The very first Strat pickups had the G string magnet .725 of an inch long, whereas the 1961 and later pickups had a G string magnet .712 of an inch long. This variance is a result of musicians switching to string sets using an unwound and (and therefore louder) G string. Newer Strat pickups have used magnets which are all the same height and protrude slightly above the top of the bobbin.

Currently Fender uses magnets which are sand cast to about .200 of an inch and ground down to a diameter of .187 of an inch. The first Strat magnets were ground on the edge. The early 1960's magnets were heavily tumbled to remove sharp edges, and they did not have a vintage look. Presently magnets are lightly tumbled.

Early Strat magnets were cast, had a rough exterior finish and were .192 of an inch in diameter, plus or minus .002. One end of the early magnets was ground so that the magnets could be easily inserted into the fiber pieces. Magnets used in the 1960's were greatly tumbled to round the ends and therefore, do not have a vintage look. Recent Strat magnets are only slightly tumbled.

2. Fiber Pieces: The bobbin of Fender single coil pickups is composed of magnets held between two pieces of vulcanized fiber. These pieces are composed of paper material saturated with resin and pressed under high pressure with the application of heat. Blanks of this material are made into pickup parts through the use of a punch press. Holes are made for the magnets, eyelets, pickup height adjustment screws, and output wires. The holes for the adjustment screws are later tapped to accept 6-32 adjustment screws. The two fiber pieces are black on early Strat pickups, but mid-sixties pickups have bottom pieces which are dark gray and often have a date on them.

3. Coil: The coil of a Stratocaster pickup is wound in the following manner: One end of a copper wire is attached to the left eyelet of a bobbin, then a coil is wound in a clockwise direction. The finishing edge of the coil wire is threaded through the right eyelet. The wound bobbin is now immersed in a hot wax bath to saturate the coil and therefore, reduce microphonics and make the coil more solid and durable. A black lead is soldered to the left eyelet and a white wire is soldered to the right eyelet.

Magnet wire for pickups is composed of electrolytic tough-pitch copper. Magnet wire is also made from aluminum, gold, as well as other metals, but copper is the most practical for pickups due to low cost and availability. Magnet wire is formed by forcing/drawing a copper billet (usually 4″ x 4″ x 36″) through a series of dies.

Strat pickups use 42 AWG gauge wire which is completely covered with insulation so as to isolate it from the wire previously wound – this prevents short out. Care must be taken when the wire is sharply bent around the end of magnets one and six, because if the insulation is broken, oxidation and crystalization can occur (which can destroy the wire and ruin a pickup). Also, if a phase switch is used (and the coil inside lead becomes hot) **and** there is a break in the insulation as the wire contacts the magnets, the following situations will occur: (1) If a string contacts a magnet, the entire circuit will short out and silence will result (if a string ground is used); (2) There will be fairly loud hum if a person touches a magnet.

Magnet wire comes with a classification that denotes the melting point of the insulation. Class 105 would mean a melting point of 105° C. Class 180 would equal 180°C. The insulation on wire used in pickups is normally Class 105 because heat is not a problem.

Fig. 64 Old Stratocaster pickups, note uneven windings.

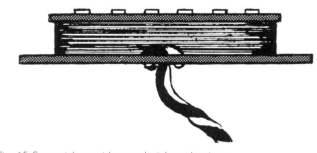

Fig. 65 Strat pickup with even height pole pieces.

STEPS IN MAKING A STRAT PICKUP

1. The top and bottom of a bobbin are joined together by six alnico magnets.
2. This assembly is dipped in lacquer to solidify it and insulate the magnets from the windings.
3. A coil of 42 gauge wire is wound on the bobbin.

MAGNETIC PICKUPS

4. The wound bobbin is immersed in a hot wax bath to solidify the coil.
5. One black and one white lead are soldered to the pickup.
6. A plastic cover is put over the pickup.

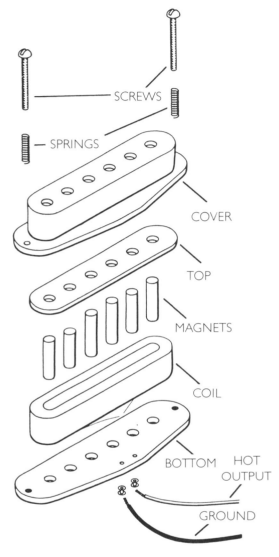

Fig. 66 Exploded view of a Stratocaster pickup.

[NOTE: Bill Lawrence has stated that "low-strength alnico V" magnets in some Strat pickups are simply full-strength alnico II. Not all early Strat pickups were type V, few people know this.]

GIBSON PICKUPS

Although Gibson was not the inventor of the electromagnetic pickup, they were the first company to make pickups popular. Before 1950, pickup manufacturing was not completely consistent. The old Gibson winding machines didn't wind to an exact number of coil turns or d.c. resistances because the machine didn't have an automatic shut-off feature. This resulted in coils of different sizes, and it's possible to find Gibson single coil pickups (the model is now called "Laid Back") with d.c. resistances from 7.5K to 9K ohms. As for magnets, no exact formula was adhered to. Gibson has used alnico 2, 4, and 8, as well as 5.

Fig. 67 Fender Starcaster.

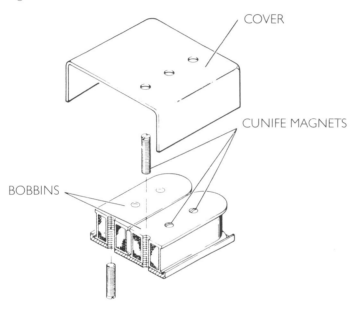

Fig. 68 Fender humbucking pickup.5

Alnico type 5 with specific characteristics wasn't called for. Often, the only qualification was that the material be a "magnet".

After 1950 automatic winders were used to wind bobbins to a set number of turns for both single and dual coil pickups. In addition, wire gauge became standardized; the wide range of d.c. resistance variance in early pickups was reduced to 2.5%. Also, magnets became standardized; in the '50's and '60's, alnico 5 was used in almost all pickups.

There is a lot of controversy about whether or not to wind coils to a set number of turns or to a specific d.c. resistance. Gibson feels that winding to a specific number of turns is the most effective method of producing a specific tone that is free of hum. Old Gibson P.A.F.'s often had about 6,500 turns and this is thought to be a magic number by some people.

When linking multiple coil pickups, Gibson primarily uses series wiring. Some exceptions to this

5. SEE PAGE 125

are the S-1 guitar and Thunderbird bass. The low impedance pickups on the Les Paul Recording are low because of the large diameter/low resistance wire. These pickups' coils are linked in series.

Most Famous Gibson Pickups

The following are descriptions of the most popular Gibson pickups. For the most part, these pickups are introduced in chronological order. Recently, Gibson created a name line of pickups which are: Laid Back, True Blues, Dirty Fingers, BJ B Jazz, and Super Humbucking.

Gibson 150 Pickup

This pickup is used on the ES-150 and the EH-150. This magnetic pickup was one of the first avidly sought after pickups and it's still in favor today. It's a single coil unit with an iron core which butts against two long bar magnets. The magnets are held in place by three screws in the top of a guitar and there is a notch in the pole piece so the plain B string isn't too loud. This pickup senses a narrow portion of the strings and produces a clear, clean sound favored by many jazz guitarists. Because of the scarcity of this pickup, some people made copies of it. This demand has become so great that Gibson has reissued it.

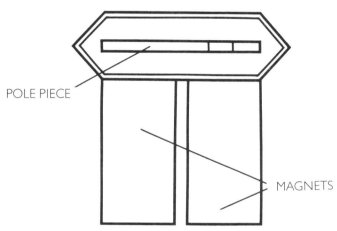

Fig. 69 Diagram of ES 150 pickup.

Fig. 70 ES 150 replica made by Duncan (empty bobbin without magnets).

Laid Back

This design is one of the first ones to be mass produced. It has been around since 1937 and it's sometimes called the "Dog Ear" or "Soap bar". This pickup uses two bar magnets under a coil wound around a clear bobbin. The magnets under the coil have like poles facing each other. The use of conductive

screws between the magnet's poles overcome the inherent repulsion of the like poles. These screws become one magnetic pole and serve to act as pole pieces. This non-humbucking pickup usually has a black or cream colored plastic cover. It was used on many instruments, including the first Les Paul guitars in 1952. Nowadays not that many people care for these non-humbucking Gibson pickups. At one time they were very popular for rhythm and blues as well as rock 'n' roll. Their popularity has since waned because they are non-humbucking and their output isn't especially high. This isn't to say that no one likes them now, because there are a substantial number of musicians that do like the sound. It's fuller than a Fender single coil pickup sound, but it's clearer than a humbucker. It has a clean sound that still packs a beefy punch. It's a versatile sound and it can be mellow, or piercing. The fact that it isn't a humbucker causes recurring noise problems for some musicians. Gibson offers this pickup on the Les Paul Pro deluxe.

The Laid Back has an induction of 7.5 henries which is very high for a single coil pickup. This is one reason the output of this pickup nearly equals that of a humbucker. The d.c. resistance is 8.3K ohms and the resonant peak is 4.78K Hz. Note how low the resonant peak is. This gives the pickup a very full sound.

Fig. 71 Laid back pickups on a Paul.

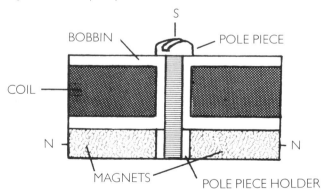

Fig. 72 Diagram of soap bar construction.

P.A.F. – The Gibson Patent-Applied-For Humbucker

The Gibson P.A.F. is the most sought after electric guitar pickup. These pickups have been sold for several hundred dollars. Many people speak of these pickups with a great deal of enthusiasm for their tone. The general feeling is that P.A.F. pickups have a good deal of power **with** clarity. The sound is capable of sustain without breaking up and the sound quality is unique in that other pickups do not possess it. The P.A.F. style pickup is still made, but the materials and manufacturing methods have changed. Some of these changes have been imposed on Gibson by suppliers, while some have been the result of Gibson's efforts to create a pickup that is consistent in quality materials and tone. The question of "Why can't they make them like they used to?", is a bit of a cliché. Yes, current standard large Gibson humbuckers don't sound exactly like an old P.A.F. but despite this fact, many players do enjoy the new ones. Are the "vintage" P.A.F. pickups worth several hundred dollars? Is it snob appeal or a decisively different tone? The answer seems to be a combination of these elements. The price of these pickups is quite high because the open market has allowed persons with money to drive up the price of these pickups. The high prices are due to the limited supply and this has led to counterfeiting of these pickups. P.A.F. pickups are the standard humbucking pickups Gibson made from 1955 to the early sixties. The initials P.A.F. stand for Patent-Applied-For. These pickups were made **after** Gibson received a patent filing number from the U.S. Department of Patents but **before** Gibson received the actual granting of a patent registration. During this interim period a manufacturer uses the term "Patent-Applied-For" or Pat. Pend. (for Patent Pending) on their work to protect the design while the wheels of the Patent Office slowly turn. In Gibson's case, the official granting of a patent number didn't occur until the late-fifties. The total number of P.A.F. pickups that exist is unknown. Some turn up every now and then, here and there. Just what qualifies a pickup to be considered a genuine P.A.F. Gibson is possibly open to question. An examination of a known P.A.F. will disclose the following features:

1. The four screws that mount the coils to the base plate are nickel plated, whereas later models have brass screws.[6]

2. There is a small square hole molded into one end of each bobbin, whereas later models have a round hole.

3. There is a small decal on the bottom of the pickup that says "Patent-Applied-For" whereas later models say "Patent Number 2,737,842".

Contrary to popular opinion, the color of the bobbins is not an indication that a pickup is a P.A.F. The first P.A.F. pickups had black colored bobbins, but then the supply of the black dye was interrupted so Gibson then started using cream colored ones. But this was done in a typical way; the new cream bobbins were dumped in with the supply of black bobbins that was running out. When bobbins were needed, workers reached for any two bobbins which resulted in a number of pickups with one black bobbin and one cream bobbin. This was not thought of as wrong because a cover was to be soldered over the bobbins. At that time almost no one was removing covers from pickups, that is quite different from today when almost everyone uses their P.A.F. with the cover off. Eventually, pickups with two cream colored bobbins became the norms after the supply of black bobbins

was exhausted. But there was a resumption of black bobbins when black dye became available. Therefore, the same mixed condition again resulted. The color story of P.A.F. bobbins can be summed up in the following manner: The original (first year) P.A.F. pickups were all black. Then cream colored bobbins were introduced. P.A.F.'s with two cream colored bobbins are presently more rare so they command the highest prices. The years 1958 through 1960 produced the most cream colored bobbins. Gibson returned to black bobbins after 1960 but cream bobbins have still been known to occur as late as 1965. The Gibson P.A.F. humbucker is now sold as the Gibson "Original Humbucking" pickup.

Fig. 73 Gibson Original Humbucker.

One point needs clarification: Not all P.A.F's are highly respected; in fact, only a portion of all P.A.F's are considered great sounding by guitar experts because these pickups were inconsistently made. A confusing fact is that a P.A.F. may sound good on one guitar but bad on another.[7]

Small Humbucker (aka Baby Humbucker)

This is a junior sized version of Gibson's standard (large) humbucker. The pickup may look like the larger model but the inside and performance are different than the larger model. The most important feature is that the induction and d.c. resistance is lower than that of the larger humbucker, and it also gives a greater amount of trebles and clarity. This is due to several factors; the most fundamental is the lower d.c. resistance. This resistance ranges from 6K to 6.5K ohms on various specimens whereas the larger pickups vary from 7.8K to 8.5K. The sacrifice for the increase in trebles and clarity in the Jr. model is a lower output. This pickup would be a good rhythm position mate for a Tele lead because of the output match. Most humbuckers have a high output and are out-of-balance used with the lower output single coil pickups like the Tele lead. If you are considering hot-rodding this pickup, respect this word of caution: This is a delicate pickup so use a very gentle touch when taking it apart. If you are interested in hot-rodding it, here are a couple of ideas: First, put a solid soft-iron pole piece in each slot of the bobbin and substitute a ceramic

6. SEE PAGE 125

7. SEE PAGE 125

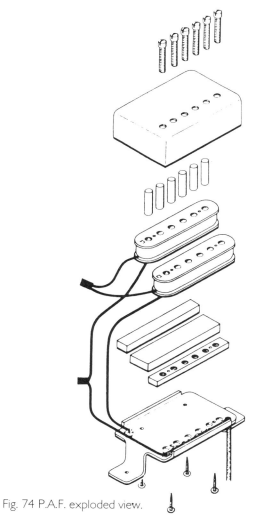

Fig. 74 P.A.F. exploded view.

Fig. 75 Iron filings showing the flux field of a humbucking pickup, side view.

magnet for the alnico one and then add four conductor shielded wiring (4+); second, stack the coils and insert a reground and remagnetized magnet into the slots and then wire as a tapped single coil pickup and insert in a Tele rhythm pickup case – it works!

Firebird

This is a powerful pickup designed for use on some Firebird models. Each coil contains its own magnet and because the magnets aren't threadable, there are no adjustable pole pieces. This pickup is powerful and

Fig. 76 Flux patterns, top view.

Fig. 77 Mini Humbucker.

clear but the clarity isn't noticed until you really crank up an amp. When played loudly it has a decidedly cleaner sound than most other pickups.

Les Paul Recording

This is a stacked double coil humbucking pickup. The strikingly clear sound of these low impedance pickups limits their popularity because it isn't a versatile sound. It's only clear and clean and it can't be driven into being fat and dirty. Also, the clear sound gives away clumsy fingering. For these reasons, they aren't popular. This is the pickup for the topnotch guitarist who wants to show his skills.

Series linking of multiple coils results in a higher impedance than parallel linking. The Les Paul Recording instruments follow the normal Gibson practice of series linking the coils of a humbucker. Les Paul Recording instruments are low impedance because they use low impedance pickups, not parallel wiring.

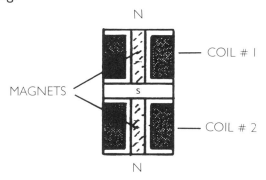

Fig. 78 Les Paul Recording pickup.

MAGNETIC PICKUPS

Johnny Smith

This pickup uses coils like those in the mini humbucker on Les Paul deluxe guitars. In a basic Johnny Smith model, the alnico 2 bar magnet is in one of the coils. The base for the pickup is a piece of soft-iron or 18% nickel steel and serves as a flux path to the pole pieces. These pole pieces extend through the other coil and screw in the base plate. This construction results in a very dimensionally thin pickup.

S-1

The individual S-1 pickup is a single coil non-humbucking pickup that uses a single bar magnet inside the center of the coil. There are no adjustable pole pieces.

The S-1 guitar has one of the most advanced pickup selections possible for electric guitars, the switching was designed by Bill Lawrence. The three single coil pickups are arranged so that there are a possibility of nine pickup combinations. Because nine selections would be too confusing to most people, Gibson has settled on four rotary selections plus an additional mode. The selections available now are:
1. Pickup #1
2. Pickups #2 & 3
3. Pickups #1 & 2 & 3 as a humbucker
4. Pickups #1 & 3 as an out-of-phase humbucker
Plus
5. Pickup #3
Older S-1 guitars offered
1. Pickups #1 & 2 Humbucking
2. Pickups #2 & 3 Humbucking
3. Pickups #1 & 2 & 3 Humbucking
4. Pickups #1 & 3 as an out-of-phase humbucker
Plus
5. Pickup #3

The reason the S-1 can get so many combinations is that the magnet to pickup #2 is of an opposite polarity to #1 and #3. This allows many humbucking possibilities, including the very rare creation of an out-of-phase humbucker. These combinations are achieved through the use of a four position rotary and a two position toggle switch.

Super Humbuckers

This fairly new pickup uses three ceramic magnets under two coils. Solid iron cores extend through the cores and butt against the magnets and there are no adjustable pole pieces. The whole unit is encapsulated in resin. Some of these pickups have multiple leads so creative switching can be facilitated.

Gibson originally used the words "Super Humbucker" to distinguish any potted Gibson pickups that use ceramic magnets (numbers 5 & 7). Today, there are Super Humbuckers that use only #5 (indox) ceramic magnets. It isn't possible to tell if a pickup is a Super Humbucker by looking at the top outside portion. However, if the pickup is removed from a guitar, you can look to see if the pickup is filled with resin. Super Humbuckers are potted in resin. Several guitars use Super Humbuckers, the S.G., L-6S deluxe, the ES-335 (and ES 325 with mini Super Humbuckers),

the EB3 (front), EB-0, and L-6S basses.

Fig. 79 Super Humbucker.

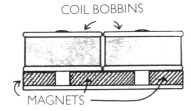

Fig. 80 Diagram of Super Humbucker construction.

Dirty Fingers

Gibson's Dirty Fingers pickup has dual exposed black coil forms, twelve gold plated screw type pole pieces, and copper grounding tape around the coils. This pickup has an inductance of 8.6 henries, d.c. resistance of 16K ohms, and a resonant peak at 6K Hz.

Fig. 81 Dirty Fingers.

True Blues

Gibson's True Blues is a low inductance Super Humbucker that uses three Indox VII ceramic magnets. It doesn't have adjustable pole pieces. The inductance of this pickup is 3.2 henries, d.c. resistance is 6K ohms, and the resonant peak is 9K Hz. Compare this to the Dirty Fingers. As the inductance goes down, the resonant peak goes up. These combined actions result in a pickup with a good deal of clear, high-end response.

Fig. 82 True Blues.

Boomerang

This humbucking pickup was created for use on Gibson's Flying V re-creation #II. The pickup consists of two coils with each coil sensing three strings. This split design gives the pickup a relatively narrow magnetic window which results in a cleaner sound than a normal parallel coil humbucker.

Each coil in this pickup uses an Indox VIII bar magnet with an iron plate on the bottom to reflect the magnetic field. These plates function much like the plate on a Telecaster lead pickup.

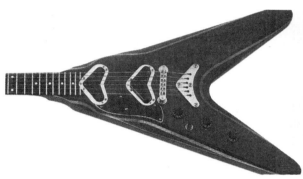

Fig. 83 Boomerang pickups.

G.R.D.

G.R.D. was founded by Charles Fox. The company makes instruments that are a bit unusual. They were one of the first to put a graphic equalizer in a guitar. Their equalizer is based on an MXR unit. The use of these devices in instruments has been very limited because all commonly available units small enough to fit into a guitar have a weak signal-to-noise ratio.

Fig. 84 G.R.D. guitar with built-in equalizers.

GRETSCH

Gretsch, an old company, entered the electric guitar business in a big way when the company joined forces with Chet Atkins. Chet was and still is, quite possibly the best guitar player in the world. Gretsch welcomed all of Chet's questions and ideas. Chet worked with Gretsch's Ray Butts to develop the Gretsch Filtertron pickup. This pickup resembles two single coil pickups joined together. There are two coils that each have six magnet slugs. The Gretsch Supertron I has a conductive bar pole piece in each of the two coils and there is a magnet under the coils. The bar pole-pieces are made of laminated iron cores to aid magnetic flux paths by reducing eddy currents and therefore giving an edge to the sound. The Supertron II has one-piece iron bar-shaped pole pieces and it has a more mellow tone than the Supertron I. All of these aforementioned pickups are humbuckers and were designed to produce a tone desired in country music.

In 1980 Gretsch came out with new solid body electrics suited for rock and country music. They use pickups designed by Bill Lawrence. They are special attenuated magnetic flux devices that produce a sparkling clear tone and a lot of volume.

Supertron I

This humbucking pickup uses laminated steel cores to provide a clearer sound. These special cores offer reduced magnetic eddy currents which contributes to clarity. The d.c. resistance is about 8K.

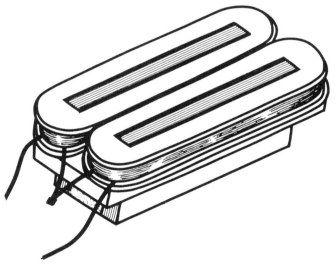

Fig. 85 Gretsch Supertron I.

GUILD

Standard Large Humbucker

This pickup is a real workhorse in that it does a lot and it doesn't cost as much as many others. Its design is similar to a Gibson standard humbucker. This Guild pickup has a d.c. resistance of about 8.5K ohms.

BILL LAWRENCE

Bill has been working with electric guitars for a long time and has worked with or for Dan Armstrong, Framus and Gibson. Up until 1972, he operated Bill's Guitar Shop in Greenwich Village, New York and in

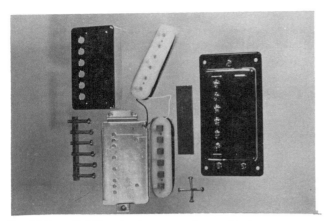

Fig. 86 Two Guild humbuckers, one disassembled.

Fig. 87 Bottom of Guild humbucker.

May of 1972 he started working for Gibson and helped design the Gibson Super Humbucker. He designed guitars for Framus and assisted Dan Armstrong in creating electric guitars for Ampeg. In 1975, he founded Lawrence Sound Research in Tennessee.

The following information concerning the history and design criteria of electric guitar circuits is based on personal discussion with Bill Lawrence.

High impedance amps were the first kind made in Germany, but it wasn't long until engineers saw the benefits of low impedance and by 1940 high impedance had lost a great deal of its popularity. In 1948 Bill was designing low impedance pickups with a d.c. resistance of 500 to 1500 ohms. One pickup he made was a dual coil humbucker, each coil was wound with 600 turns of 40 gauge wire. These coils sat on a three part U-shaped configuration of .60 inch wide alnico magnets. This was one of the world's first humbucking pickups.

It was at this time, 1958, that high impedance Fender amps were introduced in Europe and their popularity caused European guitar designers to switch back to high impedance. High impedance amps have remained popular since that time.

The sound of a pickup is dependent on inductance. A pickup with a high degree of inductance and low amount of magnetic flux will produce a mellow bass heavy tone. A pickup with low inductance and a high magnetic flux will produce a treble heavy sound.

It's **inductance**, not **d.c. resistance** which impedes highs, but since most conventional pickups use an iron load in a coil there is a strong parallel between resistance and inductance with most pickups. If a coil does not have an iron load, it's referred to as an **air coil**. An air coil has an inductance much lower than a coil with an iron or magnetic load. If you use air coils, you could make a pickup with 8K ohms d.c. resistance, but only 8.2K ohms impedance. A case in point is the Lawrence AT-170; its d.c. resistance is 14,000 ohms, but it's a mid, not high, impedance pickup. The problem of resonant peaks being in the audible range of mid-impedance pickups' output is not a problem for pickups using air coils because the resonance peak of air coils is very, very high; often it's in the upper reaches of human hearing.

The use of iron core loads in a coil can boost output, but it results in a "dirty sound" with a loss of trebles. If a conductive core in a coil is needed, a better choice is Supermalloy made by Allegheny. This material will give a cleaner sound because it "cooperates" the best with a flux field, but it isn't suitable for use as a magnet material because it doesn't retain a magnetic charge. It's this lack of retention that has it react quickly and cleanly to flux change.

As for what material to use for magnets, no material can attain a higher gauss than alnico 5 which reaches a gauss of 12,500, alnico 8 is limited to 8,000, and ceramic only reaches 4,000. What then, are the advantages of using ceramic magnets? Ceramic magnets are twice as resistant to de-magnetizing than alnico 5 making it suitable for use in like-poles-together placements because it retains its power, alnico 5 can't. Alnico 8 is somewhat between the two. Although ceramic is capable of great oerstads, its flux density is very low and Bill feels he gets all the oerstads he needs from alnico.

As for making a pickup hotter, an increase in magnetic force could do this. The exact configuration of magnets has a significant influence in this regard. Bar magnets in pickups are more efficient in creating a hotter pickup than cylindrical slugs. The sound of strings vibrating over blade type pole pieces is cleaner than the sound of strings vibrating over cylindrical magnet slugs. One problem with bar/blade pole-piece pickups is the difficulty in achieving an even volume for each string. Often the B string appears too loud because the high E is too weak.

As the Lawrence brochure says about the FT145:

A medium impedance extended range pickup for the steel string flat-top guitar (6 and 12 string) matches most high or low impedance amplifiers. Two coaxial synchron wound humbucking air coils with a high flux alnico-8 magnet in the center translate every vibration of the strings into an audio signal. You can get brilliant highs, mellow midrange, clean responsive bass . . .

The use of synchron winding helps to produce balanced outputs and this together with shielding results in quiet noise factors. The use of air coils, which are wire coils without an iron or magnet load in the center of them, results in a lowering of impedance and this allows trebles to be passed easier. However, it also results in lower induction and output.

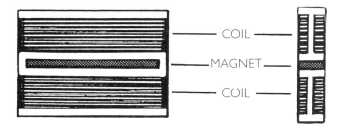

Fig. 88 Lawrence air coil pickup.

Fig. 89 Synchron wound bobbins.

Fig. 90 Lawrence pickup cases with copper foil shielding.

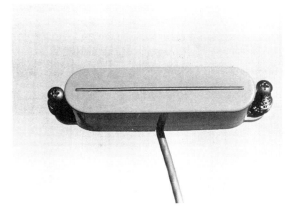

Fig. 91 The L-250, an attenuated flux version of the L-220.

L220

This is a humbucking pickup which at first glance looks just like a Strat pickup with a bar pole piece instead of six magnet slugs. The single bar, or blade, is connected to two alnico 8 magnets. The use of a blade

means there will not be a decrease of volume when bending strings. It's quite an achievement to make a humbucker that fits in the same size place as a non-humbucker.

L-500 LTS

This open coil humbucker has reduced flux strength and uses twin blade pole pieces. The base is molded plastic with conductive shielding.

These attenuated flux fields were developed after Bill studied graphs showing the gauss and oerstad figures of alnico and ceramic magnets. He came to the conclusion that nearly everyone was using the wrong material for magnets. He uses alnico in his new pickups, but not high gauss 5 or 8 because the high gauss magnets would pull the strings and interfere with their vibration. These pickups have outstanding volume and treble – a combination that is difficult to achieve.

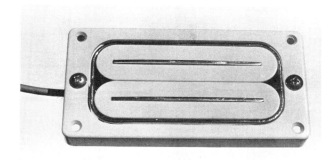

Fig. 92 L-500 LTS low flux pickup.

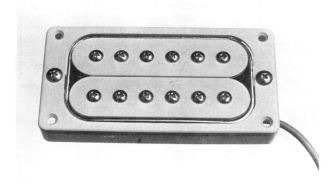

Fig. 93 L-350 LTS low flux pickup.

MIGHTY MITE

Mighty Mite offers a line of many types of pickups with both standard and radical creations. There are: Vintage pickups which endeavor to recreate the sounds of prized old Strats (the 1110 Vintage) and Les Pauls (the 1400 Vintage, a P.A.F. replica); powerful distortion pickups like the 1100 Distortion for Strats, the 1300 Distortion Humbucker for all guitars that can accept a humbucker; conventional pickups for Precision and Jazz type basses; and radical pickups like the 1900 Motherbucker and 1800 Super Stud.

MAGNETIC PICKUPS

The 1900 Motherbucker model pickup is a very versatile three coil pickup. The third coil serves a very useful purpose because almost a dozen different sounds can be achieved from one pickup. The reason for all these sounds is because of its unique construction. Although this three coil pickup is manufactured as one unit, it can be made to operate like three independent single coil pickups. The center coil has an opposite magnetic polarity from the coils on either side, and this gives a potential to achieve every possible basic phasing relations. In fact, this configuration can achieve every possible basic phasing relationship possible with a pickup. One of these wiring configurations could consist of out-of-phase coils functioning in a humbucking mode. To achieve out-of-phase/ humbucking, two coils need to have the same magnetic polarity. Since dual coil humbucking pickups have coils of opposite magnetic polarity, you cannot create an out-of-phase condition and retain the humbucking mode as you can with the 1900. If you want to get all the switching possibilities out of this pickup, it is suggested that you look at Bill Lawrence's S-1 switching system in the Gibson schematic section.

Another interesting pickup that Mighty Mite makes is the Super Stud 1800. It appears very ordinary at first glance, but closer examination will reveal a unique feature. The pole pieces in both coils of this humbucker are solid as compared to threaded screws in most humbuckers. There are some advantages and disadvantages to this design. The string-to-string volume is not adjustable, but this is a small handicap because very light gauge strings do not strictly require this provision. One advantage is that the solid slugs are more efficient in directing magnetic flux which results in a pickup with more power and delicate sensitivity.

Other Mighty Mite offerings include: A pre-wired Strat-type assembly with a phase switch for each pickup and the S-80 and S-90 active electronics circuits. The S-80 booster is capable of a 20 dB increase in gain and there is a trim pot for adjusting the amount of gain desired. The jack has a built-in ON/OFF circuit to be linked to a battery. The S-90 (made for a Strat) comes wired on a brass grounding plate. It has a pickup selector switch and three pots. The first pot is volume, the second pot is treble boost, and the third pot is bass boost. The electronic circuit could be adapted to virtually all electric guitars. It could be very useful inside an acoustic guitar that has a piezo pickup; provided that the PC board and pots are shielded.

OVERLAND EMG

Overland points out that it's very easy to get lost in a sea of technical considerations but the real challenge is not electronics technology, but rather to give the musician what he wants.

Overland makes single coil and humbucking (dual coil) electromagnetic pickups called EMG-S and EMG-H. Because EMG are distinctive initials, the Overland pickup system is often referred to as the EMG system.

These pickups are low impedance units with an op amp preamp built into the pickups. These op amps help to prevent cabling losses and boost the weak initial signal to a high level. The output is greater than 3 volts peak to peak. The voltage gate input of a tube amp can handle about 10 volts, whereas a solid state amp can accept about 7 volts. Remember, too great a boost can fry an amp.

The dual coils of the Overland humbucker are wired in parallel and this results in a low resistance/ impedance figure; it also reduces distortion, passes the trebles, and generally gives a very clear sound. Some people think a clear sound is a "thin" sound, but it doesn't have to be; you can get a clear, full sound because the fullness of a pickup's tone is dependent on the length of the string sensed by a pickup. The Overland EMG-H has a wide magnetic window which senses a fairly wide area so it gives a clear and full tone, whereas a narrow magnetic window pickup, e.g., Les Paul Recording pickup, gives a clear thin tone.

PEAVEY

Peavey pickups are fully potted and shielded. They use bar type ferrite magnets and feature non-adjustable pole pieces. The unique part of these pickups is the mounting which is accomplished through the use of four pickup height screws passing through the pickguard. These four screws provide a very secure mounting and tilt system. Two screw systems allow a pickup to flip-flop around, three screws are better, but four screws are clearly the best.

The tone control is a patented Peavey device although several companies are now using this type of system. When the pot is turned in one direction, the tone capacitor is connected to ground via the pot's wiper. The resultant sound is that of a humbucking pickup with its trebles bled to ground and the tone is bassy. When the tone pot is turned in the other direction, less of the trebles are allowed to be bled away. As the control is turned further, the center tap to the coil junction of the humbucker is gradually brought into contact with the ground connected wiper of the pot. This action grounds out (silences) one of the coils of the humbucking pickup, and this results in a very bright single coil sound. This Peavey control allows

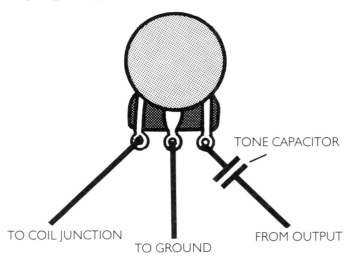

TONE CAPACITOR

TO COIL JUNCTION   TO GROUND   FROM OUTPUT

Fig. 94 Peavey rotary splitter.

for a gradual change from a humbucking sound to a single coil sound. To accomplish this smoothly, a pot with a special resistance taper is needed, and Peavey is the only company that has this special pot. A normal audio taper pot does not provide a super-smooth tonal transition.

ROWE

Rowe was one of the first builders of electro-magnetic pickups and their RHC-B was the standard pickup to put on acoustic guitars. One drawback is that it isn't humbucking, and sometimes is very difficult to mount and remove. On the plus side, however, it's relatively inexpensive, it has a built-in volume knob (a big plus), and it's nearly indestructible. It's very much like a Fender single coil pickup in that it has six alnico magnets surrounded by a single coil. The d.c. resistance is 9,000 ohms which is very high for a single coil pickup and this helps explain the pickup's high output. Rowe makes a multitude of pickups; among the most unique are both single coil and humbuckers with adjustable pole pieces.

Fig. 97 Rowe humbucker for acoustic guitars.

Fig. 95 Rowe RHC-B.

Fig. 96 Rowe pickup with threads bonded to magnets.

Rowe pickups tend to be classically conservative in design and the emphasis is often on refining a design rather than new innovations or sounds. For this reason, Rowe pickups are more dependable than flamboyant. However, some early Rowe designs were rather eccentric like the pickups used on the Martin D28-E. These pickups have screws which raised and lowered grippers attached to the cylindrical magnet slugs. See the book **The Electric Guitar** for photos of this pickup.

SCHECTER

Schecter Guitar Research is a young company which was founded by David Schecter in 1976. David has had extensive experience repairing and customizing Fender guitars and became very knowledgeable about pickup construction. He has worked with and refined tapped pickup design. Tapped pickups have two coil windings in a continuous series. The first, or inside winding, reproduces the original Fender sound, whereas the second winding in combination with the first, creates a new sound. The second sound is characterized by higher volume, more bass, and increased sustain.

Schecter makes tapped pickups for Teles, Strats, Precision and Jazz basses, and many others. Schecter also builds several types of humbucking pickups; the most unique being the Z+ and Superock humbuckers. Details regarding construction are not possible because the manufacturer retains confidentiality.

Schecter Z+ is a design that makes a humbucking pickup that has a clear treble sound. Due to the unexpected behavior of the new resin that Schecter used on their first Z+ pickups, many of these pickups have stopped working. When this malfunction was discovered, production stopped. The new Z+ pickups are now dependable and still retain the old Z+ sound.

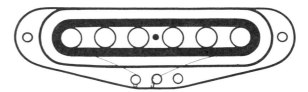
Fig. 98 First winding of a tapped pickup.

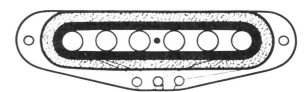
Fig. 99 Both windings of a tapped pickup.

Another Schecter innovation is their Omni Pot which is a combination potentiometer and switch. When the knob of the pot is twisted it acts as a

MAGNETIC PICKUPS

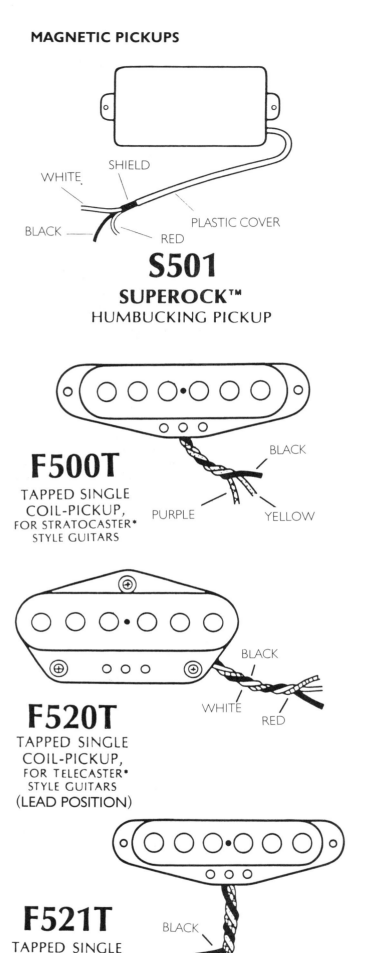

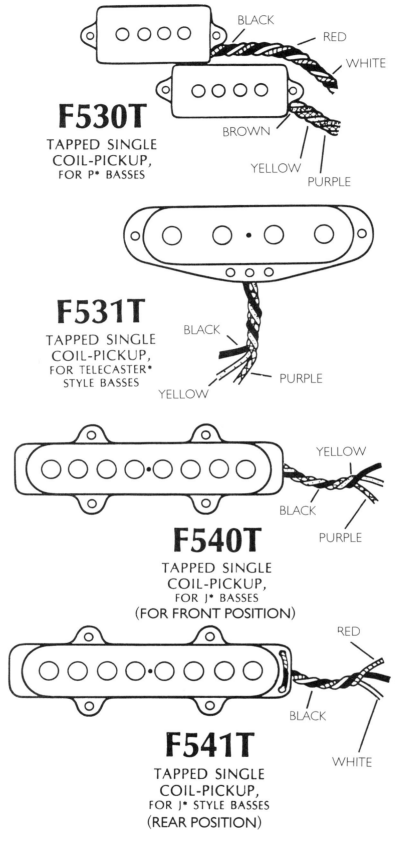

S501
SUPEROCK™
HUMBUCKING PICKUP

F500T
TAPPED SINGLE
COIL-PICKUP,
FOR STRATOCASTER*
STYLE GUITARS

F520T
TAPPED SINGLE
COIL-PICKUP,
FOR TELECASTER*
STYLE GUITARS
(LEAD POSITION)

F521T
TAPPED SINGLE
COIL-PICKUP,
FOR TELECASTER*
STYLE GUITARS
(FOR RHYTHM POSITION)

F530T
TAPPED SINGLE
COIL-PICKUP,
FOR P* BASSES

F531T
TAPPED SINGLE
COIL-PICKUP,
FOR TELECASTER*
STYLE BASSES

F540T
TAPPED SINGLE
COIL-PICKUP,
FOR J* BASSES
(FOR FRONT POSITION)

F541T
TAPPED SINGLE
COIL-PICKUP,
FOR J* STYLE BASSES
(REAR POSITION)

Fig. 100 Schecter tapped pickups (Asterisks in copy denote words that are trademarked by CBS).

Fig. 101 Schecter Z+ pickups and harness.

potentiometer and changes the volume; but when the knob is pulled out or pushed in, it acts as a switch and alters internal connections. The switch-potentiometer functions are totally independent of each other.

Schecter also makes an extensive line of guitar hardware as well as guitar bodies made from rare exotic woods.

SHADOW

The Shadow company of West Germany makes some fairly unique pickup systems and their acoustic electric model has some interesting features.

1000

This single coil pickup (which fits in a soundhole) has one very welcome feature, an output jack on the pickup which means you don't have to have an umbilical cord running out of a guitar when it's not being played. This feature was pioneered by a Micro-Frets pickup designed by Bill Lawrence.

44

This soundhole mount pickup is a humbucker with volume and tone controls. The rotating wheels on either end of the pickup connect to trimmer pots which are so small they fit inside the knobs. This is the only pickup like this in the world (to the author's knowledge).

System 360

This is the top of the line of Shadow's "Double Play" systems. The 360 uses a contact pickup and a magnetic pickup; because both function independently, they act as a stereo unit and can produce a wide range of tones. The magnetic pickup could be used to produce a full, deep bass and the contact pickup could give high trebles.

The 1979 Shadow pickups are not as fully shielded as pickups made by other companies. Some of their pickups which look like humbuckers are not, and they have a poor signal-to-noise figure. Also, the cabling is

very light duty, and if you look through the transparent orange cover of the cabling, you can see the braid gives only partial shielding.

SHERGOLD

Shergold has developed an electric guitar feature which appears logical, but it is rarely seen; that feature is modules. These modules contain the controls (electronics) of an instrument.

Module one has a single volume and tone control plus a pickup selector switch; module two has a single volume and tone control plus a pickup selector and a phase switch; module three has a volume and tone control for each pickup plus a pickup selector and a control by-pass switch; module four has stereo volume and tone controls for each pickup plus a pickup selector and by-pass switch; module five has a volume and tone control for each pickup plus a pickup selector, a phasing switch, and a coil splitting switch.

Fig. 102 Shergold modules.

STARS

Stars does not make musical instruments, but rather they specialize in making accessories for instruments made by other companies such as Gibson and Fender.

Ron Armstrong of Stars helped me in my writing of **The Electric Guitar** and here he is helping me again. The following material is based on a discussion with him.

The criteria used for judging electric guitars can be divided into the areas of magnets, coils and shielding.
Magnets

1. What type of magnets are used? Ceramic magnets have a sound similar to their structure – brittle. The trebles are much fuller than the bass. Alnico magnet pickups have more distortion and they also have an after ring that follows a note. Some people like this, some don't.

2. What is the strength of a magnet? Is the magnet old and weak, or is it new and strong?

3. What portion of a string does a magnet sense? The quality of a pickup's sound is influenced by the pickup's string sensing width, sometimes this width is called a magnetic window.

4. What is the flux transfer unit of the magnet(s)? Flux transfer is a factor in magnetic efficiency.
Coils

1. What is the tension of the coils? Tension can make a phenomenal difference in the sound of a pickup. A very loose winding gives a funky sound, whereas a tight winding gives a clean sound. Air gaps in

MAGNETIC PICKUPS

the coil somehow increase the output and this may be due to a lessened capacitance treble-shunting effect.

2. What is the gauge of wire used? Finer wire produces a more sensitive pickup.

3. How are the wire turns put on the coil? Coils can be wound to a fixed number of turns or metered to a specific d.c. resistance. Winding to a metered figure can result in a more efficient humbucking effect.

4. Are the coils balanced? A humbucker needs two balanced that are identical in specifications, resistance, etc., to work properly.

5. What is the inductance? The higher the inductance the greater the output, but the greater the loss of trebles.

6. What area of the coil is in the magnetic field? A wider area gives a fuller sound.

The following information is in reference to winding, resonant peaks, and shielding.

1. Winding: The most uniformly constructed pickups are precision wound on winding machines which eliminates human variables such as hand guided winding. New winders used by some guitar companies have the parameters mechanically set. Every three or four turns the winder fuses the windings together by spraying alcohol on the poly-bond coated wire and this results in less wire stretch.

2. Resonant Peaks: Each pickup has its own resonant peak (feedback note) which should be ultrasonic or subsonic. This peak results from the interaction of all the elements in a pickup and is influenced by henries (inductance of a coil). Generally, a high impedance coil has a near subsonic peak and a low impedance pickup is made to have an ultrasonic peak. Mid-impedance pickups have a problem in this area because their peak is often in the center of human hearing sensitivity.

3. Shielding Hints: Over two inches of wire in a single place allows audible hum to enter a circuit; therefore, shielded wire is necessary. Stars recommends using Beldon RG-174 Shielded wire because it's strong, but flexible. Shielded pots can be used, but it's often easier to paint the cavity of a solid-body with conductive paint and attach a ground wire to the paint. However, painting the inside of a vintage instrument could decrease its value.

At large mega-watt concerts the shock problem is potentially lethal when using conventional grounding techniques, and therefore people are hired to check polarity and grounds before a show.

STRING VISION

The String Vision pickup is designed for acoustic round hole guitars. It mounts quickly, easily and has a handy built-in jack so you don't have to worry about tripping on a dangling cord when the guitar isn't being played. The unique feature of this pickup is its construction and resultant mode of operation. Basically, the pickup is a non-loaded coil. The String Vision wand is used as a magnetizer. The first production run of these pickups had clear tone and fully adjustable string-to-string balance, but the low

Strings are magnetized by slowly moving the magnetic wand in a straight line across the strings at a height of 1/4".

Once magnetized you move the magnetic wand down the fret board simultaneously snapping the string. The further from the pickup the weaker the signal becomes. When the sound you're seeking has been attained simply lift the wand straight up.

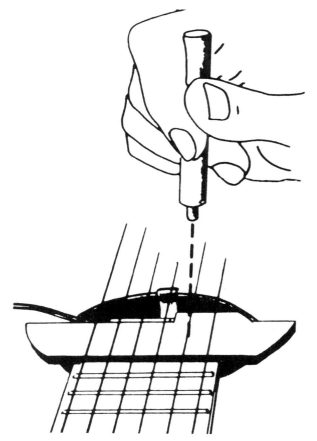

Fig. 103 Operation of String Vision pickup.

output was a handicap. New models have more output, but a preamp would help. This is not bad because a great many pickups could use the boost of a preamp. Many people misjudge this pickup by putting it on a guitar with bronze strings. This pickup needs standard electric guitar strings for full output.

VELVET HAMMER

These pickups and controls were designed by Red Rhodes. The basic pickups are simple single coil and humbucking pickups. However, Velvet Hammer has offered some rather unusual devices, two of which are listed below.

The "Stereo" Pickup

This pickup featured six individually wound coils with adjustable pole pieces for each string. The "Stereo" was pre-wired for even-odd string outputs (i.e., strings 1-3-5 go to one output, and strings 2-4-6 go to the other output).

Fig. 104 Velvet Hammer stereo pickup.

"Do-It-All" Humbucker Kit

This kit came equipped with two sub-miniature DPDT switches and two push-pull pots to replace existing volume controls. When installed along with two humbuckers the following effects are: (1) series parallel switching, (2) phasing, (3) humbucking splitting, (4) flip flopping from one coil of a humbucker to the other coil.

ELECTRIC BASS GUITARS

Electric basses have pickups and tone circuits that operate just like the components in electric guitars. The construction of the actual components for basses are different because most bass players like a cleaner, punchier sound than they would get if guitar pickups were installed in a bass. Another reason bass pickups are different from guitar pickups is that since basses commonly have four strings, a guitar pickup with six pole pieces would not give an even volume response on a bass. Guitar pickups, like the Firebird, X2 N, and Supertron could be put on a bass, but as mentioned earlier, most bass players wouldn't care for the tone.

The most popular bass pickups are those that sense only a narrow length of a string and therefore, produce a cleaner, more distinct sound. The first electric bass, the Fender Precision Bass, had a narrow width sensing single coil pickup with four alnico magnet slugs. A few years later, Fender brought out a new P-Bass pickup which is also a narrow sensing unit. It is split into two parts, each containing a single coil with four alnico slugs. (Two magnets sense each string, therefore there is no volume drop when the strings are bent.) The two pickup halves are linked as a series humbucker. The old

P-Bass style pickups are still available today and come on the Fender Telecaster Basses.

Fender's Jazz bass uses two single coil pickups that always function as single coil units. This means that the pickups do not ever function in a humbucking mode because they do not have opposite magnetic polarities. Each of the pickups has a single coil with double alnico cylindrical magnet slugs. The d.c. resistance is the same for both pickups, but the bridge pickup is wider so the magnets line up with the playing strings.

Rickenbacker's 4001 solid-body bass is another very popular bass, and it too has a narrow sensing pickup.

ALEMBIC BASS

The Alembic bass uses an interesting type of pickup. It's a humbucker with three coils, but it only uses one coil as a string sensor. The middle pickup is only a coil without a magnet and is linked to either the bridge or fretboard pickup (which are coils around ceramic magnets so either combination can be humbucking. When this pickup arrangement is used, the pickups can be humbucking but still be narrow sensing. The pickup produces a single coil sound that is very quiet and free

Fig. 105 Alembic bass.

Fig. 106 One side of Alembic PC board.

from hum. One other feature of these pickups is that they are low impedance. These low impedance devices

MAGNETIC PICKUPS

have sophisticated and respected solid state active tone and volume controls.

One slight disadvantage in the circuitry of Alembic instruments is the amount of power needed for the on-board electronics. Alembic achieves such an amazingly fine sound by using circuitry that consumes a fair amount of current. A disadvantage is that this puts a great strain (and drain) on portable power (batteries). For this reason it's practical to use an outside power source that uses a transmission cord that plugs into the instrument.

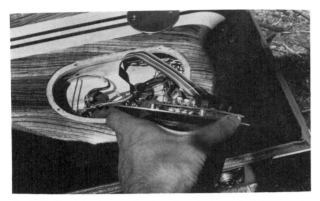

Fig. 107 Alembic electronics showing double sided PC board.

FENDER BASSES

Shown are drawings of Fender style bass pickups. The new model P-Bass is the most popular. Several

Fig. 108 Original P style bass pickup.

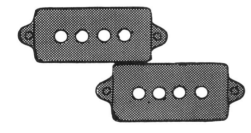

Fig. 109 Later P style bass pickup.

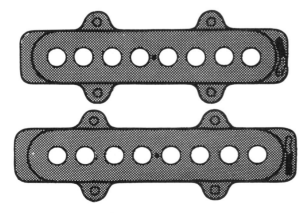

Fig. 110 Jazz style bass pickups.

non-Fender companies are making Precision/Jazz style basses using a P pickup and Jazz bridge pickup. Since this combination is gaining a great deal of popularity, we will likely see more of these in the future.

GUILD

The Guild pickup shown is composed of eight alnico slugs held by two plastic plates. A black plastic cover fits over this single coil pickup. This pickup shows how simple an effective pickup can be.

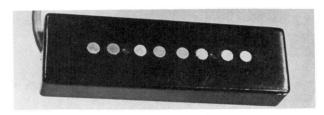

Fig. 111 Guild bass pickup in case.

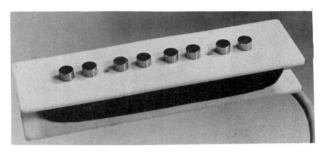

Fig. 112 Guild bass pickup without case.

RICKENBACKER

Rickenbacker non-humbucking single coil bass pickups are famous for their punch and clarity. Some people feel that all older Rickenbacker bass pickups had four cylindrical alnico magnet slugs, and that all new ones have four drive screws (steel rivets) that meet a rubberized bar magnet. However, F.C. Hall, the president of Rickenbacker, states:

"Rickenbacker makes many different types of pickups other than bass pickups. Many of our models use different pickups for each position and each pickup varies from the pickup on another model of guitar. In other words, we design pickups for the type of player we feel would use each of our guitars . . .

"You have asked if the bass pickup on the Model 4001 has changed since it was first made in 1955. The pickup is made exactly the same as it was on the first model in 1955, except we have changed the cover plate which does not affect the sound of the unit . . .

"You have asked us to explain the difference between the pickups on the model 4001 and the Model 4005. As we stated earlier, the main difference

Fig. 113 Rickenbacker bass pickup.

between these pickups is the impedance and the way they are assembled which affects the sound."

The oldest Rickenbacker bass pickups do use the double horseshoe magnet structure that Rickenbacker made famous. Newer bass pickups use a coil bobbin sitting on top of a rubberized magnet. These newer pickups use type U drive screws as pole pieces.

SCHECTER

Schecter makes basses as well as accessories for them. They offer Precision, Jazz, and P/J style instruments. Schecter's bass pickups are available in both standard and tapped modes. The Schecter tapped Precision bass pickup is a split-coil humbucker that is capable of producing two sounds when a tapped selector switch is used. This pickup could produce two additional sounds if a series/parallel selector was added to the circuit; this gives a possibility of four different sounds with one pickup.

The following is from Schecter. It describes the installation of a P/J bass assembly. This assembly gives the sound of both types of basses in one instrument.

Installing Schecter P-J* Tapped Pickup Assemblies

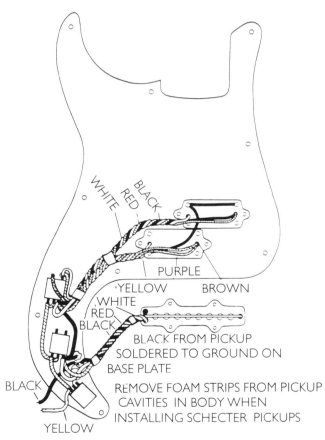

Fig. 114 Schecter bass combo.

The P-J* assembly is a custom unit that is made to fit on a P*-Bass. To install this pickup you will need to route out an area in the body to accept the J* pickup. Shown is a template drawing of the pickup cavity size and shape. The hole to feed the pickup leads through the body is constructed in the following manner. After the pickup cavity is routed,

drill a hole from the cavity to the space already routed for the controls. Use a 1/4 inch drill for this. To be able to drill the angle needed you will need a drill at least 9 inches long. A drill of this size can be bought at most large hardware stores.

This cavity should be as deep as the neck slot in the body. On Fender* instruments this is commonly 5/8 of an inch. If the neck slot is deeper the pickup cavity should be correspondingly deepened, and vice-versa. The reason for this is that the depth of the slot determines how high the neck (and so the strings) will be over the top of the body of the instrument.

Fig. 115 Template shape for a J style bass rear pickup.

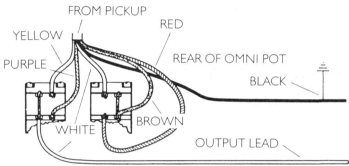

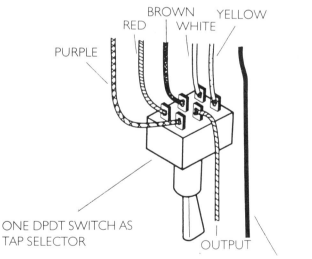

Fig. 116 Tap selectors for P style tapped pickup.

Other Bass Pickups

Many other companies make bass pickups, some highlights are: A fine bass humbucker by DiMarzio as well as a Dual Sound P-pickup; "Vintage" and super hot pickups by Duncan; Quadraphonic bass pickups by Bartolini; and bar pole piece pickups by Lawrence.

Section II

1. Hardware* Components Design and Function

WIRING

You probably know of + (positive) and − (negative) electricity terms and you have probably also heard of electric **grounds**. Electric guitars are really just about as simple as these few terms.

Fig. 25 shows a coil of wire and a magnet, this makes an elementary pickup. The coil is wound from one long piece of wire so naturally it has two ends. One end can be used as a ground and the other would be the live lead, or "hot" wire (it doesn't really get hot, it's just a term for aliveness).

On a pickup, either end of the coil winding could be ground or hot. Generally, however, the wire that comes out of the center, or inside, of the coil can be the hot wire and the end that becomes the last winding on the outside of the coil becomes the ground, but this order can be reversed. If the outside wire is a ground, the general consensus is that this produces a shielding effect.

A pickup company usually gives a clue as to which wire is which by coloring leads attached to a pickup. The common electrical color for a "hot" lead is red, and the common color for a ground lead is black. However, not everyone follows that practice. For example, Fender often uses white or yellow for a hot lead and black or blue for a ground wire; Gibson often uses white for a hot lead and black for a ground wire. Other companies may use any color such as green or purple for a hot or ground lead.

Gibson humbucking pickups are simple to figure out when taken apart. There are little black and white wires coming out of the two coils which are all inside the sealed case and can't be seen from the outside. Only a single coaxial wire coming out of the case is visible from the outside and this wire is attached to the coil wires. The outside of coaxial wire should always be the ground so it can encircle and shield the hot lead.

Grounds

The following information about grounds was written by the author for Schecter and is reproduced by their permission.

Electrical circuits use negative and positive voltages. If there is a positive voltage there has to be a negative voltage to complete the circuit. Very closely related to this is the balanced situation of having one hot lead and one ground. This is the setup in an electric guitar (or

*Hardware in electronic terminology refers to the physical equipment of a circuit or component.

bass). For an electric guitar to work, the hot lead must not have any breaks in it, and the ground circuit must not have any breaks in it. These two leads go from the pickup, through the controls, to the output jack, and are then cabled to an amplifier. The ground lead is the foundation and security of a circuit.

Diagram used to depict grounds.

Solder connections for grounds.

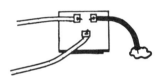

Diagram of black ground wire going from pot to a soldered ground connection.

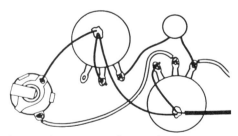

Separate wires used to connect all grounds.

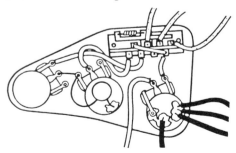

A conductive ground plate used as inter-connecting ground circuit. Ths system can be used if metal enclosed pots are used. If plastic encased pots are used you will need to add a ground connection like that shown in #3.

Fig. 117 Depiction of ground connections.

Ground connections are "common" connections. That is, all ground connections of a circuit are to be connected to each other, they join together in a commonly shared network. These interconnections of ground junctions, (also called ground joints), can take several forms. The simplest method is to just have a single bare wire soldered from one ground point to another. Another method is to use a grounding plate to make interconnections. A grounding plate is a flat piece of metal onto which guitars (or basses) controls are mounted. Ground points are soldered to the ground plate using the shortest wiring routes. For example:

1. The ground wire from a pickup can go to the ground plate.

2. The ground lug of a pot can be simply soldered to the back of a metal encased pot (if a metal cased pot is used). Since the pot is bolted up against the grounding plate, the metal case of a pot can provide the needed links between the lug on a pot which needs to be grounded and a ground connection.

This method of wiring saves time and money since no time needs to be taken to solder a separate ground connecting wire. The use of a grounding plate can look odd. There is a tendency to wonder where the ground connections are. This is of particular significance when it comes to wiring an output jack. A standard output jack has two lugs for connections. One for a hot lead, and the other for a ground lead. When a grounding plate is used there is no need to solder a ground wire to the ground lug on an output jack. The bolting of a jack against a grounding plate creates the needed connection. Still, it does look odd to many people when they see a jack lug with no obvious connection. When a grounding plate is used it is very important that all controls are bolted tightly to the grounding plate. If a component is loosely fastened it can cause a poor connection point which in turn causes hum, crackling, or no sound at all. There must be a complete unbroken path from the ground point (wire) of a pickup all the way through to the output jack.[8]

Color Codes

No two guitar electronics companies totally agree as to how to color code wires, i.e., what color the hot lead wires should be and what color the ground wires should be. White, yellow, and red are commonly used as colors of the insulation on hot leads and black is used as the color of the insulation on ground wires. There is no universal color code due to such variables as magnet orientation and direction of coil winding because when you invert the function (such as changing the direction of magnetic orientation) you could make a hot lead on one pickup behave like the ground lead on a similar pickup. For this reason, it is not advisable to rely on color as wiring clues.

The most important point about color codes is to understand what it is supposed to represent. Color codes are a short cut to help in manufacturing and consumer use. That is, it's a helpful tool only if you stick to one company's products; but if you want to use a Schecter Z+ Superock Omni Pot control harness

with a DiMarzio Super Distortion pickup and a Lawrence L-500RTS, you will have a problem. These companies do not feel they should have to provide information regarding how to mate their company's products with another's. To solve this problem you will need to determine the function of the color leads in the diMarzio and Lawrence pickups and how they correlate to the color leads of a Schecter Z+ Superock pickup in order for the pickups to mate to the Schecter Omni Pot harness. To successfully interface, i.e., combine, different companies' pickups and switches you must know the following:

a. Which colored lead is the start of coil #1.
b. Which colored lead is the end of coil #1.
c. Which colored lead is the start of coil #2.
d. Which colored lead is the end of coil #2.
e. Which colored lead is the ground lead.

Pickups are made with one of several basic wiring configurations. There are two ordinary lead configurations for single coil pickups, and six general lead configurations for humbucking pickups. The number of leads from a pickup can vary from two to eight. The more leads a pickup has, the more tonal options it can produce. When using a basic two lead pickup in a complex circuit, it will be necessary to add multiple leads to facilitate wiring. The following list can help determine what type of wiring configuration is on a pickup and what kind of tonal wiring possibilities can be achieved.

LEAD WIRING ON A PICKUP
Single Coil Pickups

Determining the function of a single coil pickup's leads is easy because of the limited number of leads and the visibility of the connections.

1. If there are two leads, one of the leads is hot and one is ground. Sometimes these functions can be inverted so an out-of-phase sound can be achieved when a second, normally wired, pickup is used. Sometimes inverting the function of the leads can produce a grounding problem and noise; experimentation is the best way to find out. A manufacturer is the best source of information as to which wire is which. The ground is generally in contact with the magnets however, and touching the magnets can be a good test to see if the correct lead is connected to a ground point. If a pickup is properly grounded and it is touched on a magnet (or case) there should be less, not more, hum.

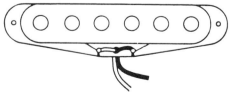

Fig. 118 Single coil pickup.

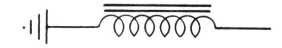

Fig. 119 Single coil schematic.

2. If there are three leads, this would be a tapped pickup. One lead would be full coil, the second would be the tap, and the third would be the ground lead.

Fig. 120 Tapped coil schematic.

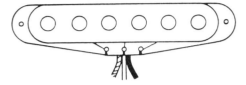

Fig. 121 Tapped pickup.

Humbucking Pickups

One way to determine the function of each lead of a pickup is to take a pickup apart and find the origin point. Sometimes it isn't possible to take a pickup apart (e.g., an encapsulated pickup) to inspect it. This problem is of little importance if you have an ohmmeter which can be used to measure d.c. resistance and so deduce the internal wiring of a pickup. Use the following steps as a guide for investigating common humbuckers.

1. If a pickup has a single coaxial lead, the braid connects to ground and the center lead is hot.

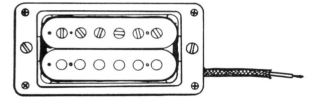

Fig. 122 Pickup with one hot lead and coaxial ground.

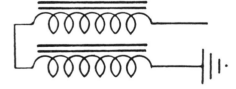

Fig. 123 Schematic of pickup above.

2. If there is a shield with two internal leads, this means that the leads are the ends of two series linked coils of a humbucker. This wiring allows in-phase or out-of-phase switching.

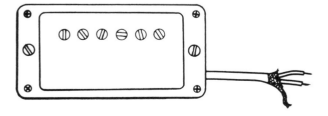

Fig. 124 Pickup with two hot leads and braided ground.

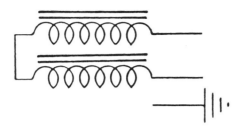

Fig. 125 Schematic of Fig. 124.

The following method can be used to determine the function of two hot leads plus one shielding lead wiring:

a. If one of the leads has a zero ohms connection to a metal bottom plate, magnet, or pole piece, that lead is ground. This lead should not have a connection to any of the remaining two leads.

b. Either of the two remaining leads could be a possible hot. Use the phase test to check which should be which.

3. If there are three leads and shield, the third lead is a center tap. To tell which is which, you must check d.c. resistances. The two outside leads will have the highest resistance and the center tap will have exactly half that resistance when connected with either of the outside leads. This configuration allows phase switching and coil splitting.

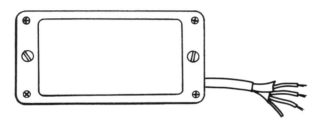

Fig. 126 Pickup with three hot leads and bare wire connecting to foil ground.

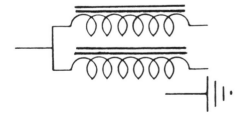

Fig. 127 Schematic of Fig. 126.

The following method can be used to determine the function of three hot leads plus one shielding lead wiring:

a. If one of the leads has a zero ohms connection to a metal bottom plate, magnet, or pole piece, that lead is ground. This lead should not have a connection to any of the remaining three leads.

b. Now hold the black probe of the ohmmeter on one of the leads and touch the red probe to each of the two remaining leads. If one of the leads gives a d.c. resistance figure of exactly half of the other, that lead will connect to the junction of both coils. If both leads give the same reading, it will mean you have the black probe connected to the coil's junction.

4. If there are four leads plus a shield, all the wires are then accessible for a normal humbucker. Two wires will be the ends of the second coil. This is easy to isolate with an ohmmeter. This wiring combination (4+) allows all wiring options without creating phase and grounding conflicts with another pickup.

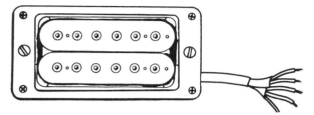

Fig. 128 Pickup with four hot leads and bare wire connecting to foil ground.

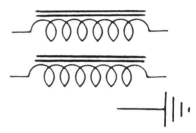

Fig. 129 Schematic of Fig. 128.

The following method can be used to determine the function of four hot leads plus one shielding lead wiring:

a. If one of the leads has a zero ohms connection to a metal bottom plate, magnet, or pole piece, that lead is ground. This lead should not have a connection to any of the remaining four leads.

b. Now hold the black probe of the ohmmeter on one of the leads and touch the red probe to each of the three remaining leads. Two of the leads will give an infinite-ohms reading, and one of the leads will give a d.c. resistance reading of 1,000 to 6,000 ohms. The two leads that give the 1 to 6K reading will be the start and finish of one coil.

c. The remaining two leads should give a reading like the two leads of step #2. These remaining leads will be the start and finish of coil #2. You have now determined the function of all five wires.

d. To determine the phase of the two leads of each of the coils, use the phase test. This test will assist you in choosing which two leads are positive and which two leads are negative; however, it can not tell which wire is from the inside of a coil, or which wire is from the outside. It takes very specialized equipment to determine this. If a pickup can not be taken apart, and you can not contact the manufacturer for specifications either lead can be used as the hot lead or the ground lead. In most cases a pickup can operate all right with the hot lead connecting to the innermost coil winding; however, sometimes this wiring can result in excess hum. If this is the case, reverse the hot and ground connections.

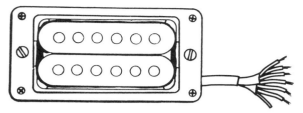

Fig. 130 Pickup with six hot leads and a bare wire connecting to a foil ground.

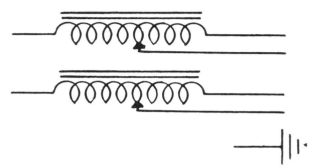

Fig. 131 Schematic of Fig. 130.

5. If you have six or seven leads you are likely to have a tapped humbucker which has three leads from each coil plus a possible ground lead from the case. A tapped humbucker would allow you to achieve about a dozen tonal variations.

6. If you have eight wires, you have a Bartolini Beast style humbucker. This pickup has two coils each with two separate windings. To better understand this, see the section on Bartolini Hi-A pickups.

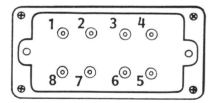

Fig. 132 Bottom of a Bartolini Beast showing eight connection pins.

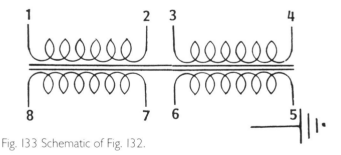

Fig. 133 Schematic of Fig. 132.

POTS
The Function of a Potentiometer
The device behind those volume and tone controls on your guitar are potentiometers; called **pots** for short. A pot is a variable resistor with three lugs.

A pickup could be wired directly to an output jack but nearly everyone would like the convenience of having volume control on a guitar. A pot is put in the line to regulate resistance of the flow of current from a

Fig. 134 Sealed and lubricated Pot.

pickup by regulating the resistance to the flow.

To get an idea as to how a pot works, imagine a tiny copper wire one mile long. Now let's say the + side of a battery is connected to the start of the wire and the − side of the battery is connected to the metal side of the base of a flashlight bulb. If the center point of the bulb is touched to the wire about an inch from the start, the current only has to travel an inch down the wire to the bulb and the bulb lights. However, if you walk down the wire fifty feet and then touch the wire . . . Hmmm, the bulb isn't glowing very brightly. Go another fifty feet and it's even dimmer. What you are now finding is that the wire's resistance is blocking the flow of current.

Because carbon is less of a conductor than copper wire, a small strip only two inches long could create a path of variable resistance. If you tapped varying lengths on this strip you could get varying amounts of current. Pots for guitars have a small carbon (or cermet or conductive plastic) path to achieve variable resistance.

Fig. 135 View of the resistance paths inside potentiometers.

If a pot changes resistance evenly, it is called a linear taper pot which means that a distance one-third of the way down increases the resistance by one-third, and if the pot is turned two-thirds the way down, the resistance increases by two-thirds.

The ear is not sensitive to sounds that change in an even progression from low to high volume (or low to high frequencies); therefore, if a volume pot were used that changed resistance in an even progression (i.e.,

linear pot) the ear would hear a sudden rise in volume which would level off as the pot was turned up. For this reason, audio taper pots are made. Their resistance change is made to conform to the hearing of the ear so that a steady increase in volume can be heard as the pot is turned up. Another reason audio taper pots are used is to ensure that the pot operation will create a non-leakage of current to ground (i.e., the third lug) when the setting is turned all the way up.

Pots can be obtained in many resistances, values from 10 ohms to 1 million ohms are used in standard devices. Electric guitars commonly use either 100K, 250K, 300K, 500K or 1 MEG ohm pots. The resistance value of a pot is related to the output of a pickup. High output pickups normally use high ohm resistance pots. The 100K (or other value) ohm refers to the total resistance when a pot is shut off. The K means to multiply by 1,000, MEG means to multiply by 1,000,000; therefore, 100K ohms means 100,000 ohms.

The value of total electrical resistance of a pot is very important because if a pot is too high in resistance, the resistance curve will be erratic. Things have not become very standardized in this respect. Single coil pickups like Fender's can adequately use 250K ohm pots. Gibson's humbuckers are more powerful pickups and used 500K pots for many years. After 7-1-73 Gibson began to use 300K volume pots and 100K tone pots. Gibson made this switch so that their guitars would have a beefier, less treble sound. However, many people now use 1 meg pots as a perfect multi-purpose pot.

Pot Turning Directions

Pots for right-handed guitars are wired so that volume, or flow, increases as the knob is turned in a **clockwise** direction. Note that normal audio taper pots are made so that the taper functions correctly **only** in one direction. When the pot turns up volume in a clockwise turning of a knob, it's correct. If you want an audio taper pot to work in the reverse direction you need a reverse audio taper pot. Remember that when you look at the bottom of pots when doing repair work, you will then want the turning action to turn in a **counter-clockwise** direction; this is done so that when the pot is inverted it will turn on in a **clockwise** direction.

Notice that there are three projections coming from the case of a pot, these projections are called lugs. The center lug goes to a wiper blade that slides along the carbon path. The other two lugs connect to each end of the carbon path. Because these lugs represent the extremes of the path, the d.c. resistance value of the pot will be the same as the d.c. resistance between these lugs.

To understand how a pot functions, hold the pot in front of you with the lugs pointing down and the shaft facing away from you. Now turn the shaft in a full clockwise direction. This will electrically connect the center lug with the lug on the right. Now turn the shaft in a full counter-clockwise direction. This will electrically connect the center lug with the lug on the left. If there is an input from a pickup going to the left lug, and an output to a jack from the center lug, the pot will then turn "on" in a counter-clockwise direction. See the three drawings. In drawing #1 the pot is full "on". Drawing #2 shows the wiper of the pot exactly half-way between the right and left lugs. In this position, the pot is half "on". In drawing #3 the clockwise rotation of the shaft results in the pot being turned off. Note: These illustrations and examples are diagrammatic of working on a pot while looking at the back. From the front of the pot, a clockwise motion turns the pot "on".

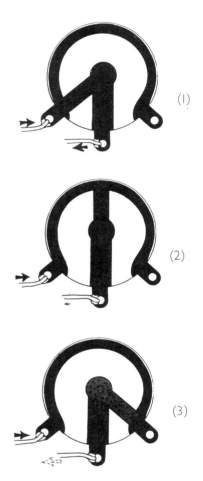

Fig. 136 The operation of a pot: (1) Pot is turned ON; (2) Pot is turned half way; (3) Pot is turned full OFF.

Types of Pots

Once there were only a few good pots made; today there are many. The following describes a good pot:

1. The conductive path inside a pot must be completely smooth – rough spots cause noise.

2. The pot should be sealed to keep out dirt and grit because contamination will make the pot crackle when it is turned.

3. The shaft should turn smoothly.

One feature that would be nice to have on a pot is a plastic shaft on which the knob fits. Unfortunately, only a few pots have a plastic mounting shaft for a knob. The plastic shaft means that metal knobs won't become part of the electric circuit and it's a good safety precaution. However, a plastic shaft can cause static

electric crackling sounds.

Shielding a pot is difficult. Some companies make covers for pots with an exit hole in the side for a coaxial wire. This helps to make a quiet, well grounded circuit. See this book's section on shielding for more information regarding the shielding of pots.

The pots used for guitars are ¼ to 2 watt pots. Because the current of a guitar's pickups is normally under ¼ watt, low wattage pots are more than adequate. Most small pots use inexpensive carbon resistance paths, but better quality pots use conductive plastic or cermet paths for longer life and smooth operation.

VOLUME POT OPERATION

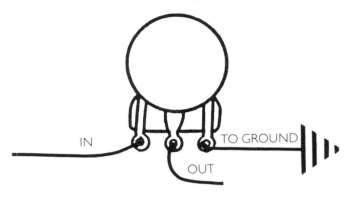

Fig. 137 Volume pot wiring.

To better understand the actual operation of a volume pot, refer to the preceding three drawings depicting a pot turned on, half way, and off. An actual volume control in a guitar will have the lug on the right wired to ground (when viewing the back of the pot). As the pot is gradually turned off, two things happen: First, resistance between the input and the output increases. Secondly, resistance between the output and the grounded lug decreases. Therefore, when a volume pot is turned off, a guitar is silenced primarily because the hot lead is shorted to ground, NOT because resistance has blocked the flow between input and output.[9]

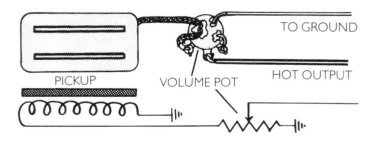

Fig. 138 Pictoral and schematic representation of a pickup and a volume control.

TONE CONTROL

The tone control is also a pot, but it has something extra – a capacitor. The following should help you understand how it works. If you connect a live hot lead wire to a ground wire, silence will result. Now, if you put a capacitor between the two wires, an interesting

9. SEE PAGE 125

HARDWARE COMPONENTS

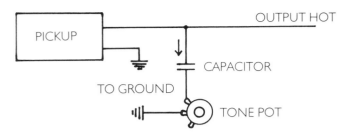

Fig. 139 The function of a tone control.

thing happens; the trebles have disappeared but the rest of the guitar's output has not. This is because trebles find it much easier to pass through the capacitor than other frequencies. If you had an on-off switch with a live lead going to a capacitor and ground, you could have two sounds: Full tone (when the switch is off) and no treble (when the switch is on). To achieve more variations, you can regulate the amount of treble that is taken away. If you use a pot instead of the switch, you can vary the amount of treble sent to ground through the capacitor. This is the tone control most guitars have. It is referred to as a **passive** control because it doesn't add anything, it can only subtract. This passive tone control just reduces treble and its specific title is treble bleed tone control.

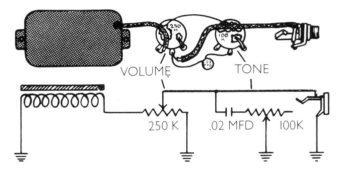

Fig. 140 Pictoral and schematic representation of a pickup with volume and tone control plus a jack.

There is another possible simple tone control, it's old and isn't used very much, it's called the treble pass tone control and it's found on Howard Robert's style guitars made by Ibanez. It is often called a bass tone control because its capacitor only allows trebles to

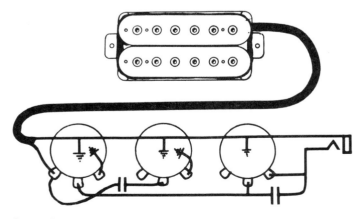

Fig. 141 Pickup with a volume, treble bleed, and treble by-pass controls.

detour the pot. Bass tones can't get through a capacitor, they have to go through the pot. In effect, the pot increases or decreases bass by producing an effect that equals the opposite of the treble bleed control.

Capacitors

Capacitors are used as a part of tone controls. They are simple, inexpensive, trouble-free devices that range in cost from 2¢ a piece and up. Only great amounts of heat or current can cause a capacitor to fail.

Just as pounds measure weight, farads measure capacitance. Capacitors are rated at a specific farad capacitance and a specific level of voltage. The voltage figure tells you how many volts the capacitor could withstand. Guitars are very low voltage, and therefore, very low voltage capacitors can be used. The higher the voltage rating, the bigger the capacitor and this is another reason for using low value (small) capacitors. When working with guitars, you should never need anything bigger than a 100 volt capacitor.

The least expensive capacitors are ceramic discs whereas the most expensive ones are made from mylar and sealed in a resin dip.

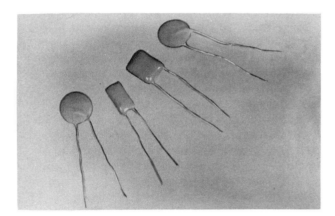

Fig. 142 Two round ceramic capacitors, and two square mylar dip capacitors.

Capacitors used in most guitar circuits range in value capacitance from .001 micro farads to .01 micro farads. A micro farad is one millionth of a farad. A .001 mf capacitor will pass only very high frequencies and some upper mid-range frequencies.

The value of a capacitor determines the amount of treble cut of a common tone control. A high value capacitor, e.g., .05, can produce a bassier tone, i.e., less treble, than a lower value, e.g., .02. Generally, single coil pickups can use a .02 micro-farad capacitor, dual coil pickups use .05 ones and basses use .05 or even a .08. However, Fender has mainly used .1 to .05 caps, and Gibson uses a lot of .02 caps.

Many people experiment with using capacitors of different values to achieve different sounds. This experimentation can't harm a guitar.

KNOBS

A good quality knob is solidly made, and it fits precisely and securely on a pot shaft. It turns totally concentrically. Metal knobs look classy, but they are electrically conductive. However, plastic knobs will sometimes crack or break. Some knobs are made with an allen keyed set-screw to affix it to a shaft. It's a good idea to make a flat spot on a shaft to receive this set-screw. Other knobs have internal ridges for being press mounted on knurled (fluted) pot shafts.

Fig. 143 Knobs for knurled shafts, and knobs for smooth shafts.

The Lore of Gibson Knobs

The knobs used on Gibson guitars have attained a mystique paralleling that of a P.A.F. pickup. This is because certain knobs are associated with certain instruments. The most sought after 1959 Sunburst Les Paul guitars have one type of knob while other Les Pauls have their own knob style.

The original "hat box" knobs on Les Pauls had sides and top that were basically flat. These knobs are similar to speed knobs being used today, but hat box knobs are taller. These knobs were molded out of clear plastic and the underneath/inside was spray painted. There are two colors used in Les Paul knobs: black or gold. Les Paul gold tops were the first Les Paul guitars to have gold knobs. All other Gibson Les Pauls, except the Custom models, also receive the gold knobs. The Custom models which came in a black finish, had black knobs. EB-1 basses used brown painted hat box knobs and it is believed by some that a few factory made Les Pauls did come with brown knobs.

In 1957 Les Pauls received bell knobs which were flat on top and did not have an insert. An insert is an emblem which designates volume or tone and is affixed into the top of a knob. Guitars made from about 1957 through 1960 had these knobs. After 1960 Gibson began to make a second style of bell knob which is slightly taller and has a recessed insert in the top. Some people remove the insert and file the top flat, but this modification does not result in true older style knobs. After making the 1960 style of bell knobs, Gibson changed again and they started to use knobs that resembled the knobs of Fender amps. This was a short-lived venture however, and Gibson soon returned to the speed knob style. Current Gibson speed knobs are shorter than early hat box knobs and they are painted on the under/inside with black or gold paint. The newest Gibson speed knobs have an internal hole size slightly smaller than older models. Because the splined shaft (also called knurled) of the pots is notched and

can be compressed, this size change is not too important. However, if you are using non-Gibson pots, you might have to drill out the hole in the knobs so the knobs can fit on the pot shafts.

Knobs can be an indication as to whether or not a guitar is a vintage instrument. However, people can switch knobs; therefore, knobs cannot be considered a totally reliable method of determining the instrument's age.

Fender Knobs

Fender knobs have not changed very much over the years. The only popular old style knobs are those on Teles. Tele knobs have changed in two ways: (1) Volume and tone controls on Teles made since 1953 have flat top metal knobs. Earlier knobs had domed tops. (2) The black plastic knob on the switch is now an oblong shape; whereas early switch knobs were round.

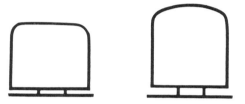

Fig. 144 New style Tele knob (left) and an old style Tele knob (right).

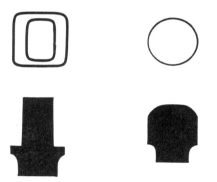

Fig. 145 New Tele switch knob (left) and old style Tele switch knob (right).

The '54 Strats had pearl-white knobs, '55 models had brittle white bakelite-type knobs, and newer Strats have simple soft white plastic ones.

TYPES OF SWITCHES
Switch Functions

The most basic switch is a lever switch which can open and close a circuit. The switch connects to a single set of wires, and it is called a **s**ingle **p**ole (SP) switch. Because the switch has two positions, one and two, it's also called a dual position switch. The technical term for each position is **throw**, so this simple switch is a **d**ouble **t**hrow or **dt** switch. The two functions are put together to make the identity of the switch specific – SPDT tells you exactly what a switch is.

If there are two sets of SPDT lugs that have parallel functions, the switch has **d**ual**p**oles and is a DP switch.

HARDWARE COMPONENTS

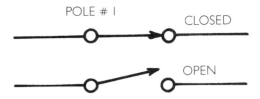

Fig. 146 Diagram of a single pole, single throw switch.

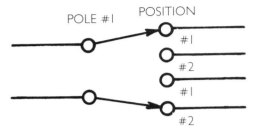

Fig. 147 Diagram of a single pole, double throw switch.

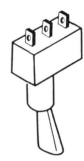

Fig. 148 SPDT switch.

If there are three possible positions, a switch has **triple throws – TT**. The pole designation comes first and it is followed by the number of throws.

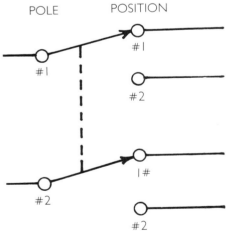

Fig. 149 Diagram of a double-pole, double-throw switch.

A pickup splitter control uses a SPDT unit; whereas a series/parallel or phase switch control uses a DPDT switch. If you use three-position toggles with a center position which is off, you could have an on-off switch. With this type of switch, the volume knob doesn't have to be turned down to obtain silence, this is very convenient when you want to leave the guitar on standby.

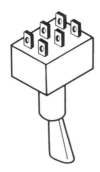

Fig. 150 DPDT switch.

The Three Position Toggle

The most common electric guitar switch is the three position toggle which is used on Les Pauls, SGs, and many, many others. It allows three selections: pickup #1, both pickups, or pickup #3. The wires go from the pickups, to the switch, and then to the controls and output.

Les Pauls take a tall switch, and thinner bodied guitars, e.g., SGs, take switches formed into a right angle.

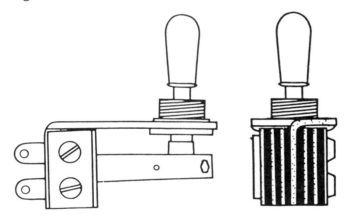

Fig. 151 Side and end view of a three position toggle switch for a Gibson SG.

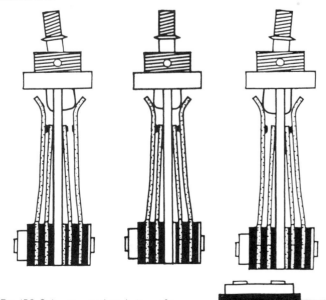

Fig. 152 Side view and end view of a three position toggle switch for Les Pauls showing the switches' three positions.

The Three Position Lever

This is used a lot by Fender and they are found on Teles and Strats. The action of this switch is similar to that of the three position toggle.

Fig. 153 Three position lever switch.

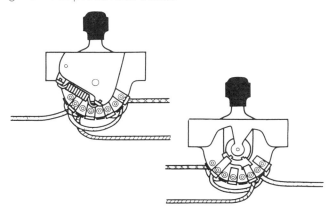

Fig. 154 Both sides of a switch for a Telecaster.

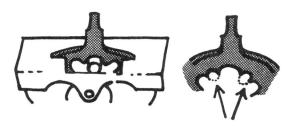

Fig. 155 Three position switch converted to a five position switch.

The Five Position Lever

This originated as a hot rod replacement item for Strats but now Fender offers it on new Strats. It allows the standard three positions, but it also offers two more; these selections are pickups 1 and 2 together, and pickups 2 and 3 together. These positions are located between positions 1 and 2, and 2 and 3 on a three-way Strat switch.

The Six Position (four pole) Rotary

Rotary switches allow the construction of switching systems too complex for one DPDT (and other similar) switches. Rotary switches are available in many configurations: One-pole twelve-throw, two-pole four-throw, four-pole six-throw, etc. One 4P6T rotary switch can provide as many switching selections as four DPDT switches.

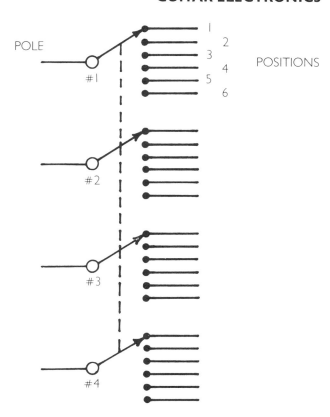

Fig. 156 Diagram of a four-pole, six-throw switch (this normally would be a rotary).

Fig. 157 Four-pole, six-throw rotary switch.

Mini Switches

These are small toggle switches and are available in many forms, e.g., two position, or three position (with or without neutral centers). These small switches are available with many pole configurations, i.e., single, double, or triple. In addition, DPDT switches are available in many contact linking configurations for special switching needs. See the chart for example.

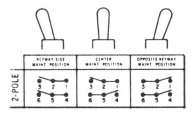

Fig. 158 Special DPDT

HARDWARE COMPONENTS

These special switches have not been fully utilized by guitar makers because the switches are not well known at this time. Many switches are expensive, one

Fig. 159 Switches: A mini toggle, and three position toggle switches.

Fig. 160 Switches: A mini toggle, a slide, and a lever.

Fig. 161 This John Judge guitar wins the switch award. There is a five position selector, switches that link each of the Schecter pickups together in series or parallel. Tapping switches, phase switches, and a tone linkage switch that connects and disconnects a Lawrence Tone Q filter. Other controls are bass cut/boost, treble cut/boost, gain, master tone and master volume. John states that it's easier to play it than to describe.

reason for this is that they are made for the strong voltages of household current and guitars don't need this, but no one makes tiny high-quality low voltage switches. When soldering, switches are not as sensitive to heat as transistors, but you should be careful not to heat one so much that you start to melt the plastic case. It is advisable to buy the switches that have plastic lever covers because this provides a layer of electrical insulation between the metal and you. This is wise because the cases of switches need to be grounded. The best way to wire a ground to a switch is to solder a ground wire to the washer that fits around the switch's threaded bushing.

JACKS

The standard jack on a high impedance guitar is a chassis-mount ¼ inch, two connector, female audio jack. Similar jacks come with three connections for stereo. Others have built-in prongs which act as on-off switches, and when a plug is inserted, an electrical connection is completed. These on-off jacks are used to eliminate the need for having to remember to turn off a preamp.

CONNECT HOT LEAD HERE

THIS CONNECTS TO HOT LEAD LUG

CONNECT GROUND HERE

Fig. 162 Mono jack.

Fig. 163 How a cord plugs into a jack.

Unfortunately, most jacks are not shielded, and guitar circuits should be completely shielded to prevent shock. Be careful when handling faulty old jacks, oftentimes the insulation between the elements compresses or breaks which can cause a shorting-out of parts that should not touch. Sometimes a jack will oxidize and short out, but this usually can be repaired by cleaning.

Fig. 164 Two Mono jacks. The one on the right has an ON/OFF connection.

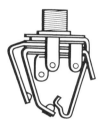

Fig. 165 Mono jack with an ON/OFF switch.

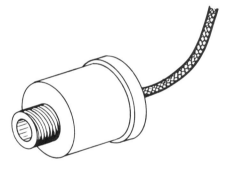

Fig. 166 Shielded jack.

Strap-jack: This is made by a company that feels there is a need for a super heavy-duty jack that doubles as a strap button. This jack is not shielded, and it's rather difficult to mount/install, but it should last about 250 years.

Fig. 167 Jacks, from left to right: A Frap end pin, a Barcus Berry end pin, and a Strapjack.

CORDS

The quality of a cord affects the quality of your sound. Hisses, hums, rattles, and crackles can all be yours with a bad cord. Regardless of price, any cord can go bad. What kind of things go bad?

1. Loose connections, causing crackles and on-off sound breaks, or sometimes resulting in no sound at all.

2. Poor shielding, causing hum and hissing.

3. Loose or broken internal wires, caused by bending or stepping on cords. This results in a loss of sound, or it can mean a microphonic sound or crackling.

Therefore, look for the following features in a new cord:

1. 100% braid shield, not a half-way slip-shod wrapping. You may have to unscrew the jacks to check the shield, and no honest music store should deny you this right.

2. Metal shielded jacks – not light-weight plastic units.

3. Secure attachments in the jacks for connecting wires. The best jacks have screws **and** solder.

4. Every part should be heavy-duty.

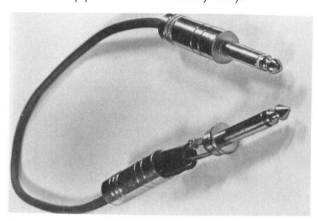

Fig. 168 Cord plug with screw terminals.

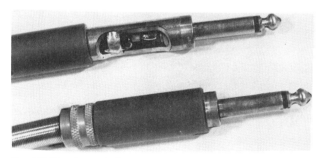

Fig. 169 Sturdy cord plug.

CORDLESS

The following information is derived from a personal discussion with John Nady, the founder of Nady systems, and printed material that he wrote.

Think of the exhilaration of playing an electric guitar while jumping, turning, and spinning; of being able to walk across a stage or studio floor without having to pay any attention to the usual tangle of cords. Imagine playing in a garden while the signals from your guitar are beamed to a recording studio. Playing cordless can give you this freedom.

Cordless units come in two styles: The first consisting of a transmitter box and antenna that attaches to a guitar strap or a belt, and then plugs into a guitar; the second type consists of transmitter box and antenna (internal) that is mounted inside a guitar. (The truss-rod could be used as an antenna if it's electrically isolated from contact with any string ground.)

Near the amp, a receiver is positioned to pick up the signals broadcast by the transmitter. A single receiver is satisfactory for about 95% of all playing situations; but more expensive dual (diversity) receivers give better performance.

Wireless transmission of sound was first achieved around the turn of the century. It wasn't until recently that the fidelity and range of wireless guitars exceeded that of guitars that use cords. The development of this cordless ideal dictated the need for development in a highly sophisticated miniaturized radio transmission system. A well designed wireless system offers several technical advantages over a cord. Cables are not ideal transmission systems for audio signals. Due to the inherent capacitance, they act as lowpass filters and lop off the highs when used with musical instrument pickups. In fact, they no longer pass true high fidelity at lengths over 5 to 10 feet. At lengths over 20 feet, the sound becomes "muddy". In addition, cables act like antennae and pick up spurious noises from light dimmers, radio signals, power lines and other external sources. Used with certain combinations of effects pedals or amps, cords often pick up nearby radio stations and CBers.

The most practical benefit of cordless operation of electric instruments is the total elimination of potential electric shock hazards. Such common shocks, caused by improperly grounded amplifiers and/or other equipment malfunctions, have even proved fatal at times (Les Harvey of Stone the Crows and Keith Relf of the Yardbirds were both electrocuted in this manner).

A well-designed wireless system generally has a usable range of about 150 feet minimum under adverse conditions, and up to 1,500 feet line-of-sight. Different applications, of course, require different operational ranges. Due to the speed of sound travel, there is an acoustic delay of about 100 milliseconds already at that distance. It is difficult for musicians to keep in time at longer distances.

There are two frequency bands most successfully utilized by today's professional wireless systems: the commercial FM (88-108 mHz) band, and the VHF business and TV channels bands (150-216 mHz). The wireless system operating in the commercial FM band are tunable so that they can be tuned to blank spots between FM stations. The VHF systems are all fixed frequency and cannot be tuned to open frequencies. For applications such as traveling musicians, live recordings, etc., where clear channel accessibility and freedom from random interference is a must in all

locales, a well-designed, frequency stable tunable system is recommended.

Distortion, frequency response, dynamic range and dropouts are the three key subjects when looking at cordless transmitter systems.

1. Distortion: Measuring distortion in any piece of electronic gear can be a numbers game, and wireless systems are no exception. Published spec's often quote a figure that represents a best case situation that may not reflect realistic in-field usage. The best new systems improve that performance to about .2 to .6% THD.

2. Dynamic Range: The greatest single breakthrough ever in the performance of wireless systems is the recent dramatic improvement in dynamic range offered by the best of the new units. Signal-to-noise was improved from a previous high of about 65dB to over 100dB. By way of comparison, a commercial FM station only registers about 70dB signal-to-noise through a high quality receiver.

3. While passing through the air from transmitter to receiver, radio waves will generally encounter a maze of reflective and absorptive obstructions. When radio waves bounce off nearby surfaces and meet in space, such that one wave's crest encounters a reflected wave's trough, a 180° cancellation occurs. A receiver antenna located at that point in space will register no received signal and a radio dropout will result. Although these null spots can occur at any receiver distance from the transmitter, they are fortunately very infrequent up to ½ to ⅔ of the system's ultimate range at any given location.

In "receiver diversity" two separate receivers and two separate antennae are employed to process the single transmitted radio signal. In a well-designed true diversity system, a totally silent comparator circuit continuously monitors the received RF signal strength of both receivers and instantaneously selects the audio output of the receiver with the stronger signal. In this way, there can be no vector cancellation of the received signals.

Since cordless systems have improved, it seems only a matter of time until many instruments are factory wired for cordless operation or at least come with an empty compartment for placement of a transmitter. Although rock musicians have been the first to

Fig. 170 Nady cordless transmitter equipment.

enthusiastically welcome cordless transmitters, it would seem likely that more conservative musicians will eventually become "secret" users. What better musical device could bluegrass players have than a transmitter. A whole group could look like they were playing acoustic instruments when in fact, the guitar, banjo, mandolin, and fiddle would all be wired for playing "electric".

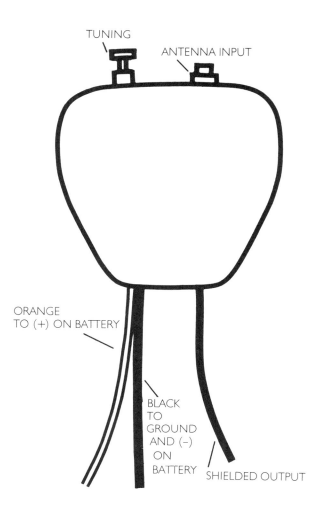

Fig. 171 Actual size of a Nady cordless transmitter.

AMPS & SPEAKERS

Amps – Solid State & Tube

It is necessary to know some things about amps because you need to match a pickup's impedance and an amp's impedance for the best in sound and amplifier operation.

The first amplifiers used vacuum tubes, or to use the Great Britain term – valves. These devices have a high impedance, and for this reason, devices designed to plug into tube amps were also designed to be high impedance.

Leo Fender is largely responsible for the creation and popularity of the guitar amplifier. His early designs for tube amps are still revered, and the Fender company continues to make tube amps which are similar to his original designs.

Because of the use of high impedance amps, high impedance pickups became the norm. Until circa 1970, nearly all guitars were high impedance units. The transistor really changed things because the transistor is basically low impedance.

Solid state amps are by nature lower impedance than tube amps. They are admirably suited for use with low impedance pickups and preamps. Nowadays with the use of solid state preamps and other transistor based circuits, solid state power amplifiers are bound to become more popular.

Speakers

Speakers need some comment because they are the last link of the pickup chain. We hear the sound of a pickup and judge it from a speaker. Speakers come in many sizes and designs, and even identical speakers can be as variable as pickups. To evaluate pickups, it's best to hear them all using the same guitar, amp, and speakers. Small speakers give more crisp, high notes, large speakers give more solid, low notes. Generally, large magnet structures give more fidelity and more power. Hi-fi speakers can not take the demands placed on them by musical instruments.

2. Servicing Electric Guitar Circuits

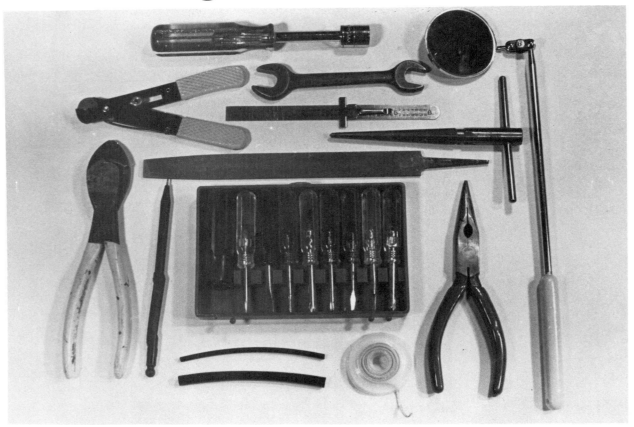

Fig. 172 Tools for working on electric guitars.

TOOLS & EQUIPMENT

Tools

Working on guitars requires few tools. Listed below are the basic tools and what they are used for.

Soldering gun – for melting solder to make heavy-duty metal connections. A small gun of 100 to 200 watts is adequate. Large soldering guns are too clumsy to handle deftly. A light built into the front of a gun helps you to see what you are doing; very helpful when working inside a guitar.

Soldering Iron – for soldering electric guitar connections. A small soldering pencil is hot enough to adequately solder most joints and doesn't get too hot when used on transistors.

Solder – use only rosin core solder for electrical work. Do not use acid core. Acid will cause corrosion and poor connections.

Wire Cutter/Strippers – for cutting and stripping wire. Get a fairly good adjustable tool.

Needle Nose Pliers – these insulated pliers hold little wires in tight spaces when soldering. They are also useful for crimping wire prior to soldering, and affixing solderless fittings.

Box-end Wrenches – for tightening and loosening nuts, holding pots, switches, and jacks.

Socket Wrench – for tightening and loosening nuts holding pots, switches, and the recessed jacks on some electric guitars such as Telecasters.

Small Screwdrivers – for adjusting the height and pole pieces on pickups.

Allen Keys – for adjusting pole pieces.

De-soldering Tool – it "drinks" pools of excess solder.

File – a small file is useful in removing the "non-stick" surface on the back of metal pots.

Jumper Cables – for testing out a possible wiring plan before soldering. Also good for checking out faulty connections when doing repairs.

Ohmmeter – one that reads up to 500,000 is needed for checking pots. Most pickups have a d.c. resistance of 4,000 to 13,000 ohms. An ohmmeter is excellent for discovering "half-bad" circuits, and other elusive problems.

Soldering

The standard method of forming electrical connections for electric guitars is soldering. Solder is a soft metal alloy composed of tin and lead with the addition of flux. Flux is the substance that helps solder flow and stick. There are two basic types of flux: acid based and rosin based. Acid flux is often based on nitric acid which chemically scours clean the metal to be soldered. This is important because clean metals accept solder much more readily. Unfortunately, the scouring action of acid flux results in residues and when these residues combine with the solder, it can form corrosion whenever an electrical current passes through the soldered joint. This corrosion interferes with the free flow of electrical current; therefore, acid flux is not recommended for soldering electrical connections because it will eventually result in guitar malfunctions. Rosin flux, which has a resin core, is milder in action than acid flux, and it is based on resins, like tree resin. It is non-corrosive when subjected to electrical currents. It is the author's experience that Multicore brand rosin core solder for transistors is so superior to other solders that it is heartily recommended for all electric guitar work. This solder has five internal cores of resin which makes for more distribution of flux when soldering. It also has a lower melting temperature than normal solder. This means that soldering can be done more quickly (lower temperature) and more evenly (core distribution).

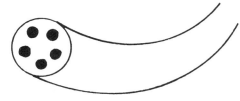

Fig. 173 Multi-core solder.

Some metals repel solder, in this case you can buy extra flux which will help solder stick. Using more heat can also help form joints if the metal is highly repellant. Many components for electric guitars come housed in stainless steel cases, and because stainless steel is very difficult to solder, it is advisable to solder to a washer which fits on a shaft of the component.

The following tips on soldering are from a Schecter bulletin written by the author:
If you want to you can construct soldered connections. If you do choose to solder it is advised that you use heat shrink insulation. Solder connections can be constructed following this method:

1. Slip a piece of heat shrink over one of the wires to be joined and **move it several inches away** from the connection to be soldered. (This is so the shrink won't get hot from the soldering.)
2. Gently twist the two wires together as they are laid end to end.
3. Heat the junction and then bring solder into contact with the hot connection.
4. When the solder has cooled, slide the heat shrink over the joint.
5. Heat the tubing with a flame. A butane lighter is perfect. A match will leave black soot.

A final piece of heat shrink could be used to hold a bundle of connections together. If this is desired, it would be necessary to have slipped a large piece of heat shrink around all the wires before they are connected. Heat shrink can not work if it is slit and wrapped around a joint. Heat shrink is a very strong durable aid to wire connection. It is far superior to

using electricians' tape.

Heat Shrink Installation

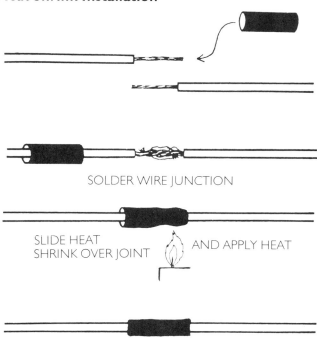

SOLDER WIRE JUNCTION

SLIDE HEAT SHRINK OVER JOINT   AND APPLY HEAT

Fig. 174 Using heat shrink.

To make hooking up a SCHECTER pickup assembly as easy as possible, SCHECTER provides wire twist caps. Use a twist cap in the following way:

1. Take the two wires to be joined.
2. Twist the bare ends together.
3. Place and push down the twist cap over the junction using a rotating motion. The plastic wire cap will thread itself down onto the wires and provide a secure connection that is properly insulated.

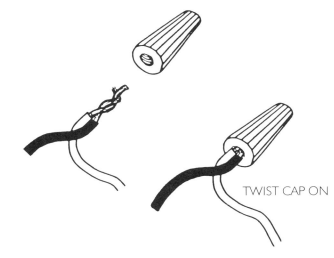

TWIST CAP ON

Fig. 175 Installation of wire twist nuts.

Wire

An assortment of wire recommended is:
(1) miniature coaxial phonocartridge wire for the intricate wiring of phase switches etc.; (2) single strand wire in an assortment of variously colored insulation jackets, for ground connections; (3) multiple stranded

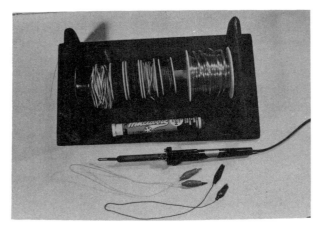

Fig. 176 Assortment of wire.

wire in an assortment of variously colored insulation jackets, for wiring where unshielded wire is desired; (4) coaxial wire, for wiring where shielded wire is desired; (5) multi-lead shielded wire with foil shield, for wiring circuits where the ground and hot leads are switched, such as a phase switch. If a standard coaxial wire were used, the outside braid would become an unshielded hot lead when the switch was thrown.

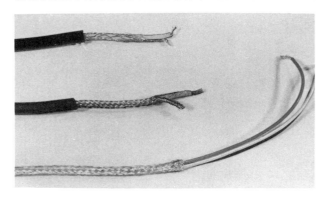

Fig. 177 Coaxial wire, from top to bottom: (1) Very inexpensive wire; (2) Very high quality coaxial wire; (3) Multi-lead shielded wire.

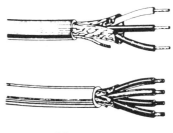

BELDFOIL
100% Shield Coverage

Fig. 178 Three and four conductor foil shielded wires.

Using an Ohmmeter

You are underestimating yourself if you think an ohmmeter is something strange and hard to understand. An ohmmeter is really a "must" if you want to work with pickups. They aren't hard to use or understand, and they don't cost very much. You can get one that will do the job for as low as sixteen dollars.

An ohmmeter is used to:
1. Check to see if pickups are working properly.
2. Check to see if pots are working properly.
3. Check to see if all the wiring is working properly.

Taking a few minutes to learn some ohmmeter basics will save you days of trial and error experiments.

For our use, only one facet of a VOM is needed. (VOM stands for **V**olt, **O**hm, **M**eter.) These devices are test machines which test several things, such as volts and ohms, and they are referred to as either VOMs or multitesters. However, the only function we are concerned with is measuring ohms, and to make things even easier, we only have to check d.c. (direct current) ohms. Ohms are measuring units of resistance, and resistance is the amount of force which resists the flow of an electrical current. The measurement of resistance is very important because we can use it to check parts and circuits to see if the current is able to flow as it should by checking ohms. If the ohm reading between the two outside lugs of a 250,000 ohm pot is 1,000,000 ohms, we can safely guess that the pot is broken inside, for it should be 250,000 ohms. Likewise, if one coil of a dual coil humbucking pickup reads 4,000 ohms and the other reads 2,500 ohms, we know something is wrong, and we don't have to guess. If one reading is below what it should be, we then know there is a short in the wiring because the d.c. resistance in the coils of a humbucking pickup must be equal to each other.

How To Use A Multitester

The first thing noticeable on a multitester is a dial-like meter window with many numbers, division lines and a needle which points to the different numbers. Notice that there are several differently colored arcs with numbers on them, we are only interested in the one that says **ohms**. There may be one or two knobs that select the function that a meter will register, but in guitar electronics the basic concern is d.c. ohms – not volts or anything else. There will be several numbers and codes on the ohm function switch that read like 1, 10x, 100x, 1000x; this notation is a multiplier. If a scale reads 1, and if the needle points to 500 ohms, then multiply it by 1. This is simple, it registers 500 ohms. However, if the selector is turned to 10x, 500 ohms must then be multiplied by 10 which equals 5,000 ohms. For shorthand, that could be written as 5K ohms (K stands for 1,000 in electronics terminology).

Because you will be testing parts with d.c. resistance of up to 500,000 ohms, you will want a meter that goes up to at least this amount. If a meter just goes to 500K that number will most likely be crammed at the end of the scale where it's hard to read. When you buy a meter, check how hard it is to read the following amounts of ohms: 3,000, 5,000, 7,000, 8,500, 13,000, 16,000, 250,000, 500,000. These are the readings for many common guitar parts. The lower figures are resistances of pickups; whereas the two high ones are pots.

To get a reading from a meter, touch a probe (there are two) to either point of something to be measured. If the two probes are touched together, the scale should read no resistance no matter what the ohm selector multiplier may be. If the two probes are held apart in the air, the scale should read, infinite ohms. Most meters have an infinite ohms adjust knob and a "no" (zero) resistance adjust knob. There really is no reason to buy a superduper meter, you need not spend more than about $16 to $50 (U.S.A. currency). Digital readout meters are easy to read when you look for one value, but if you are trying to see how smoothly a pot changes resistances (when a knob shaft is turned), it's better to watch a moving needle.

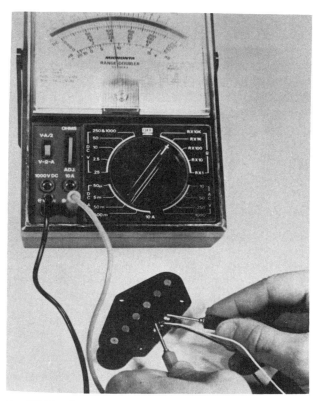

Fig. 179 The three photos show how to use an ohmmeter: The first photo shows an infinite ohms reading, the second photo shows a zero ohms reading, and the third photo shows checking the d.c. resistance of a pickup.

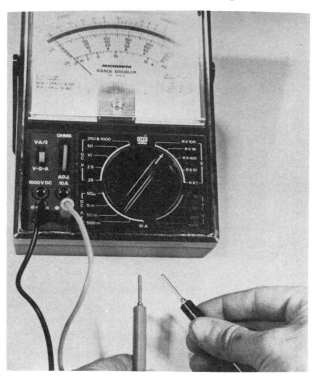

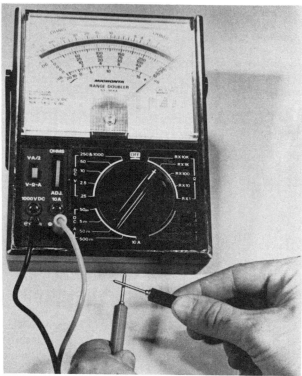

SHIELDING

Shielding is the use of conductive material to electronically insulate a component. A conductive shield can intercept noise producing electrical signals by conducting the signals to a ground point. Any unshielded signal carrying conductor can pick up hum and noise. Guitars need to be completely shielded in order to provide the best signal-to-noise ratio and safe operation.

Shielding Against A Shocking Experience

Some guitar companies don't do a proper shielding job. Many new guitars are well shielded, but there are many old guitars that require additional shielding. Proper shielding involves surrounding a guitar's electronic components with an insulating cover that is connected to ground. Because this can become expensive to manufacturers, a few guitar companies have not bothered to shield instruments. To compensate for this, they run a ground wire to the bridge. The bridge connects to the strings, and guess who connects to the strings? That's right – You! You become the ground shield that the companies don't care to install.

Every once in a while you hear about a guitar player being electrocuted while playing a guitar. How does this happen if a guitar cannot generate high voltage? Well, the truth is that it isn't the guitar which produces the shock, it only allows it to happen. This is how it works: Imagine you are playing a guitar and singing into a mic. Now, if your sound systems are plugged into two-prong outlets, the plugs can go in either way. If your guitar amp is plugged in so that the ground connects to the left prong, and the mic's amp is plugged in so that the ground connects with the right prong of the power cord – watch out! This situation results in a reverse ground condition; and if you hold the guitar's neck and strings in one hand and grab the mic with the other hand, you become part of a current carrying circuit. You very well may go out in a blaze of glory – forget the encore!

For your own protection, take off the ground wire that goes to the bridge. The guitar could hum very loudly with the bridge ground disconnected. Don't despair, just go through and completely shield and properly ground all electronic components. Although a humbucking pickup can cancel hum noise, all other wiring and exposed conductive surfaces in a guitar can cause noise.

Single pickup guitars present a perplexing shielding/grounding problem because they are not humbucking; therefore, they cannot be totally hum-free through the use of shielding. A ground wire to the bridge is necessary for quiet operation.

Some guitar companies specialize in expensive single-coil pickup guitars which use a string ground. These instruments are often sold to experienced professional guitarists who are very aware of the possibility of shock hazard and so are in little danger. It is hoped that this book will help inform the guitarists about the shock hazards of guitars and instill cautious behavior. Guitars can benefit from isolated ground circuits, but even guitars without them, e.g., single-coil pickup guitars, can be safe when prudence is practised.

Shielding generally consists of: (1) a metal or foil cover that shields the pickup, (2) braided or foil shielded connecting wire, (3) a shielded control compartment, and (4) a shielded output jack.

Covers for Shielding

All covers should be electrically conductive; but they should not be attracted to a magnet; therefore, they should not be iron, steel, or nickel. They could be solid aluminum, copper, brass, gold, or even a silver, copper, or carbon conductive paint. A steel cover would interfere with the string signal and distort the flux field of the magnet. A pickup cover should be thin so that it doesn't interfere or slightly distort any signal of the strings. Gibson makes nickel silver cases, but they are a bit thick; new ones are .028 of an inch thick, old ones are .022 of an inch thick. The heavy cases are made to protect guitars that get rough treatment. These cases do not significantly alter the magnetic field of a pickup.

A shield can be as thin as .005 of an inch and still be effective. It just so happens that this is the thickness of heavy duty aluminum foil. Aha! The problem here is that pickups covered with aluminum foil look shoddy. You should really have a plastic exterior cover for appearance sake.

Some musicians take the metal covers off their humbucking pickups in an attempt to gain power and a more rock 'n' roll sound.[10] Most covers (tops) are

10. SEE PAGE 125

soldered to a mounting base with two spots of solder. The common way to remove the top requires a soldering gun (not pencil) and a de-soldering tool which can remove the solder lump after you melt it. Without this tool you may be tempted to try bending the case sides to break the solder bond. This could hurt the pickup if you're clumsy, and it is very easy to rip the fine wires of the coils. The photo shows the best way to remove a cover; using a Dremel with a saw blade to cut through the solder which holds the cover to the base.

The sound you get by having the covers off will be louder and brighter, but you will also have a bit more hum because you have removed the cover which provided shielding.

Fig. 180 Removing a cover of a humbucking pickup.

Single coil pickups are not humbucking; therefore, they are not capable of truly quiet operation, but they still can benefit from a shielded cover. Fender Telecasters have a metal cover shield which fits over their single coil rhythm pickups. The lead pickups are covered by a grounding plate. Covers provide a more quiet operation with less background noise. Fender Stratocasters also have single coil pickups, but the covers on these pickups are of a non-conductive plastic and do not assist shielding. If the inside of these covers were painted with conductive paint and connected to a ground lead, they could form an electrical shield.

All pickups, whether single coil or humbucking, can benefit from the shielding provided by covers.

Fig. 181 Open top and closed top pickup covers sold by DiMarzio.

One problem some players experience with uncovered, hot rod single coil pickups is that they are too big to fit under the stock pickup cases, and the high E or low E can catch on the lip of the bobbin. This can be a problem for Strat owners who use high output replacement pickups and play in a very vigorous manner. In this situation, the only answer is to cast a pickup within a mold so the final product has a solid, smooth exterior. Check the pickups on a Gibson S-I for an example of this solution.

Shielded Wire

It is very important that the wires going from the pickups to the controls and then to the output, be shielded so that only the sound of the strings is heard because unshielded wire can act like an antenna and pick up noise. Shielded wire consists of a conducting wire(s) surrounded by a braided wire or metal foil shield. Inexpensive coaxial braided wire has a miserly shield that is only half there. Be careful when buying wire, it's wise to remove an inch of the outside plastic so that you can see how good the braided shield is. Remember, it should be braided, not just a few loosely woven strands of copper. The braid should cover 100% of the surface.

Fig. 182 Coaxial wire with a braided shield.

Gibson once used a coaxial wire known as Lenzite. This wire consisted of a bare-wire braided shield, and under this was a cotton liner that wrapped around the plastic insulated hot lead. This wire is now very hard to find, but it's worth looking for because it offers one significant advantage: you can solder to the metal braid and the plastic insulation will not melt because the cotton liner keeps the heat from penetrating through the wire. Nowadays the outside plastic sleeve must be stripped off the outside of most coaxial wires, and it's important to be very careful when soldering the braid to a pot because there is no cotton liner. This means that the heat goes directly to the internal plastic casing and melts it, allowing the center wire to contact the outside braid. There is now a short, which can't be seen, inside the wire, and the only way the short can be located is to use an ohmmeter. So remember – **solder with care!** If you are doing a lot of wiring, **check each wire connection after you solder it.**

In the last few years, multiconductor four-lead shielded wire has become popular. The shield is usually 100%, and the wire is small and flexible. This wire is available with one, two, three, four or more colored leads.

Shielded Controls

Just as pickups need to be grounded, so must all other components of an electronic circuit. This includes pots, switches, etc. The most practical grounding method is to solder a grounding wire to the lock-washer which fits over the threaded bushing of the component.

The hard-to-shield parts are open wire connections at pots, switches, and jacks; all of which add up to several inches of unshielded wire and hum. One

solution is to have everything encased in metal containers with only coaxial wire between the containers. Gibson has done this with some guitars, and one of the first guitars to receive complete shielding was the Gibson ES-I75C. It's phenomenal how free of external noise this instrument is. The pickups are shielded, and the pots and jack are also completely shielded. Shown are the parts necessary to accomplish this shielding. It's well worth the extra time and expense.

Fig. 183 A shielding can for a pot.

Gibson has recently become one of the leaders in effective shielding. The new Les Pauls with humbuckers are a good example: (1) the pickups are completely shielded with a shielded coaxial wire going to the control pots; (2) a foil-shielded multi-lead wire goes from the shielded pots to a shielded toggle switch; (3) a shielded output then goes from a switch to an output jack enclosed in a shielded canister; (4) there is no ground wire going to the strings, and this prevents accidental electrocution; (5) the grounding and shielding are perfect, and even the pots have plastic insulating knobs.

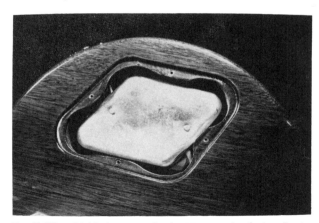

Fig. 184 The shielded tone and volume controls of a Les Paul.

Unfortunately, Gibson's Les Pauls with single coil pickups (and virtually all single coil pickup guitars) still have a ground wire connected to the bridge which connects to the strings and player. Single coil pickups have an inherent hum problem, and without the ground wire to the bridge, the guitar will be unplayable in certain situations.

Fig. 185 The shielded switch of a Les Paul.

Another method of shielding is to paint the guitar's control compartment cavity with conductive paint, then attach connection wire to ground. There are several types of paint that can be used for this purpose: silver, copper, and carbon. The silver paint works very well but is quite expensive. Generally, only two coats are necessary to form an adequate shield. Copper is less expensive than silver, but it requires five or six coats to form an adequate shield. Carbon conductive paint is the newest material for painted shielding, and it is becoming very popular. It's reasonable in cost, waterbase, and easy to see when an adequate amount has been applied. The carbon paint is black and is painted on until a solid black surface is achieved.

Fender recently began applying conductive carbon paint to the internal cavities of their instruments. This coating serves as an efficient conductive shield for the instrument's electrical conductors. This shielding results in a more hum-free instrument as well as being safer to operate.

Shielded Output Jacks

A shielded jack is a jack encased in a metal can, and this can is connected to ground. These jacks have a hole into which a shielded wire can be inserted. A shielding can prevents the connection wires of the jack from receiving unwanted noise.

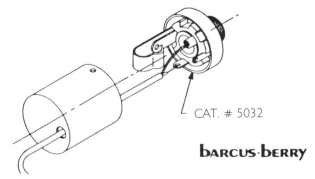

CAT. # 5032

barcus-berry

Fig. 186 Shielded jack w/ON-OFF.

SHIELDING PROCEDURES

The following information describes the methods used to shield guitars:

1. Shield the pickups: Use a metal cover or a plastic cover lined with foil. Watch out so that the shielding material doesn't come in connection with any hot lead.

This can happen quite easily with the exposed lead connection joints on Fender pickups. Bring all grounds to a single point so as to eliminate ground loops and resultant hum.

2. Attach coaxial or multi-lead wiring.

3. Use a shielded switch. You may have to make a box to hold it.

4. Use shielded pots, or shield the control compartment. II

5. Use a shielded output jack.

6. Use plastic knobs. Metal knobs can act as conductors.

7. Recheck and make sure that the shielding is connected to the ground connection of the jack, and that no ground ever touches a hot lead, even when the pickups are switched out-of-phase.

8. Remove the ground wire to the bridge, and live a long and happy life with a hum-free guitar.

SQUEALS AND FEEDBACK: MICROPHONICS IN PICKUPS

Squeals and feedback are a result of a pickup being microphonic. The best method to use in dealing with this problem is: potting and saturating.

Potting

Potting a pickup means encasing it in a solid material, e.g., epoxy resin. Potting helps reduce the possibility of microphonics. Microphonics occur when any integral part of a pickup loosens and becomes a source of internal magnetic induction. When the insides of a pickup are loose enough to move, the pickup can start to behave like a microphone. In fact, if you speak into a pickup that is internally loose, you can hear your voice through the amplifier. One way to overcome this problem is to encapsulate the internal structure in resin. When hardened, resin reduces internal shifting.

Fig. 187 Resin potted Super Humbucker.

The most common procedure for potting is as follows: First, a pickup cover (also called a can) is half filled with a resin such as epoxy. Then the coil bobbins and magnet/pole piece structure is lowered into the cover. More resin is poured until the cover is full. At this point, the resin is allowed to harden. [Note: Most epoxy resins will not properly harden below 65° Fahrenheit. Also remember that epoxy must be

II. SEE PAGE 125

thoroughly mixed so pockets of non-mixed, non-hardening materials do not exist.]

After a pickup is potted it cannot be taken apart. If a single lead humbucker is potted, it cannot be changed to multi-lead. Therefore, you should anticipate what type of wiring you may want in the future before you pot the pickup. If you want multi-leads, the following two procedures can achieve this: (1) Multi-lead wire can be soldered to the wire ends of each coil before potting. This will result in the pickup end of the output wire being securely anchored in the potting material. (2) Soldering lugs can be connected to the ends of the coil wires, and these lugs can protrude above the surface of the potting material. Connection wires can then be soldered to the lugs whenever desired.

Coil Saturation

By itself, potting is only able to reduce a minor portion of microphonic susceptibility in a pickup. The best way to reduce this susceptibility is to solidify the wire coils. Solidifying coils is often called saturation. Sometimes it is incorrectly called potting. For clarity sake, the term potting should be reserved for the encapsulation of magnets, pole pieces, and wound coils.

To combat the source of pickup microphonics, it's necessary to solidify the coils of a pickup before potting them. Few humbuckers are made with solidified coils. Solidifying coils is done by impregnating a coil with a substance that will create solidarity. Wax is the most common material used.

As of the writing of this book the author knows of only one company that saturates the coils of all of its pickups, that company is Schecter. The following information will describe the procedure. First, wound bobbins are suspended in a framework, and the bobbins (coils) are then submerged in a vat of heated synthetic beeswax for one hour. It takes this long for wax to fully penetrate 100% of the coil windings. The synthetic beeswax is used because it adheres very well to the wire, hardens without becoming brittle, and melts at higher temperatures of 170°F. Normal paraffin isn't used because it's very brittle at cool temperatures, and it has a melting point which is considered too low – 130°-140°F.

The humbucking pickups made by many companies are notorious for their microphonic behavior. Attempting to wax saturate these pickups' coils is **very** tricky because the plastic bobbins on which the coils are wound often melt at 140°-150°F. It is possible to saturate wound bobbins in melted 130° paraffin if caution is used. It isn't practical to saturate humbucking pickup bobbins in melted synthetic beeswax because of the high temperature. The plastic bobbins of nearly all humbucking pickups are made from some type of ABS plastic. This material cannot withstand high temperatures. When a bobbin is immersed in 170° synthetic beeswax, it will begin to disintegrate in 30 to 60 seconds. To successfully saturate a wound plastic bobbin, use the following procedure:

1. Remove cover if present.

2. Remove mounting screws. There are usually four of them under the base plate.
3. Unwrap connections of lead output to coil leads. Unwrap joined coil leads if present.
4. Unsolder these connections.
5. Separate wound bobbins from the rest of the pickup.
6. Very carefully unwrap and remove tape from around the outside of the wound bobbins.
7. Suspend bobbins in a bath of 130°-135°F wax for one hour if possible. Check often to see if bobbins are warping or melting.
8. Remove bobbin and let cool.
9. Reassemble pickup.

Wax saturating single coil pickups is usually very easy because these pickups do not normally use a temperature sensitive plastic bobbin form. Usually the bobbin is constructed out of vulcanized fiber board and alnico magnet slugs. This type of assembly can take the degree of heat needed to melt even synthetic beeswax.

Feedback From Loud Volumes

When playing electric guitars at loud volumes in front of powerful amps, feedback and squeal can be very annoying problems. The cause for this is usually a pickup that is creating microphonics. (See the section on microphonics.)[12]

The use of metal pickguards is introducing a new source of feedback and squeal because these metal plates vibrate when subjected to sound waves coming from speakers. The resultant howl can seem to be a mystery to people not familiar with feedback. Aluminum is the worst offender; brass pickguards are about one-third as susceptible to plate feedback. There are several things that can be done to combat this problem, all involve dampening the motion of the plate. Some people have had success with putting tiny rubber "O" rings under the pickguard's mounting screws. Other people have had success with putting a very thin (one-eighth inch) slab of soft foam padding under the pickguard. This foam crushes down to about one-thirty second of an inch. The surest way to eliminate the vibrations is to spread liquid silicone rubber under the pickguard. This does dampen the plate, but it also glues it down so firmly that it might bend when removing it for servicing. If you use silicone rubber, use it sparingly.[13]

REPAIRING ELECTRIC GUITARS

Nearly every time an electric guitar stops working it's because of a broken wire somewhere in the guitar. In these cases it's easy to see what's wrong if you examine all the inter-connected wires. The most common problem source is the output jack. It seems that the wires that connect to a jack keep breaking loose. This happens because the nut that holds the jack vibrates loose. This condition is due to the frequency of plugging and unplugging the cord. To eliminate this problem, it's a good idea to add Lock-Tite (available at auto parts stores) to the threads of parts that tend to loosen. Typical parts that loosen are the output jack, pots, and switches. The loose nut problem also affects

12. 13. SEE PAGE 125

SERVICING ELECTRIC GUITAR CIRCUITS

switches, especially rotary switches because people turn the knobs too forcefully. Likewise with pots, if they are not secured, they turn and break the wires off the lugs. Another thing that could happen is that twisted wires can short out against each other which causes intermittent sound and hum.

Three-way toggle switches are notorious for causing several problems. The most common complaint is that they don't stay in positions #1 and #3; they keep slipping back to position #2 (the center). In this case, you can either replace the switch or try to bend the contacts so that the contacts stay where they should. If you have a pair of needle nose pliers, you can bend back the contact that doesn't firmly mate with the switch lever. This is much easier to see than to explain.

Soldered connections done by a guitar manufacturer are usually good, but sometimes a cracked joint will cause the sound to flicker on and off. A good solder joint looks shiny like chrome, whereas a poor joint looks like dull pitted silver; this condition is usually the result of solder not being hot enough. This cold solder joint is more prone to failure because it is crumbly and brittle. Another solder problem is too much heat which can cook the insides of pots, switches and pickups. Fortunately, pots and switches are heavy-duty units.

When checking out a nonfunctioning electric guitar with a pickup, don't jump to conclusions as to what is malfunctioning. The number one reason for an electric guitar not working properly is a defective cord. Yes, the cord, not the guitar. Make sure your cords are not defective; check them with an ohmmeter. Stepping on a cord can cause it to break on the inside, and pulling it can break the connections on the plug ends. Another common cause of "guitar" failure, is an amp that doesn't work properly.

The following is a guide for pinpointing the problem of an electric guitar that doesn't work correctly:

Symptom: No sound at all.
Possible Diagnosis: Broken hot lead. Check for a broken lead.

Symptom: Loud hum, but no string sound.
Possible Diagnosis: Broken ground connection.

Symptom: Crackling sound.
Possible Diagnosis: Loose connection on pot, jack, or other component.

Symptom: Gritty, scratchy sound when tone or volume are touched.
Possible Diagnosis: Check for dust or dirt in a pot. The pot could be worn out.

Symptom: Low volume.
Possible Diagnosis: Pickup is too far from the strings, or bronze acoustic strings are being used on an electric guitar, or there is a short in the pickup. Also check to see if grease, silicone rubber, or some other insulating material is on the output jack. Check if there is a broken pot path. All these conditions can be checked with an ohm section of the multitester.

Symptom: Tone control doesn't work.
Possible Diagnosis: Broken connection, or wrong value capacitor. Most single coil pickups use a .02 up to a .05 capacitor. Humbuckers use a .05 to a .01 microfarad capacitor.

CHOOSING THE RIGHT POT FOR A GIBSON LES PAUL

If you want to replace defective pots in a Les Paul or upgrade the pot quality, you could encounter some tricky problems. The main problem is fitting standard pots into the changing thickness of the violin-shaped curved top. Standard pots for Fender guitars with a 1/4 inch or 3/8 inch threaded bushing will not fit into a Les Paul because these pots are made for mounting through a pickguard and not through a thick wooden top of a guitar. The Nashville made models pose a problem because the depth of the hole through which the pot shaft bushings go through is inconsistent, whereas in older Les Pauls the depth for each hole remains the same. In Nashville made models, the two holes near the edge go through 9/32 of an inch of wood; the hole nearest the center goes through 15/32 of an inch; and the remaining hole goes through 12/32 of an inch. Therefore, pots suitable for a Fender guitar with a threaded bushing of 1/4 of an inch cannot work in these Nashville Pauls. Pots with a 1/2 inch bushing could work for three of the controls but an 1/8 of an inch of wood would have to be carved out around the hole of the pot closest to the center. A simple solution is to use extra long threaded pots and have a nut on the shaft adjusted so that only a desired amount of the shaft can fit through the hole. You should not have a problem if you use pots with bushings of 7/8 of an inch. This problems of selecting pots with the correct length bushing is greatly simplified when working with older Les Pauls. Older Les Pauls like '59 classics take pots with 1/2 inch long threaded bushings for all four positions.

The Schecter Z+/Superock harness uses Omni

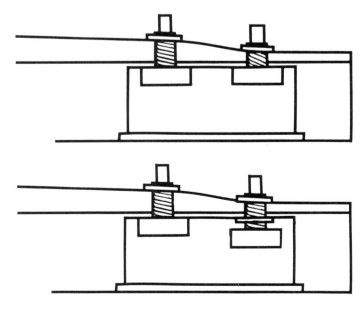

Fig. 188 How to fit pots through a changing thickness top.

Pots, and this harness assembly fits right into older Les Pauls. The Omni Pots provide coil splitting, series/parallel and phase changing. You can achieve all this without having to drill one hole or carve out any wood. Quite an attractive feature to a "sunburst tiger-stripe" '59 Paul owner. However, owners of newer Pauls may have a problem because they may have to route out a deeper control compartment and some may even have to make a new brass grounding plate because the Omni Pot's threaded bushings are only ½ inch long.

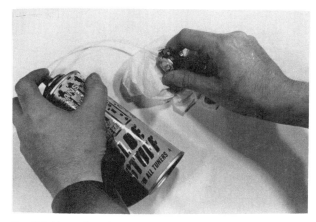

Fig. 189 Using Blue Stuff.

Servicing Pots

Sometimes a pot makes a crackling sound when it is turned. That would mean that there is dirt in it, or it is charged with static electricity, or the resistance path is worn out. There are many brands of solvent spray cleaners that can be squirted into an open pot to rinse it out. A superior product is "Bluestuff" which cleans and also contains a non-conductive lubricant that helps produce a smooth-turning pot.

Before installing a pot in a complicated circuit, it's a good idea to check it out on an ohmmeter. Look to see if the needle moves smoothly. If it jumps erratically, the pot is defective. Checking things beforehand with an ohmmeter can save a lot of grief.

Fig. 190 The information in this book can help prevent repair destruction like that which has occurred with this vintage instrument.

3. Hot Rodding Electric Guitars

Before the advent of specially made pickups by companies like: DiMarzio, Lawrence, Hi-A, Schecter, Duncan, etc., altering standard pickups started to become common. One of the first hot rodding alterations to pickups was to replace the single alnico magnet with a ceramic one.[14] This resulted in an increase in the power of the magnetic field which increased the induction of the pickup's coils, and therefore increased the output of the pickup. A Gibson pickup modified in the manner will have an increase in volume, especially in the mid-range and trebles. Gibson saw that this was what people wanted, and came out with their version of a hot rod pickup – the Super Humbucker, it uses three ceramic magnets.

The magnets are an integral part of the internal structure of Fender single coil pickups and cannot be removed without damaging the coil; therefore, the only effective way of boosting a stock Tele or Strat is to install a preamp. Many companies make preamps that are small enough to fit in the control compartment of Fender and other guitars.

There are many other guitar alterations for more tonal variation. The following information describes how to achieve more versatility from an electric guitar.

CHOOSING A SPECIALTY PICKUP

There are some strong opinions about what is the "right" sound. It is a valid point that any sound you like is right. What has been traditionally the type of sound for a particular music, changes throughout the years. The electric guitar was once ignored or treated like an outcast, but today it is embraced by all types of music. Many people have taken the sound of one type of instrument and introduced it to other audiences. However, there is a limit to what can or will be accepted as a change because there are some firm traditions. Telecasters have a "country" sound, and Les Pauls are really "rock" guitars, etc. Some musicians are able to interest people in the sound of an instrument used for another style music, such as a country electric guitar being used in hard rock 'n' roll. It's a challenge of originality and creativity. However, there are some things that would be difficult to accomplish successfully – such as playing classical music on rock guitars.

Generally, acoustic based music (e.g., bluegrass) demands an acoustic type sound which can be obtained by using contact pickups. Progressive bluegrass, folk, and simple country music may call for acoustic sounding electromagnetic pickups on acoustic instruments which give the clear, sharp twang of single coil pickups. Rock music uses a lot of full, heavy sounds, and often requires high impedance/high output humbuckers. Just remember there is no rule that says "this music" must have "this kind of sound", or that you must use "this kind" of pickup.

As for practical considerations of what pickup to use, check the descriptions of pickups, and such factors as cost, quality of tone, durability, ease of installation and usage.

Installing An Electro-Magnetic Pickup On An Acoustic Guitar
1. Loosen the strings.
2. Place pickup in soundhole.
3. Tape output cord in place.

If you want to permanently install a pickup on a guitar, you could use a Barcus Berry end-pin for a non-conspicuous jack, or you could drill a hole in the side of the lower bout and install a 1/4 inch output jack.

Installing A Replacement Pickup In A Solid Body Guitar
1. Remove the strings.
2. Remove the cover plate and unsolder the present pickup from its first connection which could be either the switch or a volume pot.
3. Remove the pickup mounting ring with the pickup attached.
4. Separate the pickup and mounting ring.
5. Install new pickup on mounting ring.
6. Solder the lead from the new pickup to the proper place.
7. Install the screws holding the mounting ring.
8. Put strings back on.
9. Adjust height of pickup and pole pieces.

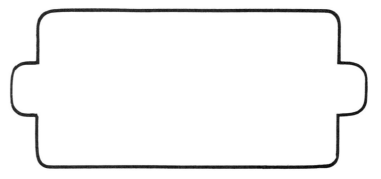

Fig. 191 Template shape for routing a hole for a humbucking pickup.

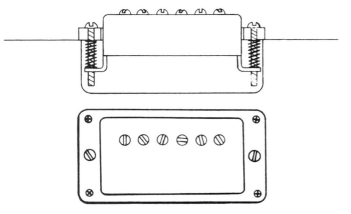

Fig. 192 Pickup using a mounting ring.

Mounting Rings

Pickups mount either on a pickguard or on mounting rings. Mounting rings are attached to the top of a guitar and provide support for a pickup. This procedure means that the pickup is not directly attached to an instrument but rather, to a mounting ring. Nearly all large humbucking pickups use mounting rings. If you are working with mounting rings, you may have noticed their many different heights and angles. One convenience of mounting rings is that they are easily removed which facilitates pickup repairs.

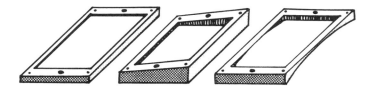

Fig. 193 Mounting rings, from left to right: On left, for a guitar with a totally flat top; in the middle, for a guitar with an angled neck, and on the right, for a guitar with a curved top.

Some instruments use a modified ring concept. In this situation, a pickup is mounted to a pickguard which has a cut-out the same size as the pickup. The pickguard mounts to the guitar, and the pickup fits within the cut-out. Therefore, the pickguard becomes a mounting ring. Fender guitars use this system. It may not offer all the convenience of a detachable mounting ring, but it's effective and less expensive.

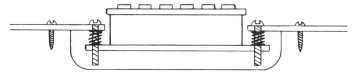

Fig. 194 Pickup mounted on a pickguard.

There are a few electric guitars and basses which eliminate both mounting rings or pickguards by having pickups screwed or bolted into place. Probably the most common instruments with this feature are the Gibson guitars with single coil pickups. In this set-up, each pickup is held down by two long screws.

Adjusting Pickups For Desired Volume

Pickups need to be close to the strings for full fidelity because it's the strings' movement that activates the pickup. Missing notes can result from having the pickup too far from the string. After pickups are as close as possible without the fretted string hitting them, or causing a dampening of the strings, adjust the pole pieces to adjust string-to-string volume. Shown is the basic pattern of pole piece adjustment when using strings with or without a wound G string. Plain strings are louder than wound.

A screw driver is used to raise the pole piece or lower it; turning clockwise lowers it; turning counterclockwise raises it. The top of the pole piece should never be below the surface of the pickup, nor should it be more than one-eighth of an inch above the surface. Be careful not to turn it too far because it could fall out.

One sensitivity adjustment that cannot be achieved

Fig. 195 Adjusting the height of a pickup.

Fig. 196 Adjusting pole pieces of a pickup.

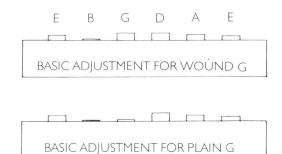

Fig. 197 Pole piece adjustment.

is the drop in volume that is experienced when bending strings. This drop is the result of the string being pushed out of the area of a pole piece which can be an annoying problem on Strats. For this reason (as well as others) Bill Lawrence came out with pickups that have full width pole pieces.

COIL REWINDING

Some people, when working on their pickups, break the fine wire of the coils. Other people have new guitars and want "the old sound". Both are candidates for pickup rewinding.

You could try rewinding the coils yourself by hand, but it's difficult because the wire breaks very easily. Therefore, you must wind very slowly, and this makes it a tedious process. It could take a whole day or two to wind just one pickup. Also, you can't buy just a small amount of wire because it's commonly sold in minimum one to five-pound spools. A five-pound spool could cost $50 and will wind approximately seventy single coil pickups or fifty sets of twin coils for humbucking pickups. So after you have made a winding jig and bought all the supplies, you will have a lot of time and money tied up in a project that requires the skill of experience. It's better to have pickup rewinding carried out by someone set up to do it, for example: Seymour Duncan. He could rewind defective coils or put a custom gauged winding on your pickup's coil bobbin.

Tele lead pickups used coil wire that was of a different gauge than that which is used today, and some guitarists want that finer gauge so as to recapture the "vintage" sound. If an owner of a rare expensive electric guitar finds that his pickup's coils have become defective, he won't like the idea of having to use new pickups because that would greatly reduce the value of the instrument. The solution to this problem is to have his old pickup bobbins rewound. Another advantage of rewinding is that custom designs can be fabricated. If you design your own pickups, you could have a coil winder make any kind of coil you desired. An owner of a guitar could make magnet assemblies himself which could be of interest to those with a Stratocaster because they could have a pickup made with an opposite magnetic polarity to that which is standard. This pickup could then be used as a replacement for the stock middle pickup. This combination means that a Strat could function as three independent single coil pickups in the following manner: #1 and #2 pickups linked together as a humbucker in-phase; the #2 and #3 linked together as a humbucker in-phase; or #1 and #3 linked together as a humbucking pickup out-of-phase. Any of these humbucking configurations could be series or parallel linked. In addition, there is still the option of using the pickups individually so a true Stratocaster sound could be obtained. This would give a total of over 8 tonal possibilities.

A few closing notes on what makes a good coil: (1) the wire should be wound tightly and evenly. Unless the coil is 100% saturated for solidarity, loose windings make for poor performance and microphonics, (2) there should be a guard against moisture penetrating the coil because moisture in a coil increases its capacitance and limits the output. The most simple guard is to dip a coil in wax, but the most secure method is to saturate the coil with epoxy resin, and make sure the resin doesn't melt the insulation of the wire. A shorted-out coil beautifully encased in a ruby red resin is only fit to be a paper weight.

Saturating coils in resin can be tricky. It's often difficult to get resin to penetrate to the inner windings of a coil. It's the inner windings that are the main agents in causing feedback because they vibrate against the magnet(s).

WHEN TO USE MULTI-LEAD WIRING

The earliest pickups came with two leads: a ground lead and a hot output lead. Most single coil pickups had two separate unshielded wires. Most humbuckers had a single coaxial wire; the outside braid was the ground,

and the inside wire was a shielded hot lead.

In time, people began to add new wiring configurations. If someone wanted one humbucker to be out-of-phase with another, one of the pickups would need three leads. The first lead would be a ground, the second lead could be hot lead #1, and the third lead could be hot lead #2. Since phasing involves switching the polarity of the pickup, there is a need for two (preferably shielded) hot leads that could be inverted. One would be hot and one would be ground. Pickup companies therefore, began supplying humbuckers with two shielded leads and a ground. But then people began to split humbuckers because they wanted that "Fender" sound. This necessitated a lead connection to the junction of the two coils so that one coil could be grounded out of operation. At this time, pickup companies began making humbuckers with three shielded leads plus a ground. Then people started linking humbuckers to series/parallel switches to get more tonal possibilities. It is preferable to have four independent leads plus a ground. Each coil has two leads (a beginning and end of the wire winding), and a humbucker has two coils; four leads gives access to all wiring possibilities. The ground should be separate so there is freedom to use any wire as a hot lead.

Many companies are now making humbuckers with 4+ (four leads plus a ground) wiring which allows for a complete wiring freedom. If you have a humbucker with less than the 4+ layout, you may want to take apart the pickup and attach multiple leads to it. The number of leads needed depends on the functions you plan on using. However, if you are taking the time to rewire a pickup, it is suggested that you install the 4+ wiring so that in the future you can use leads you presently might not have use for.

Shown in a photo is a pickup with four separate coaxial wires attached. This is believed to reduce the incidence of capacitance and inductance losses. This type of cabling is quite extreme, and currently no companies are actively using it. However, many companies are offering 4+ wiring which is a good alternative to four separate leads.

The braided shield 4+ wire is the heaviest duty but is stiff to bend around tight corners and is rather large. Foil shielded 4+ wire is better for small spaces because it is smaller in diameter and is more flexible. Foil usually gives 100% shield, whereas braided shield varies

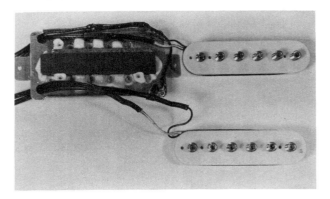

Fig. 198 Two coil pickups can have four leads.

(from 50% to 95% shield coverage).

Now that you have your pickup apart you are probably wondering how to connect the leads. There is no universal color code, but you could follow Di Marzio's example since their 4+ wiring is the most common. However, the author feels that hot leads should always have a "hot" color, and ground leads should always have a "cold" color. So when you are trying to determine what wire goes to where, you have complete freedom, but remember what you did. You should keep a schematic of your connections for future reference. See the section on color codes for a full explanation on what several companies are doing with their pickups. In conclusion: color coding is useless if you don't remember what connects to what!

ADVANCED WIRING CIRCUITS

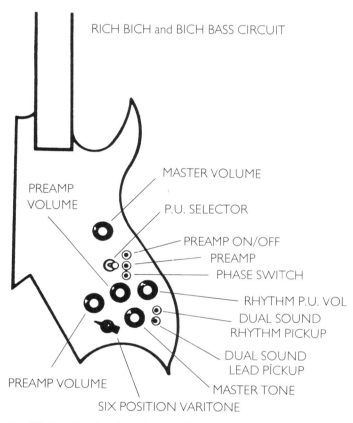

RICH BICH and BICH BASS CIRCUIT

MASTER VOLUME

PREAMP VOLUME

P.U. SELECTOR

PREAMP ON/OFF

PREAMP

PHASE SWITCH

RHYTHM P.U. VOL

DUAL SOUND RHYTHM PICKUP

DUAL SOUND LEAD PICKUP

PREAMP VOLUME

MASTER TONE

SIX POSITION VARITONE

Fig. 199 A multitude of switching and control possibilities of a guitar.

By-Pass Control

When the output of a pickup is routed through a switch, volume pot and tone pot, there is a degradation of the signal. The full power and brilliance of an electric guitar is impeded. For this reason, some musicians like

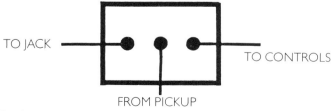

TO JACK

TO CONTROLS

FROM PICKUP

Fig. 200 By-pass switch.

the option of playing straight to an amp with no components in the way of the signal. A simple SPDT switch can be used as a selector to route the signal to the controls, or by-pass them and send the signal to the guitar jack. This is fine if an amp can handle the full output, and if a musician doesn't mind the lack of on-board controls.

Phasing

Importance Of Phasing

When you are working on a guitar with several pickups, it's necessary to know the phase relationship (which wire is the ground lead and which wire is the hot lead) of those pickups. If you don't know the phasing, it will be difficult to correctly wire the guitar. You will most likely end up with an instrument that creates only a loud hum or has a "nasalish" tone or has no sound at all.

It isn't that simple to determine phase relationships of an individual pickup, much less that of several pickups; especially when they are made by several different companies. Phase relationships involve several factors:

1. Which magnetic polarity (or polarities when referring to a humbucker) is the top of the pickup?[15]

2. Which direction was the coil wound?

3. Which side of the bobbin is the top, and which side is the bottom?

Even simple single coil pickups, like those made by Fender, can be tricky. Most of the time the magnets in these pickups have a south pole orientation for the top. But occasionally a pickup with a north orientation, or a reverse wound coil, is encountered. This can cause a playing problem, i.e., unwanted out-of-phase sounds.

If one pickup is out-of-phase with another, there isn't always a simple remedy. If you decide to use a hot lead as the ground and the ground lead as the hot, you may create a grounding problem. Ground leads are often connected to the case and/or magnet(s). Whereas hot leads don't connect to a ground point at all. If a ground lead and hot lead are reversed, the most likely result will be a pickup with a very high degree of hum because the case and/or magnets will now be an unshielded hot lead. This is a particular problem when wiring two pickups to a phase switch circuit, or when wiring two pickups to a series/parallel switching circuit.

In some situations it's possible to add "coming" and "going" leads to a pickup's coil(s) which are independent of a ground lead. The coming lead would be connected to the wire coming from the inside of the coil. The going lead would be connected to the wire on the outside of the coil. This would assure that grounding problems are averted when using complex switching networks. However, switching leads to solve phasing problems may not always be the solution because this situation may require reversing the magnetic orientation of the pickup. This reversing is easy to do. Just take the magnet (if it comes apart), or the whole pickup (if it's a single coil with alnico slugs) to anyone with a magnetizer. It's a very simple operation.

15. SEE PAGE 125

HOT RODDING

Phase Test

Using an oscilloscope is the professional way of determining phase, but this tool is very expensive. A more economical method to determine pickup phase is to use only a magnet, screwdriver, resistor, and ohmmeter: Switch the ohmmeter to d.c. ohms and hook up the pickup. Make sure the needle is in a centered position on the scale so you can see its motion clearly. If the needle is off center, it can be centered by using a resistor in series with the pickup. For example, if you have a 9,000 ohm pickup, and 20,000 ohms would be the center of the scale, use an 11,000 (or 10,000 for simplicity sake) ohm resistor. Now the needle should be standing straight up (or nearly so). Wave the magnet (preferably a bar magnet) in one direction closely over the pickup. You will notice that the needle of the ohmmeter will be deflected either right or left. Your only concern will be the first, or major deflection. Tapping the pickup with a screwdriver can be used in place of waving a magnet. This is an easier method for some people to use.

If all pickups deflect the needle in the same direction (always right or always left) the pickups are in-phase. If the deflections are in opposite directions, the pickups are out-of-phase.

Out-Of-Phase Wiring Of Pickups

When pickups are wired out-of-phase, you get a treble, hollow sound. This type of sound has been made famous by B.B. King.

Phase relationships apply to any pickup system that uses two or more signal sources. These sources can be the two coils of a humbucker, or two separate single coil pickups, or a combination of other types of pickups.

For the sake of simplicity, the function of two single coil pickups will be explained. A two-coil system is in-phase if both pickups receive the string's motion signal in the same way. That is, when the string moves toward the pickups, both the pickups become charged with a positive voltage. When the string vibrates away from the pickups, a negative voltage is induced. This sameness of pickup behavior will occur if both pickups have the same magnetic pole on their top side and are wired the same.

Now, if the pickups are four inches apart; the full fundamental note of a string could be 24 inches, the second harmonic would be six inches and the third harmonic would be three inches.* Note that the third harmonic will be shorter than the distance between the pickups which means that as the string is vibrating in short waves, one part of the string will be going down towards one pickup while another part of the string will be raising over the other pickups. This results in the pickups sensing opposite things. When these senses are joined, the two signals pretty much cancel each other out. The result is that you don't hear all the high pitched short wave overtones.

*A string also has many other vibrational patterns. See *Tuning Your Guitar,* by Donald Brosnac.

Now, if the hot lead and the ground lead are switched, an interesting thing happens. In this situation, the long wave tones of the string are mostly cancelled, and it's the short (shorter than 4 inches) high overtones that sing through. This is called out-of-phase.

Two pickups can be wired to be out-of-phase. This wiring is easy to do on a Telecaster, but to be out-of-phase, it's best that both pickups have a matched output. The two pickups on a Tele are different. A classic out-of-phase system is that found on the Gibson ES-355 played by B.B. King. This guitar has a switch that controls phase. When the switch is up, (and both pickups are on) both pickups work together in an out-of-phase condition. Gibson is now putting these switches on new ES-335's.

A phase switch's main function is to invert the relationship of both the ground and hot lead coming out of one pickup. One single coil pickup can be so linked to another, and the same holds true with two humbuckers, or even the two coils in a humbucker. The major disadvantage of having a humbucker out-of-phase with itself is that it's no longer humbucking.

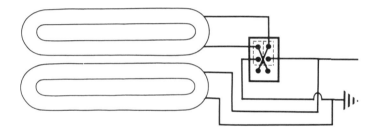

Fig. 201 Two coils in-phase

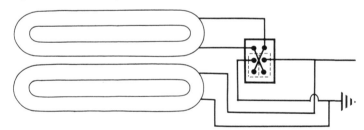

Fig. 202 Two coils out-of-phase.

Because out-of-phase reduces the low notes (which have a lot of energy) there is a loss of volume when switched to out-of-phase. This can be a bother because you have to readjust your volume when you switch

Fig. 203 Two DPDT switches, one with a cross-over necessary for phase switching.

between phase relationships. The closer the pickup elements are, the greater the out-of-phase effect, and the greater the drop in volume. A humbucker out-of-phase with itself will give the greatest change of sound, but the volume in out-of-phase will be reduced to about one-half.

Series/Parallel Switching

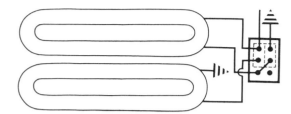

Fig. 204 Humbucker in parallel.

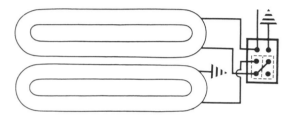

Fig. 205 Humbucker in series.

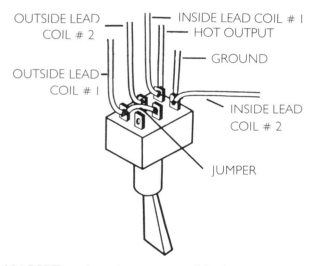

Fig. 206 DPDT switch used as a series parallel selector.

Earlier in this book the operation and tonal difference of series and parallel wiring were covered. In this section, diagrams of switches for series/parallel linking are given. The most common switch for this purpose is a DPDT switch; however, an Omni Pot is valuable for this use because no hole has to be drilled for a switch.

Splitter Switches

Splitter switches are used with dual coil pickups, i.e., humbuckers. If you want the extra tonal possibility of a single coil "Fender" sound from a humbucker, you can simply use only one coil of the pickup. All you need to do is add a switch that allows only one coil to be engaged. That is, you split the pickup. The only drawback of this new single coil sound is that it is not humbucking.

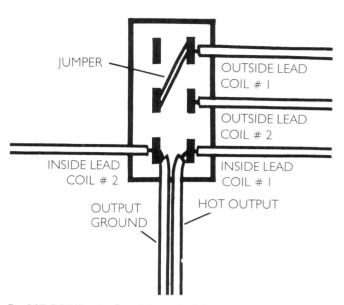

Fig. 207 DPDT series/parallel switch, DiMarzio style.

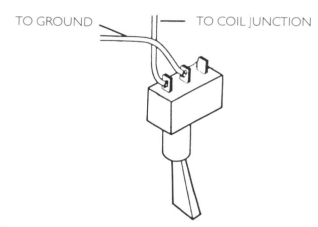

Fig. 208 An SPDT splitter switch.

A simple DPDT switch will allow the splitting of a coil. A DPDT position will allow three selections: (1) coil #1, (2) both coils as a series humbucker, and (3) coil #2.

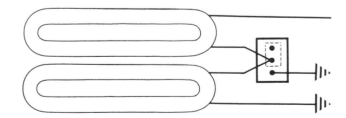

Fig. 209 Humbucker with both coils on.

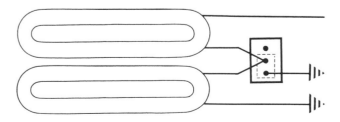

Fig. 210 Humbucker with only coil # 1 on.

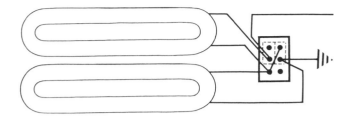

Fig. 211 Humbucker with only coil # 1 on.

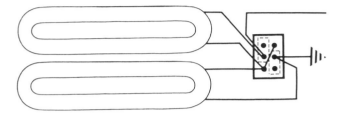

Fig. 212 Humbucker with both coils on.

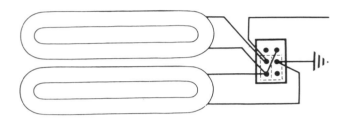

Fig. 213 Humbucker with only coil # 2 on.

Stereo

Stereo means getting two separate sounds from your guitar at one time. You could plug a single pickup guitar into two separate amps but that would not be stereo because stereo requires two separate signals. Therefore, to have stereo you need two pickups, each connected to its own amp, or any other means of creating two separate signals (i.e., a single pickup which is divided, such as the Ovation Acoustic Stereo pickups). Rickenbacker, Gibson, Ovation, Alembic, and others offer stereo guitars and basses.

There are several ways to achieve stereo. One way is to split a dual coil pickup, but this isn't very popular

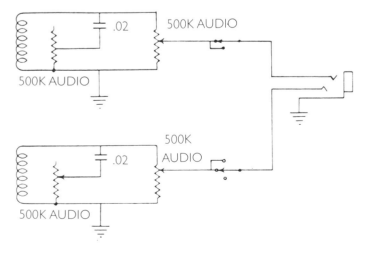

Fig. 214 Two pickup stereo.

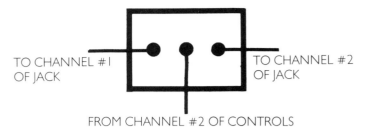

TO CHANNEL #1 OF JACK

TO CHANNEL #2 OF JACK

FROM CHANNEL #2 OF CONTROLS

Fig. 215 Switch needed for combining both channels when using a mono cord.

because then the pickup wouldn't be humbucking; therefore, using two humbuckers is preferable.

When playing in stereo, a musician can create a very full, unique sound by setting the tone differently for each of the pickups. This is stereo at its best. However, this is not extensively used because of the complications involved. The author has built interesting acoustic electrics that use magnetic pickups for bass tones and Hot Dots for treble tones.

A note on two magnetic pickup systems using dual controls: If there are two pickups, each having a volume control, and if everything is wired in monaural, the volume knobs will **not** act independently. When one volume is turned down, both pickups will be affected. The only way to avoid this is to go stereo.

Fig. 216 Two stereo CTS pots, the type used by Ovation.

Tapped Pickup

Tapped pickups are special single coil pickups. The coil is wound about half way, and then the lead wire is

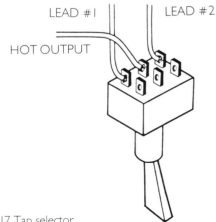

LEAD #1   LEAD #2

HOT OUTPUT

Fig. 217 Tap selector.

brought out to a junction point where it is soldered. A second lead is soldered to this junction, and a second coil is wound on top of the first. This gives three separate leads: (1) a ground lead from the inside of the coil, (2) a hot lead from the end of the first winding, and (3) a hot lead from the end of the second winding.

The first hot lead, connected to the lower resistance small coil, will give a bright clear sound. The second hot lead, connected to the higher resistance of the complete coil windings, will give a full, solid sound.

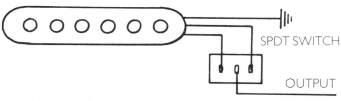

Fig. 218 Pickup and a tapping selector.

Varitone

Varitone is a tone device that offers a variety of tones and is based on the idea of using several capacitors for passing varying amounts of trebles.

If a certain capacitor of X value is used, all frequencies above Y frequency will flow through it. For example, the smaller the number value of a capacitor, the higher the frequency the capacitor passes. A varitone device gives the choice of several capacitors, so that we have a variety of tonal possibilities.

A common varitone design uses five capacitors and one coil choke all of which are attached to a six-

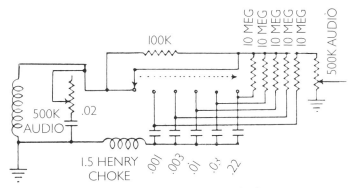

Fig. 219 Varitone circuit, see Gibson schematic for full details.

position rotary switch. The capacitor and coil are each attached to separate lugs of a rotary switch. The switch allows a player to choose whatever tone position he desires.

The coil is used as a tone filter similar to capacitors. A coil passes basses easier to ground, and this gives a thinner, treble tone. The biggest capacitor consumes (or drains) the most in trebles, the smallest passes the least. The coil is after the smallest capacitor. The whole assembly produces evenly changing tone steps.

You can select any of the six positions of the control. If you use the position linked to the coil, you will get the most treble, whereas the position linked to the smallest capacitor gives slightly less treble. There is a progressive change in tone from the first position to the last position. [Note: A varitone control always

needs to be used in conjunction with a tone control pot. Remember that a varitone control simply replaces the single capacitor of a normal tone control.]

Volume Control Extras

The Fender Telecaster uses a .001 mf capacitor between the input and output of the volume pot. This addition allows the trebles to be retained when playing at low volume settings. Schecter uses a .001 mf capacitor and a 150K ohm resistor so that the high fidelity is assured at low volume settings.

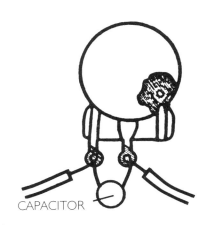

Fig. 220 Using a .001 capacitor on a volume control.

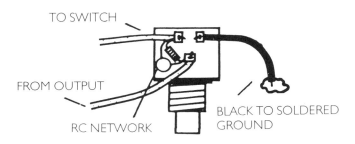

Fig. 221 Using a .001 capacitor and a 150K ohm resistor on a volume pot.

COMBINATION CIRCUITS

This switching system uses one humbucking pickup or two equal single coil pickups with opposite magnetic polarities. The choices are: Humbucking series in-phase, humbucking parallel in-phase, only coil #1, only coil #2, series out-of-phase, parallel out-of-phase.

Fig. 222 Four-pole six-position rotary switch used in combination circuits.

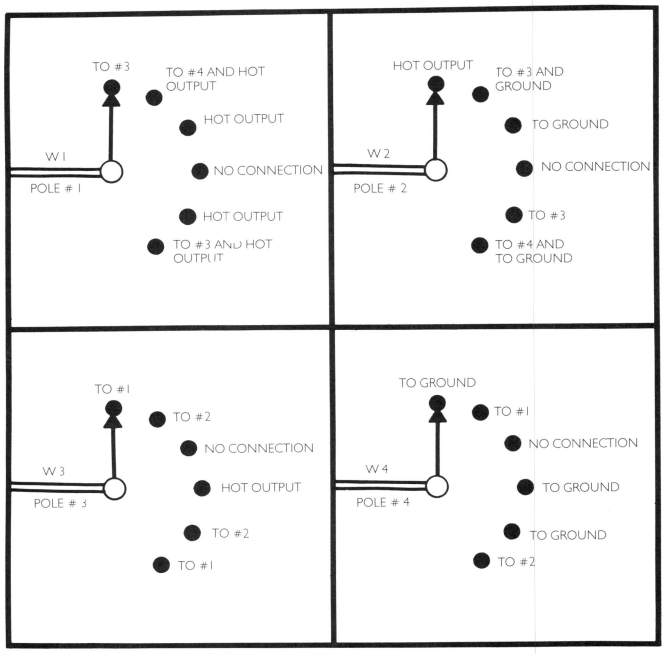

Fig. 223 Six selectable linkages for use with a four hot lead humbucker.

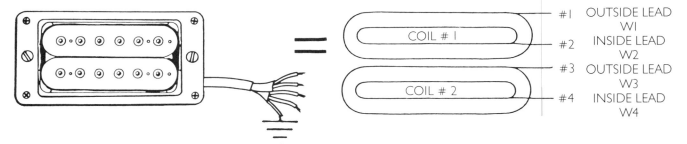

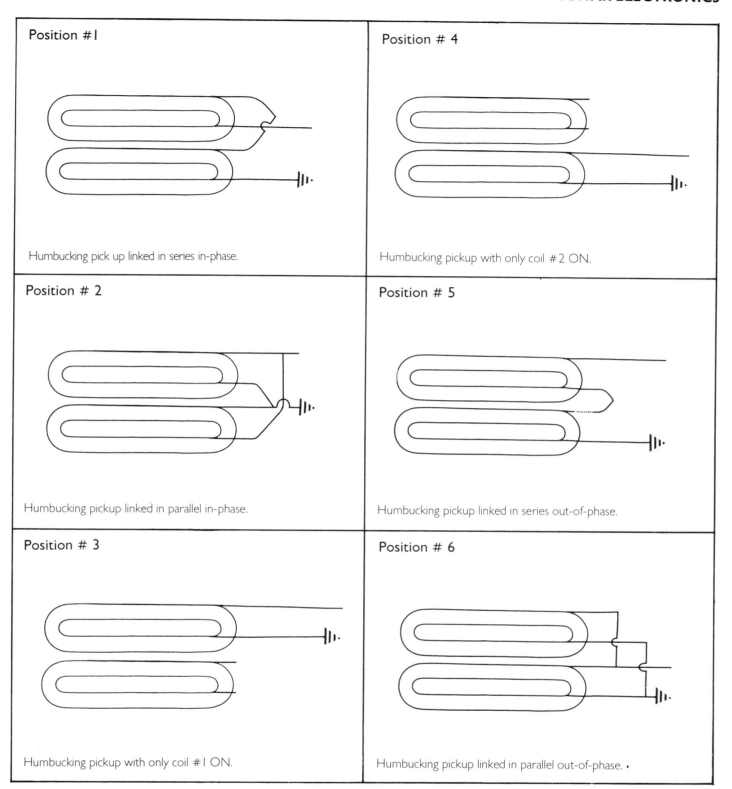

Position #1

Humbucking pick up linked in series in-phase.

Position # 2

Humbucking pickup linked in parallel in-phase.

Position # 3

Humbucking pickup with only coil #1 ON.

Position # 4

Humbucking pickup with only coil #2 ON.

Position # 5

Humbucking pickup linked in series out-of-phase.

Position # 6

Humbucking pickup linked in parallel out-of-phase. .

Fig. 224 Selectable linkages.

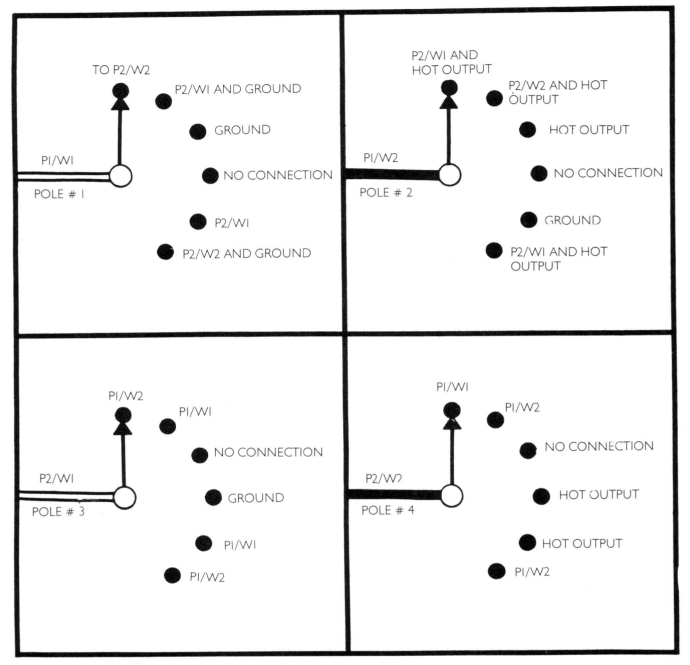

Fig. 225 Six selection switching for use with two pickups (humbuckers are shown).

This switching system uses two single coil pickups or two humbucking pickups. The choices are: pickup one, pickup two, both in series, both in parallel, both linked out-of-phase parallel, or both linked out-of-phase series.

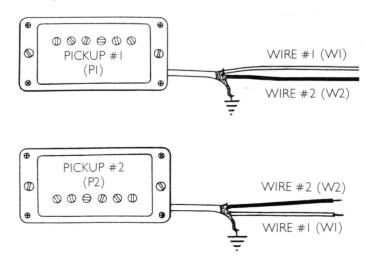

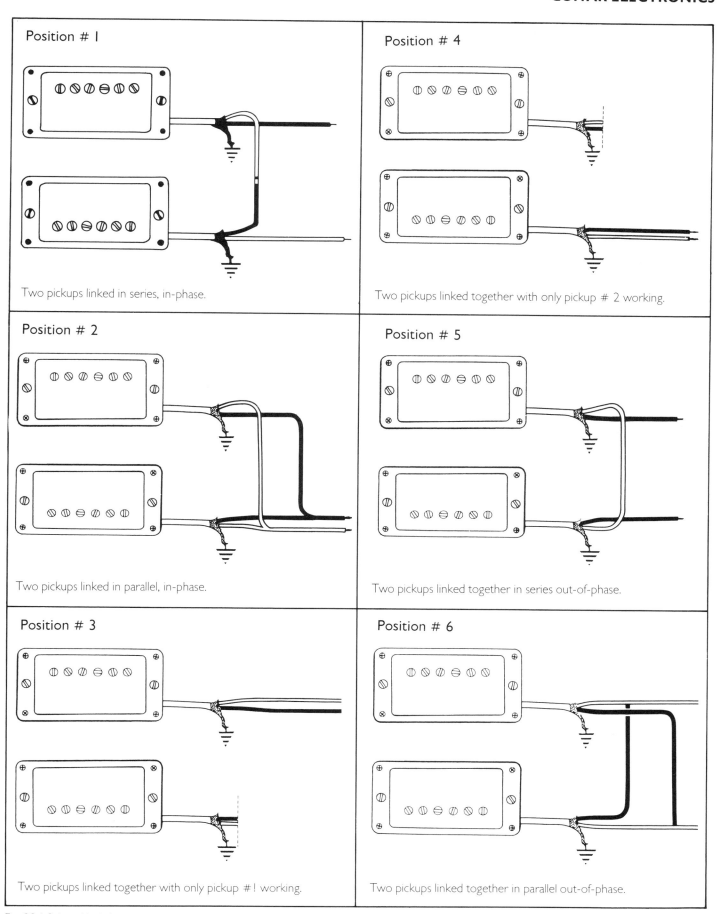

Position # 1

Two pickups linked in series, in-phase.

Position # 2

Two pickups linked in parallel, in-phase.

Position # 3

Two pickups linked together with only pickup #! working.

Position # 4

Two pickups linked together with only pickup # 2 working.

Position # 5

Two pickups linked together in series out-of-phase.

Position # 6

Two pickups linked together in parallel out-of-phase.

Fig. 226 Selectable linkages.

HOT RODDING

INSTALLING SOUND MODIFIERS IN GUITARS

Some musicians prefer to have effects built into their instruments instead of plugging cords into boxes on the floor. The advent of practical cordless systems, i.e., Nady, etc., make internal effects extremely practical. Gretsch, Gibson, Music Man, Electra, Fresher, and others, make guitars equipped with built-in sound modifiers. The Fresher guitar has one of the most extensive control panels, it includes: phase shifter, auto-wah, sustainer, distortion, and booster. The electra features plug-in-and-plug-out sound modifier modules. Gibson's R-D Artist has one of the most advanced tonal circuits ever designed for a guitar. This is not surprising since it received the expertise of Mr Moog.

Because cordless guitar operation seems to be the eventual mode of electric instruments, it could be well worthwhile for repairmen and musicians to become familiar with the installation of sound modifiers into guitars and basses. Shown below is a simple schematic of wiring a black box into an electric guitar circuit. Most other devices can be wired into an electric guitar's circuitry with equal simplicity.

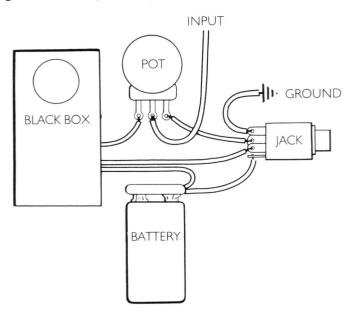

Fig. 227 Wiring of a black box into a guitar circuit with a volume knob to control the effect of the box.

LC NETWORKS

You have learned how a capacitor can be used for a tone control. The capacitor allows treble to be leaked away to ground which leaves only the bass sound. With further study, it can be learned how a capacitor can be used as a treble pass bass control in the pseudo Howard Robert's circuit shown. If a choke (coil) is added to the treble by-pass circuit, something of profound importance is created – a tonal circuit with a wide frequency range. This is what is used on the real Gibson Howard Robert's guitar.

If a capacitor and a choke are wired in series, watch what happens: A capacitor lets trebles through easier than low frequencies, and a choke allows low frequencies to pass through easier than trebles. If a

capacitor allows only frequencies over 1000 Hz pass, and the choke allows only frequencies under 200 Hz pass, the capacitor-choke assembly has then become a mid-range filter. Now we would have a precise set of tone controls: a treble control, a bass control, and a mid-range.

If you are wondering how values of capacitors and chokes are determined, it's not a hit or miss experiment, it all follows a very precise, simple formula. However, before getting into the formula, it's advisable to get acquainted with the accepted electronic term for the filter system: inductance/capacitance system. The international symbol for inductance is L, the symbol for capacitance is C. Together they form what is called an LC system or network. An LC system focuses on a specific frequency band, and the band width of frequencies affected is called the Q band, or simply – Q. If a large capacitor and a small inductor are used, the band width will be broad. If a small capacitor and a large inductor are used, the band width will be narrow. The formula for LC systems is:

$$L = \frac{1}{(2\pi F)^2 \, C}$$

Explanation: L is the inductance in henries. π is Pi, which for our purposes can be rounded to 3.146. F is the frequency you want to center on. C is the value of a capacitor in Farads. For example, if you want a narrow band filter to center on 400 Hz, you can do the following: Start with a small capacitor, which automatically means you will have a narrow band effect. What value capacitor? A common .01 MFD one can be used. Now you must change the .01 micro farad to full farads. .01 MFD equals .0000001, or 10 to the minus 7. Now you have 2 times 3.146 times 400 (for the frequency 400 Hz). Now square that value and multiply this number by the C value of .0000001. Then find the (1) reciprocal of this figure. The answer to this is 1.58, the value of the inductor in henries. In summary, a .01 MFD capacitor and a 1.58 henry choke will create a narrow band 400 Hz filter.

Fig. 228 LC network.

These LC networks can be created for many frequencies. They are one of the most basic electronic circuits, but they are not seen too often on guitars. There is a growing demand for more variety in musical tones, and the use of LC systems is bound to grow.

The following information about the behavior of chokes and LC networks, is from Bill Lawrence and describes his L and Q filters:

"The Lawrence Tone-L-Filter is a fully shielded humbucking inductance coil. Wired like a capacitor to a tone control you can gradually clean up the sound of your humbucking pickup till you get that crisp, clean sound of a single coil pickup . . . If you replace the tone control with a two position on/off switch, you will have two sounds similar to a split coil wiring without losing the humbucking effect . . . The Tone-Q-Filter is a fully shielded humbucking inductance coil tuned with a fixed capacitor . . . The T-Q-F replaces the capacitor at the tone control . . . While the capacitor cuts off the highs and makes your tone muddy, the T-Q-F gives you that sweet and mellow tone."

Fig. 229 Lawrence tone control using an LC network.

ELECTRONIC VOLUME AND TONE CONTROLS

Electron Tubes

"Solid State Electronics", this term is used to differentiate between old fashioned vacuum tube circuits (or valve, the English term), and modern transistor circuits. Tubes are a naturally high impedance device; whereas transistors are low or mid-impedance. There are three main elements in a tube; the first is the cathode, the second is the grid, and the third is the plate.

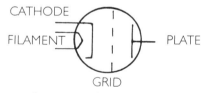

Fig. 230 Diagram of a vacuum tube.

A tube functions as follows: When a cathode is heated by the filament, a current is discharged and tries to get to the plate. A grid is placed in the path of this activity and if it weren't for the grid, the current would simply jump the gap. When a positive current is passed to the grid, any negative current of the cathode would become attracted to it, and vice versa. In this way, a small charge to a grid can control an enormous flow of current between a cathode and a plate. Note that the C (cathode) to P (plate) flow will become a duplicate of the charges that the grid is subject to. Therefore, if a pickup is connected to the grid, the signal from the strings will modulate the C/P flow. If the C/P flow is of higher strength than the grid current, it then becomes the basic amplifier circuit. Tubes are very versatile, but they do have several limitations. First, they consume a lot of power, and a cathode must be very hot to work. This heating provided by a filament takes a lot of energy, much more than batteries could commonly

supply. All this heat can cause serious problems when a tube circuit is in a small space. Second, tubes are very hard to make small. Third, they burn out in time and are prone to breakage.

When electronic circuits were first put into early electric guitars, they were only tube circuits, and this created many problems. Heat and space were the most critical. Rickenbacker once offered a guitar with a tube circuit (they used hearing aid tubes) inside it, and they deserve an award for a gallant experiment. It is much easier to put electronic circuits in guitars since the invention of transistors.

SOLID STATE ELECTRONICS

Transistors are just one part of solid state electronics. Any solid devices that are used in electronics can be called solid state, and this includes resistors, capacitors, and diodes. All of these devices use a solid material that reacts in a set way to an electric flow.

Transistors are a solid version of a tube, and there are three elements in a transistor that correspond to the (1) cathode, (2) grid, and (3) plate in a tube. The elements in a transistor are called the (1) emitter, (2) base, and (3) collector. Current flowing to the base regulates the E/C flow (emitter to collector). The transistor has changed electronics because it has several very attractive features: It's inexpensive to make, it's durable, it requires very low current (batteries can be used) and it's small in size. It's simple to make a complete transistor based amplifier circuit that is 1"×1"×1", and powered by a simple 9 volt battery. In other words, it's easy to make solid state circuits that fit into a guitar.

If a small solid state amp is put in a guitar, the guitar must have a normal instrument amplifier to create

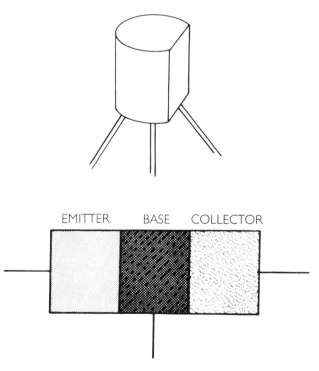

Fig. 231 Transistor and the elements of which it is made.

85

audible sound. Because this type of small booster amp comes before a main amp, it's called a preamplifier, or preamp for short.

The transistor design and usage has been improved in the last few years. Now integrated circuits, or ICs, are available and they consist of networks of transistors, diodes, resistors, and capacitors. These tiny creations help get even more into a tiny space. The IC offers more reliability than that obtainable with discrete components. Up to 50% of all circuit failures within circuits that use discrete components, e.g., transistors, diodes, and resistors are caused by faulty interconnections. Another reliability factor affecting ICs, is the closeness of the components within a silicon wafer, this allows small signal/low power operation. This low power means less heat, and less heat results in low internal temperatures and extended component life.

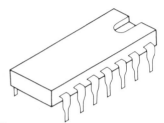

Fig. 232 An IC.

You may ask, "Why put an electronic circuit in a guitar?" The most basic reason is to just amplify the sound so the instrument is louder. The basic sound of most Fender guitars is brilliant, but not too loud. Many people put preamps in Stratocasters so their guitars will be as loud as a guitar with a hot humbucking pickup. Several companies make small boosters that can be fitted to a guitar. A boosted instrument could mean you could use a smaller, less expensive main amp, but a boosted instrument could strain an amp.

Solid state active controls can change the frequency response of a guitar much more than passive controls. If a passive treble bleed tone control is used, it can only reduce high frequencies. If passive treble, mid-range, and bass controls are used, they can only cut sections out of the frequency response curve, but they cannot fill out a deficient bass or treble. Active filters have three advantages over passive filters: (1) active filters are easily tunable through selectable resistor and capacitor networks; (2) active filters basically are high Z in, and low Z out; (3) active filters are less expensive in mass manufacturing than passive systems which rely on chokes (coils).

Solid state electronics can give tone controls which boost or cut a frequency response. Because the amplifier sections of these electronic networks boost the signal they are called active, and tone controls which boost sections of a frequency output are called **active controls**.

There are three basic active tone shaping circuits. These are: (1) A low-pass circuit, which only effects low frequencies; (2) a high-pass circuit which only effects high frequencies; and (3) a band-pass circuit

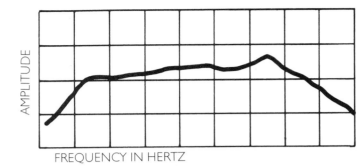

Fig. 233 Frequency response curve.

which can adjust to different frequency bands. The high and low pass are probably easier to understand, but the band-pass may be more difficult to comprehend. A band-pass control is set for a specific band and width which is predetermined by manufacturer or designer of a specific unit. Depending on the unit, the band **width** can sometimes be adjusted by the owner/operator. For example, if you have a 1,000 Hz moveable band, it can be moved up the frequency ladder to affect only frequencies of 3,000 to 4,000 Hz; or it can be moved down so it works only on frequencies of 500 to 1,500 Hz.

If a guitar had several band-pass controls, it could get cluttered because each control would need one knob to place the band, and another knob to control the volume of that band. If you wonder what a band-pass system sounds like, use a Wah-wah pedal; these devices act as band-pass units. In one position, only the bass is strong; in the middle position, it's mid-rangy; and in the last position, it's in the treble frequencies. Sophisticated band-pass devices are sometimes called parametric equalizers.

The greatest potential in using active electronics is in creating equalizers. In some "active" controls, the basic tonal profile of a signal keeps its general shape

Fig. 234 Ovation bass with a built-in equalizer.

even when there is a boost. More sophisticated active controls can be adjusted to boost very weak bass or treble signals. In other words, an advanced active low frequency control can make a guitar sound like a bass; whereas a high frequency control can pick up weak harmonics and boost them so you get a high piercing, ringing sound. This then, is the reason there is so much interest in active controls. Some are successful, others don't do much. Sometimes a company implies that their passive controls are something more special, i.e., active controls.

Active controls are generally a bit expensive, but as electronics skills advance, and competition increases, the prices fall. At one time, you had to get one part of a circuit here, and another part there; then you had to figure out how to put it together. It's only natural that many companies are now manufacturing complete circuits that bolt right into a guitar.

DC-EQ

Fig. 235 G.R.D. with built-in equalizers.

BARTOLINI

Another interesting Bartolini device, is their "Chip" which is a one transistor preamp capable of a gain of 100. Bill chose to base this device on a transistor instead of an op amp because op amps drop off trebles at high gain. Although the "Chip" is a simple unit, it can provide many exotic options, such as three-way (treble mid-bass) tone controls or even a parametric equalizer.

R.A. GRESCO

This company makes active electronics for instruments. They make one unit called "A.T.C." that boosts or cuts trebles and bass. Their "Force" unit is a preamp which gives a very high amount of gain with a flat response. Their "Tone Cube" is a LC network tone filter. The remarkable feature of these units is their small size. The A.T.C. is barely larger than two pennies; their small size is important because room inside a guitar is limited. To make a circuit exceedingly small and still operate satisfactorily is the mark of a skilled electronics designer.

FRE-AX

This company makes solid state volume control units that are made to replace standard pots in a guitar. These units consist of volume, treble-bass, and mid-range controls.

Fig. 236 Fre-ax active controls.

POWER POTS

The Power Pots company makes a number of solid state devices that fit into many electric guitars without a great deal of installation effort. The most simple unit is a combination volume pot and preamp; the most advanced is an active volume and tone control unit that features six tone shaping notch filters.

Fig. 237 The first Power Pot.

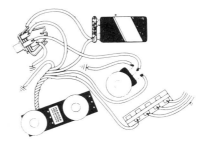

Fig. 238 Power Pots' Activestrat.

HOT RODDING

STARS

The Stars company makes several active electronic devices.

Fig. 239 Stars active volume unit.

DiMarzio, Phoenix, and many others also make active controls for guitars and basses.

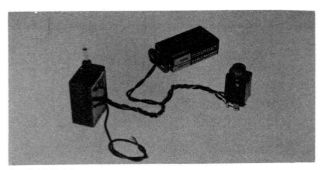

Fig. 240 DiMarzio active volume control.

FOR LEFTIES AND JIMI HENDRIX FANS

Jimi was one of the most respected of all guitar players. Because of this, many musicians want to learn how to play like him. One of the first things a fan of Jimi learns, is that Jimi was left-handed. The most interesting part about this was the fact that he played a right-handed Stratocaster upside down, i.e., the control knobs and tremolo bar were on the upper side. The positioning of the controls, tremolo arm, and cut-aways all influenced his playing and so contributed to his sound. Many right-handed guitarists find that playing a left-handed Strat helps them get "experienced". For this reason, information for left-handed players is important to many right-handed players.

Left-handed guitars take different components and wiring than right-handed instruments. Most guitars use audio taper pots; left-handed guitars would need reverse audio taper pots. A linear taper pot is the same from either end so there is no right or left taper; it can be used interchangeably with right or left-handed guitars. The wiring for left-handed pots must be reversed from what is used on right-handed pots. Switches must also be transposed.

Some pickups with nonadjustable pole pieces are meant only for use on right-handed guitars because these pickups have fixed pole pieces that give balanced string-to-string volume. These fixed pole pieces are constructed in a staggered height arrangement with each pole piece sensing just one string. On a normal guitar the high E string is too low in volume, and the B and G strings are too loud. To balance the output of these strings, the pole piece for the E string is taller than normal, and the pole pieces for the B and G strings are shorter. This means that the string-to-string balance will be vastly uneven due to the fact that the strings are put on in reverse order in left-handed guitars. Fender's staggered height single coil pickups are made to equalize string-to-string volume. If a staggered pickup for a right-handed guitar is put on a left-handed guitar, the string-to-string volume balance will be odd to say the least.

Anyone looking for a left-handed guitar should be aware that Fender and Duncan both make left-handed pickups.

In summary: The closer a pole piece is to the strings, the louder that string will be. Taller pole pieces increase volume and shorter pole pieces decrease volume.

SCHECTER OMNI POTS

Basically all pots are very similar in that they all are simple variable resistors. One exception to this is the Schecter Omni Pot which is a combination of a potentiometer and switch. The following information is from a Schecter technical bulletin written by the author when he worked for Schecter.

Schecter Omni Pots Are Unique

How would you like to have the benefit of having switches for phasing, splitting, series-parallel, and tapping your pickups? And have this without resorting to drilling even one hole in your prized guitar? You can have all of this with Schecter Omni Pots.

The Omni Pot is a sophisticated, yet simple, electronic device specially made to Schecter demands. It is a combination of two elements: a finely crafted sealed and lubricated potentiometer, joined together with a versatile switch. Just the switch itself equals four simple toggle units or one double pole double throw switch. It is able to create exotic wiring selections simply.

The shaft that holds the knob is a two-way control. Pull the knob on a shaft and one of the switch positions is selected, push the knob/shaft in and the other switch selection is achieved. Now turn the knob. The shaft rotates the pot elements controlling either volume or tone. The turning (pot motion) and the push-pull (switch motion) are completely independent of each other.

The pot section is totally sealed in a block of non-conductive polymer. Most common pots are round. They have three in-line tabs. The center tab connects to the wiper in the pot. On an Omni Pot the wiper is located separate from the two tabs for the ends of the resistance paths. It is located a little bit closer to the shaft and it is positioned at an angle 90° from the other two tabs.

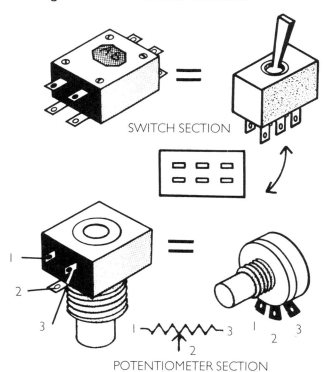

SWITCH SECTION

POTENTIOMETER SECTION

Fig. 241 Omni Pot construction features.

Omni Pots come in two configurations: the first (MO43), has a ⅜ inch threaded section for installation onto pickguards. The shaft is solid on this unit and it is perfect for accepting dome knobs and other set-key knobs. The second (MO47), has a ½ inch long threaded section for mounting through the thicker tops of Les Paul type instruments. This unit also has a knurled (fluted) shaft for mating with Gibson speed knobs.

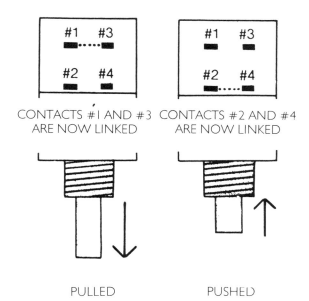

#1 #3

#2 #4

CONTACTS #1 AND #3 ARE NOW LINKED

#1 #3

#2 #4

CONTACTS #2 AND #4 ARE NOW LINKED

PULLED   PUSHED

THE FOUR CONTACTS OF THE OTHER SIDE ACT IN THE SAME FASHION

Fig. 242 Omni Pot switch function.

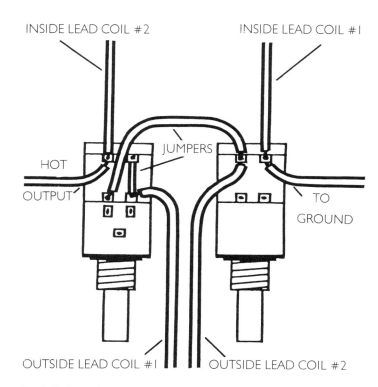

INSIDE LEAD COIL #2   INSIDE LEAD COIL #1

JUMPERS

HOT

OUTPUT

TO

GROUND

OUTSIDE LEAD COIL #1   OUTSIDE LEAD COIL #2

Fig. 243 Omni Pot used as a series/parallel switch.

Section III

Schematics and Technical Information

READING SCHEMATICS

Shown is a chart of drawing symbols used in electronic circuit schematics. Note that the drawings represent a simplified depiction of a component. Even though some schematics do not use standardized symbols, most are easy to understand.

Many schematics show a simple coil for a representation of a pickup. A humbucker would actually be shown as two coils with loads. The reason for an incomplete drawing of a coil is mainly to save time and make a more simple drawing.

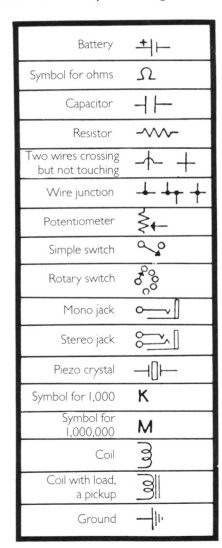

Battery	
Symbol for ohms	Ω
Capacitor	
Resistor	
Two wires crossing but not touching	
Wire junction	
Potentiometer	
Simple switch	
Rotary switch	
Mono jack	
Stereo jack	
Piezo crystal	
Symbol for 1,000	K
Symbol for 1,000,000	M
Coil	
Coil with load, a pickup	
Ground	

Fig. 244 Schematic symbols

BARCUS-BERRY®

LOCATE THE HOLE:

Be sure you are installing the Hot-Dot in the correct place. With a center punch, locate a hole ¼ inch from the saddle of the bridge on the treble side of the instrument. It is important that the saddle of the bridge point directly at this hole.

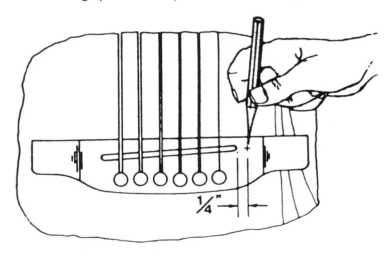

DRILL – TWO STEPS:

The actual hole for the Hot-Dot is drilled in two stages. With the larger drill bit, size No. 10, drill into the bridge at the spot located in step one. DO NOT DRILL ENTIRELY THROUGH THE INSTRUMENT WITH THE LARGER BIT, AS THIS COULD WEAKEN ANY BRACE THAT MIGHT EXIST UNDER THE BRIDGE. Now, with the smaller drill bit, size No. 38, continue the hole through the top of the instrument to provide a passage for the Hot-Dot cord.

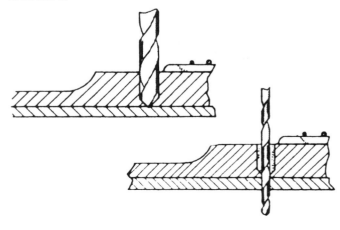

EPOXY INSERTION:

Before proceeding with the next step, inspect the Hot-Dot, if you have not already done so, and notice that it has one flat side. This flat side must face the saddle of the bridge when the Hot-Dot is installed. Keeping this in mind, cover the outside of the Hot-Dot body with epoxy, catalog No. 5090,

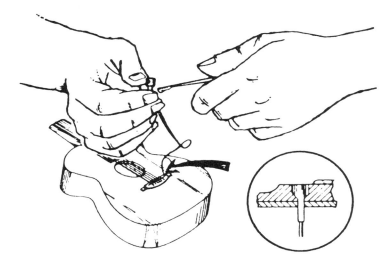

and press it gently into place. The top of the Hot-Dot may either be flush with the top of the bridge or slightly countersunk to allow for a decorative pearl inlay, catalog No. 5095.

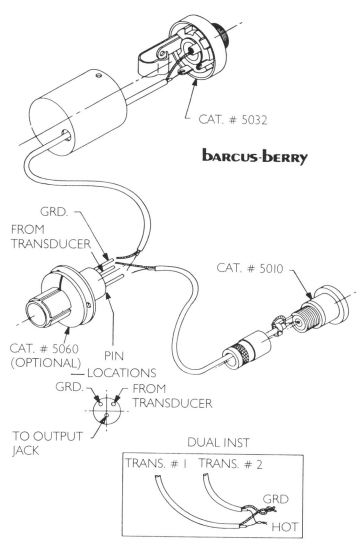

CAT. # 5032

barcus-berry

GRD.
FROM TRANSDUCER

CAT. # 5010

CAT. # 5060 (OPTIONAL)

PIN LOCATIONS

GRD. FROM TRANSDUCER

TO OUTPUT JACK

DUAL INST
TRANS. # 1 TRANS. # 2
GRD
HOT

CAUTION!

STRAP JACK INSTALLATION:

There are several available output jack accessories which can be utilized with the Hot-Dot. The following installation is recommended. The strap button jack (endpin), catalog No. 5010, used in conjunction with the Hot-Dot will preserve the clean over-all appearance of the acoustic instrument. First remove the original endpin and enlarge the hole to 25/64 inch. Fish the Hot-Dot cord through the endpin hole. Separate the jack cap from the jack itself and slide this cap over the cord with the threaded end facing outwards. Press the cap into the

ORIENTATION:

At this point, make sure that the Hot-Dot has been installed with the flat side facing the saddle of the bridge. This must be done for the Hot-Dot to function properly. If necessary, use a flat toothpick to position the Hot-Dot until the epoxy becomes sufficiently hard to hold it in place. If this is done, completely fill the hole after removing the toothpick as any unfilled space on the flat side will reduce the output level of the Hot-Dot.

SCHEMATICS

endpin hole until it is flush with the outer surface of the instrument. Trim the cord to a length of 5 inches and solder the strap jack as shown in the illustration.

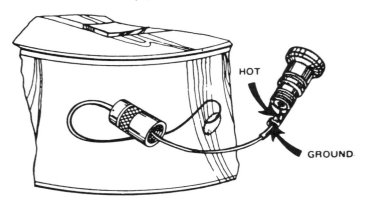

After soldering the connections, turn the strap jack four revolutions in the counter-clockwise direction and screw into the jack cap. This will allow the cord to be un-twisted after installation.

OPTIONAL DUAL INSTALLATION:

For optimum performance, **two** Hot-Dots may be installed. If this is desired, place the second Hot-Dot on the bass side of the bridge, again with the flat side facing the saddle. This cannot be over-emphasized as it is mandatory for proper operation. Notice that the Hot-Dots are color coded. The brown and black coatings signify opposing polarity. Make sure to use one of each color in the dual installation.

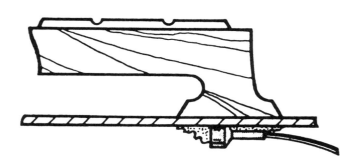

HOT-DOT BANJO INSTALLATION:

The Hot-Dot installation for banjo is quick and easy, and provides excellent results. First, ensure that the inside surface of the head directly under the treble foot of the bridge is clean. For improved adhesion, slightly roughen this surface with extra fine sandpaper. Apply epoxy, catalog No. 5090, to the flat side of the Hot-Dot and press it firmly to the head under the treble foot of the bridge as shown in the illustration. The Hot-Dot may be held in place with masking or other suitable tape. The cord can be threaded through the resonator to the output jack and bracket, catalog No. 5040 and No. 5045 respectively.

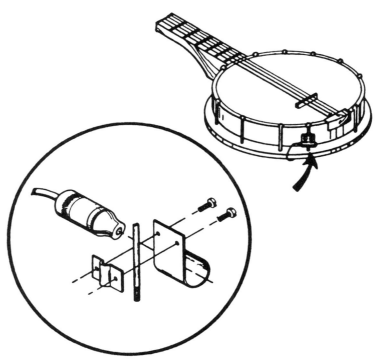

BARTOLINI

The Chip

The Chip is a miniature audio preamplifier. It is hand made from selected discrete components. The Chip has a maximum gain of 100 and full audio frequency response (±1 db 20 to 20000 Hz). It is fully shielded and its noise and hum levels are extremely low. It requires a standard 9 Volt battery and has very low battery drain (less than 160 microamperes). Since its output impedance is 200 KΩ, it can be used with all high and low impedance pickups and dynamic microphones. It is ideal for electronic instrument preamplification since its size allows easy installation in most electric guitars and basses.

The Chip is not an operational amplifier and most op.amp. feedback circuitry cannot be used with this preamplifier. We recommend the following circuits:

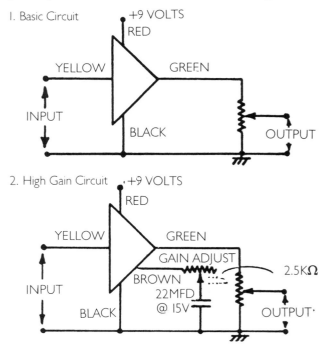

3. Treble Cut

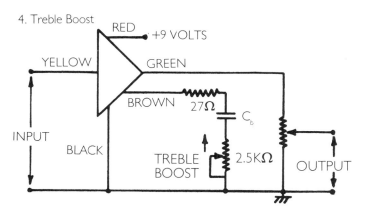

Distortion – Sustain (Fuzz)

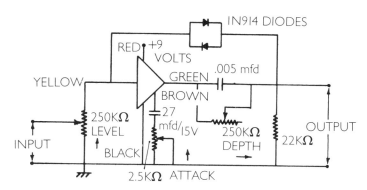

4. Treble Boost

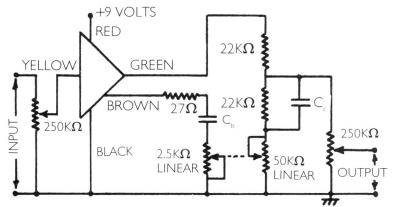

Wah-Wah

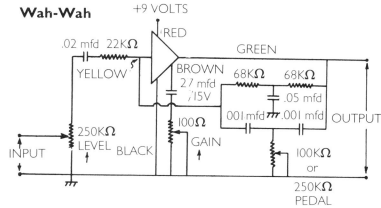

5. Single Control Treble Boost and Cut

BARTOLINI BEAST II

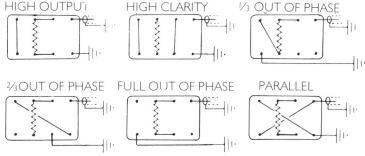

6. Bass-Mid-Treble Tone Controls

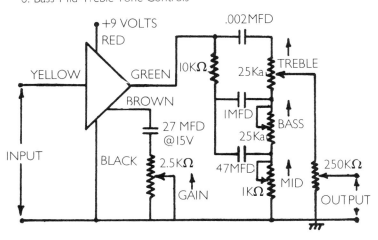

DIMARZIO

Installing 4-Conductor Pickups

General Instructions

Many of the players reading this sheet will be using our pickup to replace an old pickup. If you are among them, try to do the following:

Remove your old pickup carefully. It is better to unsolder your original pickup cleanly than to cut its wire, because installing the new pickup will be much easier with a clean connection. Make a note of exactly where the old pickup was connected, as in most cases the new one will go to the same place.

A soldering iron with a fine tip (25 to 45 watts) is preferable to a gun. If you intend to use a miniature switch with the pickup, try to be as clean as possible with the solder connections to avoid short circuits or damage to the switch.

SCHEMATICS

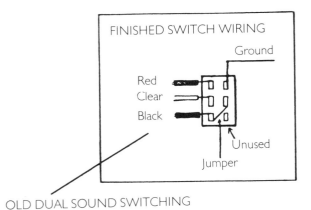

FINISHED SWITCH WIRING

Ground
Red
Clear
Black
Unused
Jumper

OLD DUAL SOUND SWITCHING

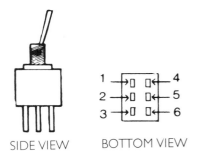

SIDE VIEW   BOTTOM VIEW

A final note: if you haven't had any experience with wiring before, or feel unsure of what to do, consider having a professional do the work, the extra expense involved may save you a good deal of trouble in playing a properly functioning instrument.

DiMarzio 4-Conductor Pickup Instructions

4 wire humbucking pickups can be wired in a great variety of ways. We cannot cover every possibility here, but any further information required can be obtained by writing to our Technical Department at the address shown on this sheet.

Basic Instructions

The color code of the 4 wire pickup is as follows: red, black, green and white. The actual arrangement of the coils is:

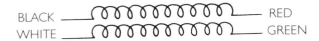

BLACK _____ RED
WHITE _____ GREEN

The simplest way to wire the pickup is for the standard, series humbucking sound. This can be done by first soldering the **black** and **white** wires together. The solder connection should be covered with tape, so the connection does not touch any other part of the circuit. The **red** wire is then soldered to the hot connection in the guitar's circuit. In most cases where you are replacing an old pickup, the **red** wire will be soldered to the same place the hot, or center wire of the old pickup was connected to. The **green** wire is soldered to ground, as is the bare wire. Usually, this connection is made to the back of a control.

If you install this pickup in a two-pickup instrument and find the pickups to be out of phase when on together, simply wire the **red** wire to ground, and the **green** wire to hot.

Dual Sound

If you want dual sound capabilities, you will need a double pole, double-throw miniature switch. This switch is available from DiMarzio, Inc., through your dealers.

The switch should be installed in the control compartment. Placement between the output jack and tone control is recommended. The hole size is ¼ inch. Refer to the first illustration. It shows 6 poles on the bottom of the switch, arbitrarily numbered 1-6.

This wiring will produce two sounds. One is the same as the sound just covered, that is, with the pickup coils in series for maximum power. The second sound is made with the coils in parallel, which will produce slightly less power, with more highs and an overall 'cleaner' sound. This is not exactly the same effect as turning off one coil, but we recommend it more strongly because it produces less noise. Turning off a coil means your pickup is no longer humbucking, and does not cancel 60-cycle hum. Dual Sound wiring keeps both coils on, and still cancels this hum. A double-pole, double throw miniature switch is required for this option, and the wiring looks like this:

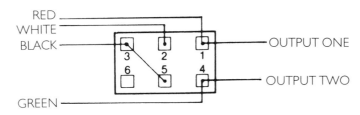

RED
WHITE
BLACK   OUTPUT ONE

GREEN   OUTPUT TWO

Solder the RED wire from the pickup to pin No. 1 of the mini-switch. Solder the WHITE wire to pin No. 2. Solder the BLACK wire to pin No. 3, and then solder a short connection from pin No. 3, to pin No. 5. Solder the GREEN wire to pin No. 4. Be sure the GREEN wire does **not** make contact with any other pin, or with any "hot" connection in the guitar.

You are now ready to connect the switch to the volume control. For this, you will need a short length of wire, similar to the colored wires in the pickup cable. Solder a wire from pin No. 1 of the mini-switch to the leg that your old pickup was soldered to. Be careful not to break the contact that is made on most guitars between this leg of the volume control and the tone control. Solder a wire from pin No. 4 to any good ground. This can be to the back of the pot itself. Be sure this wire does not make contact with any other pin on the switch, or with any "hot" connection in the instrument. Try to keep both of the wires from pins 1 and 4 as short as possible, to minimize any chance of noise. The wiring is now complete, and the bass can be reassembled.

Be sure to make the jumper connection between poles 3 and 5 of the switch. The wire labelled OUTPUT ONE should be the hot output, connected to the same place your original pickup was soldered to. The wire labelled OUTPUT TWO is soldered to ground. To reverse the phase of the pickup, reverse these two wires: OUTPUT ONE will go to ground, and OUTPUT TWO to hot. The bare wire from the 4-conductor cable is soldered to ground.

Phase Switch

This is how to wire the pickup to a phase switch. The switch is the same type as that for dual sound switching – double pole, double throw.

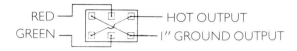

If you want to wire the pickup to a dual sound switch and a phase switch, first wire the pickup to the dual sound switch the same way as shown in the dual instructions, then connect the dual sound switch to the phase switch like this:

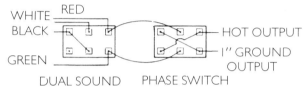

The wire labelled HOT OUTPUT is connected to the same spot as the original pickup. The wire labelled GROUND OUTPUT is soldered to a ground connection, like the back of a control. The bare wire from the 4-conductor cable should also be soldered to ground.

Single Coil Switching

There are several ways of turning off one coil of your pickup. First, a switch can be used. It can be the same type as is used for dual sound or phase reverse (double pole, double throw miniature), or a simpler single pole, double throw switch. The diagram shows the double pole type, as that is our standard switch.

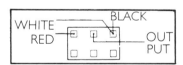

The wire labelled OUTPUT is the hot connection, and is soldered to the same place your original pickup was. The GREEN wire from the pickup must be soldered to ground, along with the bare wire.

The switch shown above is the double pole type. One side of the switch is not being used, so if you like you can have two pickups go from double to single coil on one switch, like this:

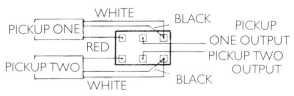

Again the GREEN wire from the pickups, and also the bare wire must go to ground. If you want to

combine a phase switch with a single coil switch, the diagram would be this:

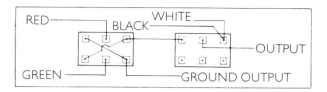

An interesting feature of this arrangement is that the phase switch has two functions. When two pickups are on together, it performs its normal task, but when the pickup shown above is on alone, and the single coil switch is on, the position of the phase switch determines which of the two coils is turned off giving a subtle variation in tone.

How to Wire a PAF for Phase Switching

If your guitar is wired so that you can select 2 pickups at the same time (as in Les Paul-style guitars and many other U.S. models) additional tonal variations can be obtained by fitting a phase switch to one of the pickups. For phase switching 4-conductor pickups see above. For DiMarzio 2-conductor screened cable pickups, wire as in diagram.

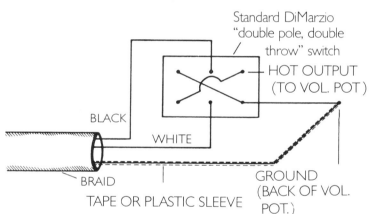

Installing the P-Bass Pickup

Part I

A) The first step is to remove the original pickup. This can be accomplished by the following: unscrew all screws fastening the pickguard to the bass, and lift the pickguard carefully from the instrument. You will have to loosen the strings to accomplish this. Now remove the 4 screws holding the original pickup in place. You can now disconnect the pickup by unsoldering the **two** wires that connect it to the bass. Unsolder the two wires furthest from the pickup; one wire should be disconnected where it is soldered to the volume pot, and the other where it connects to the brass plate underneath the pickup. The pickup can now be removed from the bass. Both halves of the original pickup can be left connected together.

Now install the P-Bass pickup: draw all four wires from the P-Bass through to the control compartment, and then screw the two halves of the pickup into the bass. It does not matter which side the two halves sit in.

SCHEMATICS

B) Solder the **red** wire to the same leg of the volume pot the original pickup was connected to. Solder the **green** wire to ground, preferably the back of the pot. Solder the white and black wire together. You should then put a piece of tape on this solder connection, to make sure it does not make contact with any other part of the circuit. You can now replace the pickguard, retune the strings and adjust the heights of the P-Bass sections to suit taste. Fine adjustments can be made with the pole pieces.

Fender

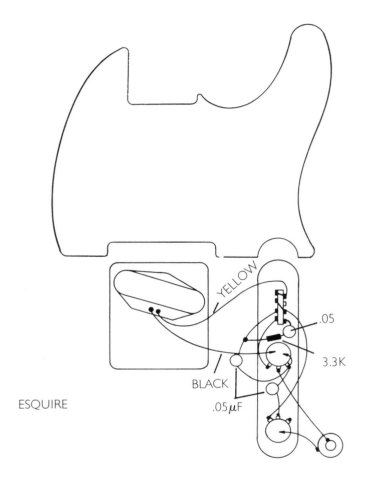

ESQUIRE

Telecaster Custom

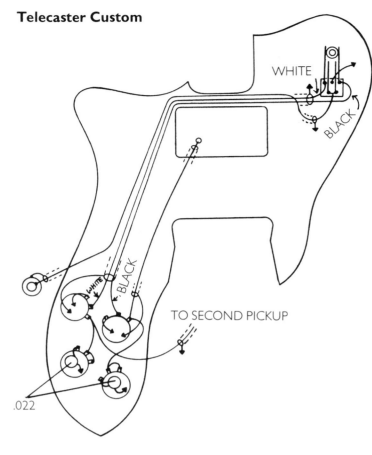

Jazzmaster

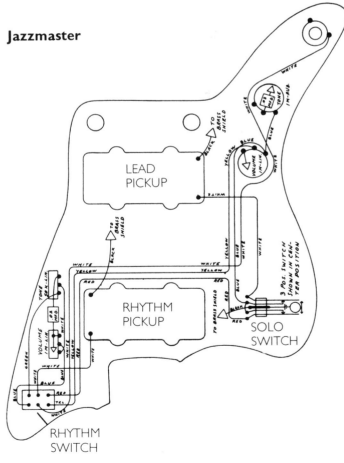

Broadcaster ('53 Tele)

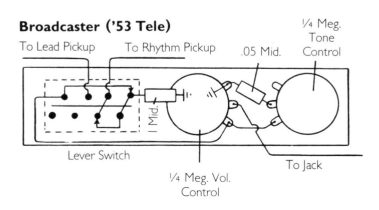

Fender "Jaguar" wiring diagram   DRAWN AUG. 7, 1962

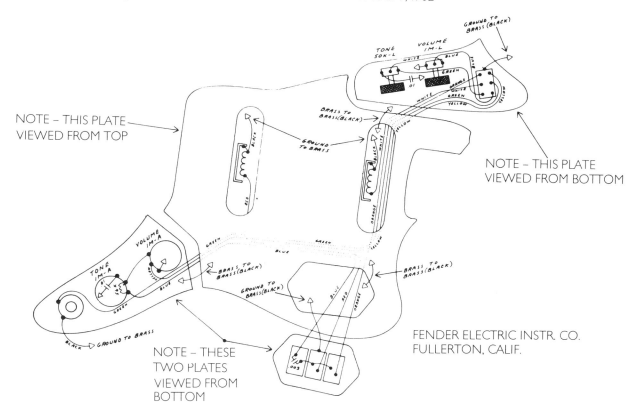

NOTE – THIS PLATE
VIEWED FROM TOP

NOTE – THIS PLATE
VIEWED FROM BOTTOM

NOTE – THESE
TWO PLATES
VIEWED FROM
BOTTOM

FENDER ELECTRIC INSTR. CO.
FULLERTON, CALIF.

Mustang

Stratocaster

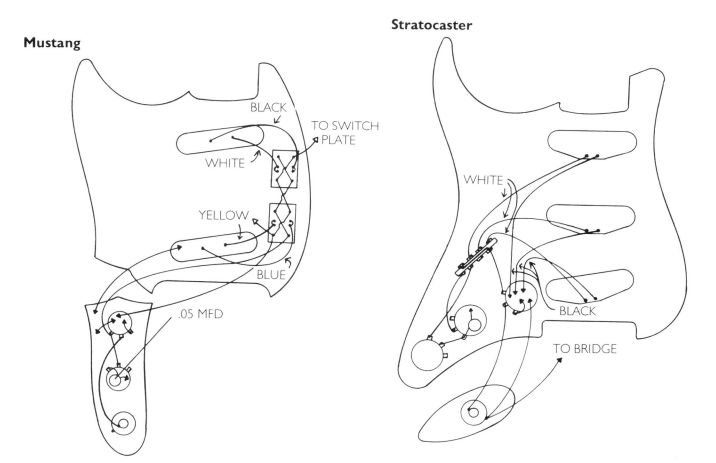

97

SCHEMATICS

Standard Strat Switch

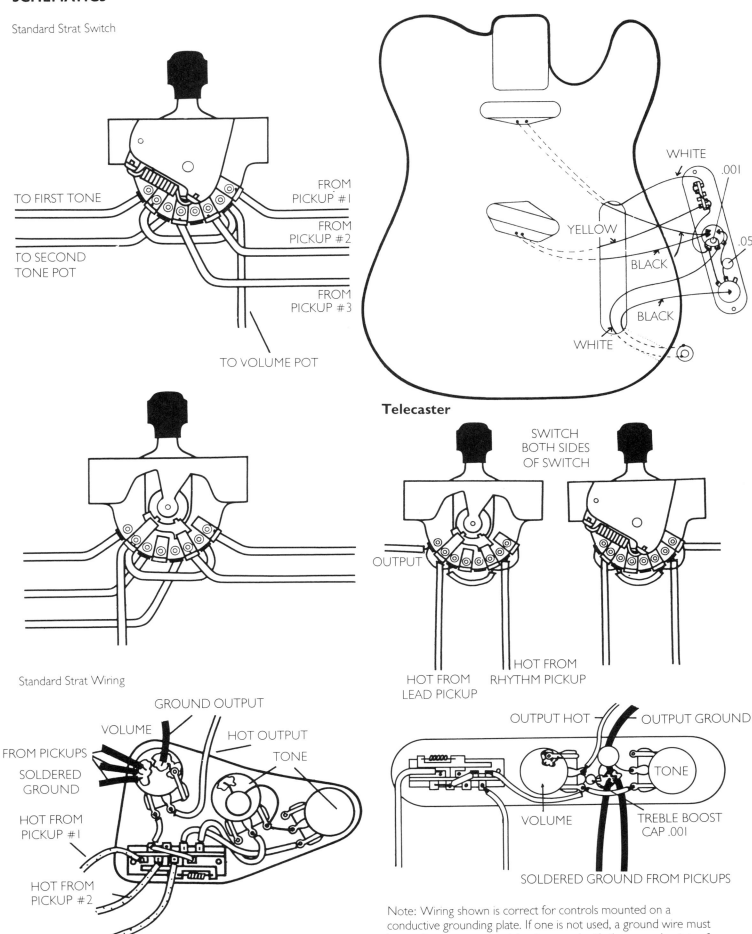

TO FIRST TONE

FROM PICKUP #1

FROM PICKUP #2

TO SECOND TONE POT

FROM PICKUP #3

TO VOLUME POT

WHITE

.001

YELLOW

BLACK

.05

BLACK

WHITE

Telecaster

SWITCH BOTH SIDES OF SWITCH

OUTPUT

HOT FROM LEAD PICKUP

HOT FROM RHYTHM PICKUP

Standard Strat Wiring

GROUND OUTPUT

VOLUME

HOT OUTPUT

FROM PICKUPS

TONE

SOLDERED GROUND

HOT FROM PICKUP #1

HOT FROM PICKUP #2

HOT FROM PICKUP #3

OUTPUT HOT

OUTPUT GROUND

TONE

VOLUME

TREBLE BOOST CAP .001

SOLDERED GROUND FROM PICKUPS

Note: Wiring shown is correct for controls mounted on a conductive grounding plate. If one is not used, a ground wire must be used to connect the pickup's ground with the ground points of the pots and output jack.

P-Bass

Gibson

**Solid Body
Double Neck
Guitar 1965**

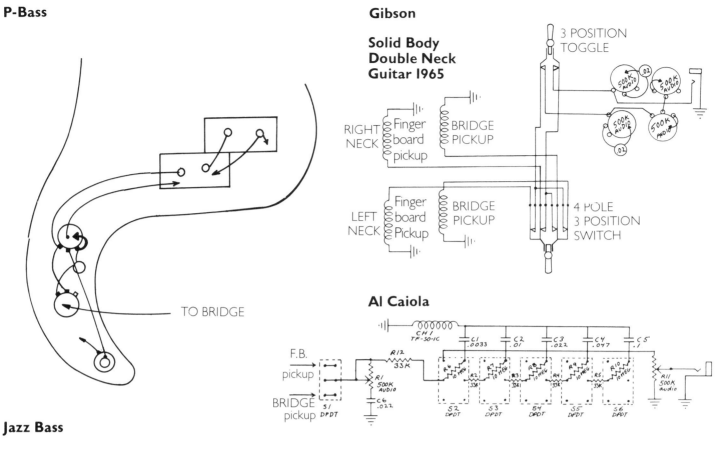

TO BRIDGE

3 POSITION
TOGGLE

RIGHT NECK — Finger board pickup — BRIDGE PICKUP

LEFT NECK — Finger board Pickup — BRIDGE PICKUP

4 POLE
3 POSITION
SWITCH

Al Caiola

F.B. pickup

BRIDGE pickup

S1 DPDT

Jazz Bass

1965

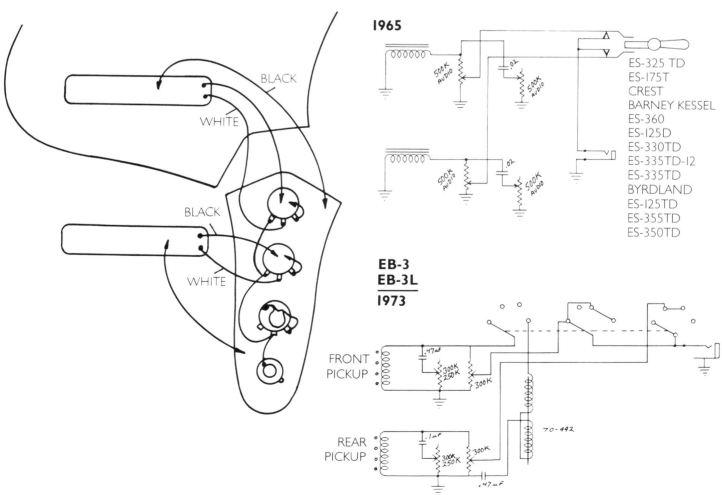

BLACK

WHITE

BLACK

WHITE

ES-325 TD
ES-175T
CREST
BARNEY KESSEL
ES-360
ES-125D
ES-330TD
ES-335TD-12
ES-335TD
BYRDLAND
ES-125TD
ES-355TD
ES-350TD

**EB-3
EB-3L
1973**

FRONT PICKUP

REAR PICKUP

SCHEMATICS

EB-3
EB-3L
1974

ES-340

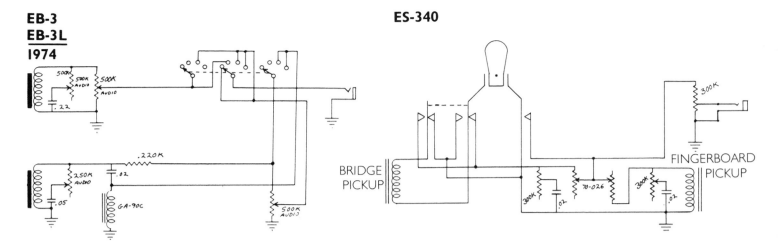

BRIDGE PICKUP

FINGERBOARD PICKUP

EB-4

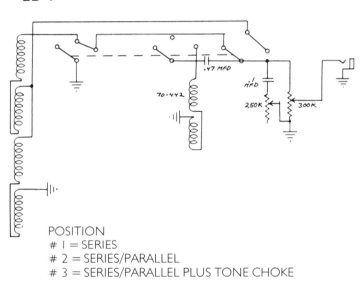

POSITION
1 = SERIES
2 = SERIES/PARALLEL
3 = SERIES/PARALLEL PLUS TONE CHOKE

Firebird 3 Pickup 1965

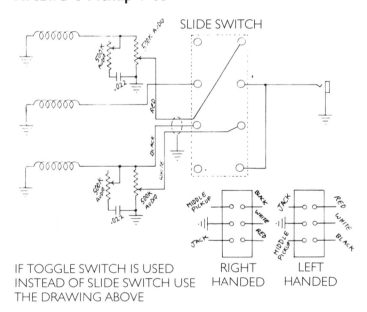

SLIDE SWITCH

IF TOGGLE SWITCH IS USED
INSTEAD OF SLIDE SWITCH USE
THE DRAWING ABOVE

RIGHT HANDED   LEFT HANDED

ES-335 with Coil Tap 1974

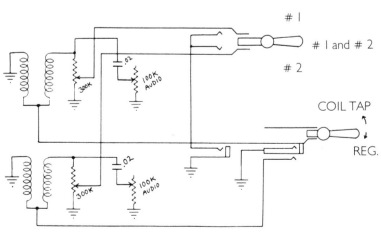

1

1 and # 2

2

COIL TAP

REG.

Firebird 2 Pickup 1965

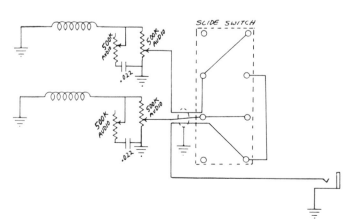

SLIDE SWITCH

ES-5

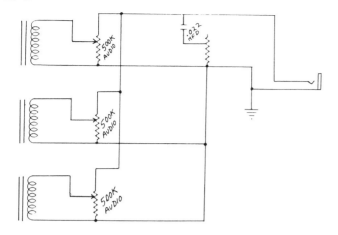

Johnny Smith Double Pickup 1965

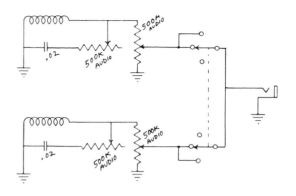

Flying V 1967

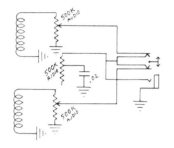

Howard Roberts 1974

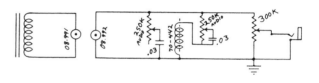

Johnny Smith Stereo

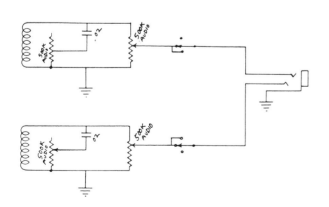

L6-S 1973

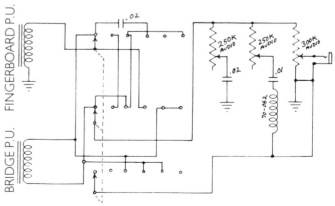

POSITION
1 BOTH – SERIES – IN PHASE
2 FINGERBOARD – –
3 BOTH – PARALLEL – IN PHASE
4 BOTH – PARALLEL – OUT OF PHASE
5 BRIDGE – –
6 BOTH – SERIES – OUT OF PHASE

SCHEMATICS

Les Paul Controls 1954

Controls In A Les Paul

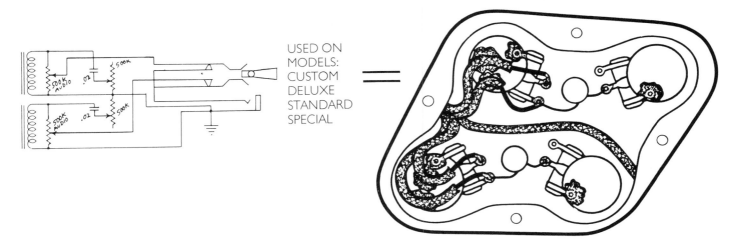

USED ON
MODELS:
CUSTOM
DELUXE
STANDARD
SPECIAL

Les Paul Professional 1970

Les Paul Recording 1977

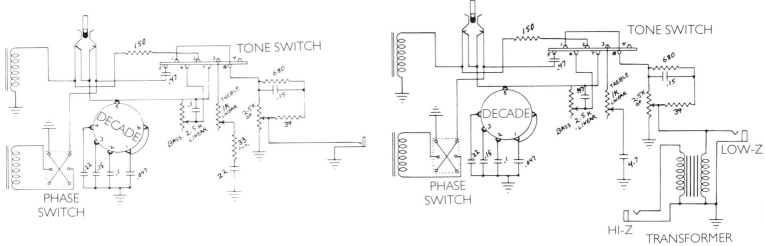

Les Paul Personal 1970

Les Paul Signature Bass

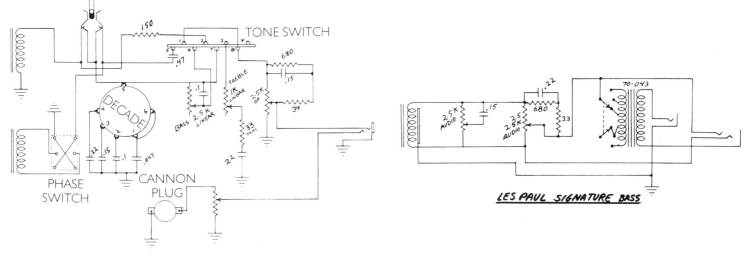

Les Paul Recording 1971

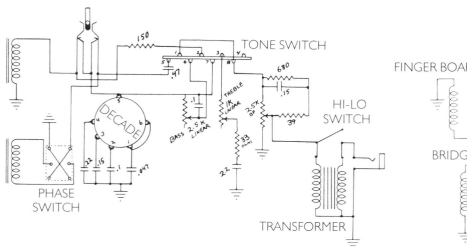

Marauder 1975

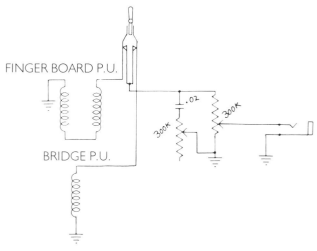

Les Paul Signature Guitar 1973

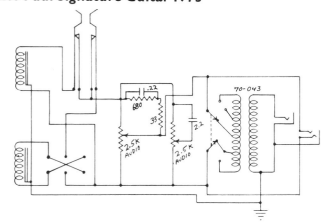

Melody Maker D 1965

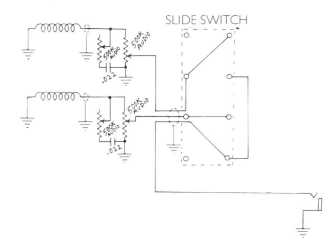

Les Paul Triumph Bass 1972

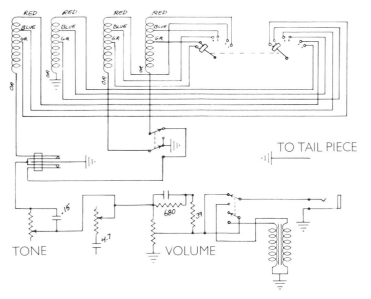

RD77 Standard Guitar 1977

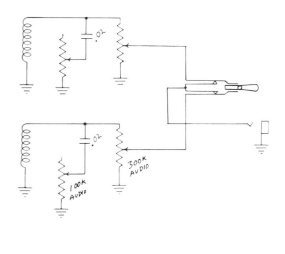

SCHEMATICS

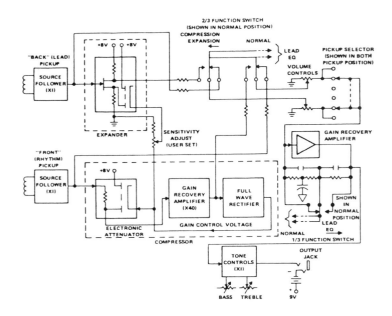

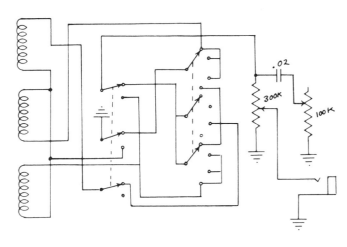

RD-77 Standard Bass 1977

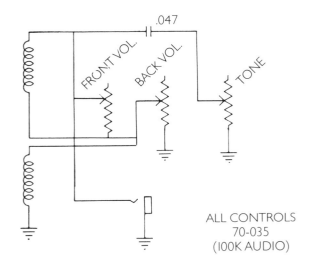

ALL CONTROLS
70-035
(100K AUDIO)

Thunderbird II 1974

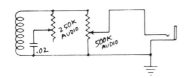

Thunderbird III 1974

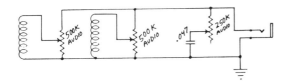

SG-1 1974

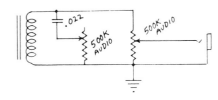

Thunderbird "76" 1979

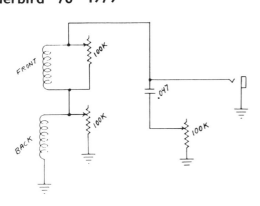

SG-200 w/Humbuckers 1975
(Ground Shielding of Pickups to Lug)

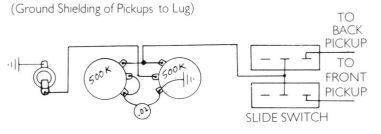

Varitone Circuit Chip 1974

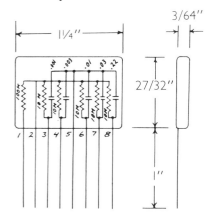

Super Chet

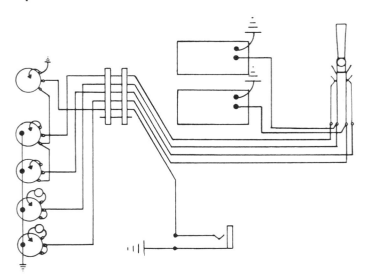

Varitone Stereo

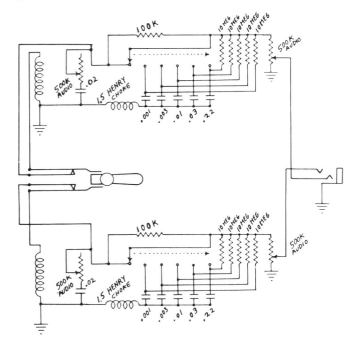

Stereo Harness

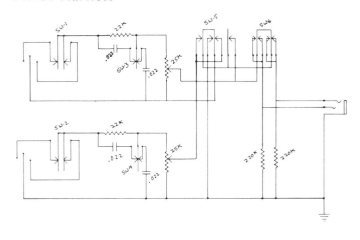

Varitone – Monaural, 1961

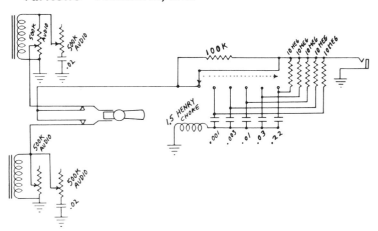

Compressor/Phaser

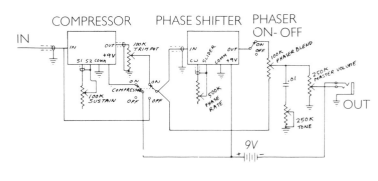

SCHEMATICS

Lawrence

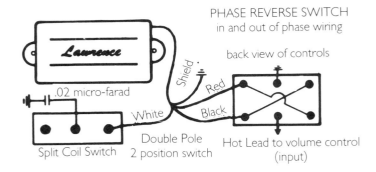

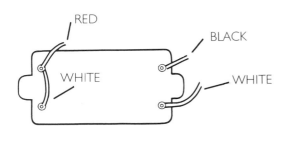

Mighty Mite Humbucker

Lawrence replacement pickups are equipped with 2 conductors and shield for IN PHASE and OUT OF PHASE wiring – OUT OF PHASE means that one pickup has positive polarity while the other has negative polarity. The change of polarity on a single pickup does not affect the sound and output of this pickup. Most pickups have positive polarity.

POSITIVE POLARITY – Connect black conductor and shield to ground and use red conductor as hot lead.

NEGATIVE POLARITY – Connect red conductor and shield to ground and use black conductor as hot lead.

SPLIT COIL WINDING – Lawrence pickups are equipped with an additional white conductor for a split coil two sound wiring. By using a .02 microfarad capacitor in the circuit you avoid volume loss and you maintain the humbucking effect.

IMPORTANT – To maintain the extreme low noise level of Lawrence pickups you should shield all circuitry.

Mighty Mite Strat Style Pickup Assembly With Phase Switches

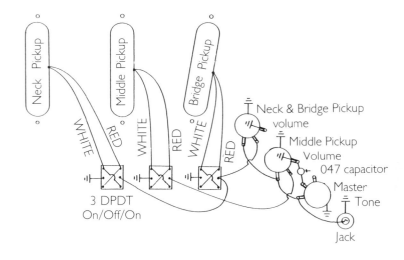

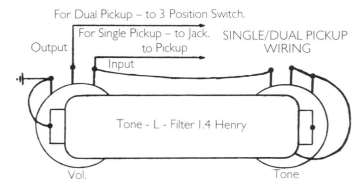

The Tone-L-Filter is a 1.4 Henry humbucking inductance coil. Wired to a tone control you can gradually clean up the sound of your hot humbucking pickup without losing the humbucking effect. By replacing the lead between volume and tone control with a .02 Micro Farad capacitor you can gradually get a sweet mellow sound without getting muddy.

L – Volume is a 1 Meg special taper for the volume control.

L – Tone is a 1 Meg special audio taper for the tone control.

TEST CONDITIONS FOR MIGHTY MITE PICKUPS

Inductance measurement:

General radio RLC bridge model 1657
Accuracy: 0.2%
Measurements made at 1000 Hz with "Series R" setting
DC resistance measurements:
Hewlett Packard model 3476A
Digital multimeter
Accuracy: 0.5%

AC impedance measurements:
Signal source: Interstate Electronics Corp. model F33
Signal generator

Voltage measurements: Hewlett Packard 3476A
Digital multimeter
Accuracy: 1.5%

Current measurements: (current is calculated from measurement of voltage across 1.00K ohm. 1% resistor using Hewlett Packard 3476A)
Accuracy: 2.0%

Signal source: Interstate Electronics Corp model F33
Signal generator set to square wave output, 10VP-P, 500 Hz, OV DC offset.

Waveform observation:
Tektronix oscilloscope model 464 (or equiv.) with P6054A, 10X probe, 12.5 PF capacitance

test #	test description	"Vintage Humbucking" (Model 1400)			"Distortion Humbucking" (Model 1300)		
		Split Coil	Humbucker	Dual Sound	Split Coil	Humbucker	Dual Sound
		A	A	B	A	A	B
1	DC Resistance (ohms)	4.42K	8.85K	2.22K	6.81K	13.61K	3.40K
2	Inductance @ 1000 Hz (henrys)	2.24	5.26	1.31	3.34	7.69	1.92
3	Impedance (ohms)						
3a	@ 50Hz	4.45K	9.10K	2.27K	6.95K	13.91K	3.48K
3b	@ 100 Hz	4.70K	9.58K	2.39K	7.24K	14.64K	3.65K
3c	@ 500 Hz	8.95K	19.91K	4.97K	13.44K	29.60K	7.35K
3d	@ 1000 Hz	15.20K	35.00K	8.80K	23.00K	52.50K	12.94K
3e	@ 2500 Hz	34.90K	83.20K	20.30K	53.30K	124.50K	30.00K
4	Self Resonant Freq.	12.80KHz	10.00KHz	13.90KHz	10.10KHz	8.33KHz	10.60KHz

test #	test description	Vintage Strat	Distortion Strat	Tele Lead	Tele-R	P/Bass	Jazz Bass
1	DC Resistance (ohms)	7.19K	11.97K	16.60K	8.86K	7.40K	7.75K
2	Inductance @ 1000 Hz (henrys)	2.74	5.73	8.58	3.924	4.43	3.76
3	Impedance (ohms)						
3a	@ 50 Hz	7.28K	12.16K	16.90K	8.98K	7.57K	7.85K
3b	@ 100 Hz	7.24K	12.35K	17.50K	9.14K	7.91K	8.04K
3c	@ 500 Hz	11.39K	20.80K	31.80K	13.80K	15.80K	13.05K
3d	@ 1000 Hz	18.70K	35.90K	56.80K	22.20K	28.50K	21.90K
3e	@ 2500 Hz	47.00K	98.60K	161.40K	57.20K	74.20K	57.7K
4	Self Resonant Freq.	10.40KHz	6.66KHz	6.06KHz	9.09KHz	8.19KHz	9.43KHz

SCHEMATICS

MODEL	12 STRING VIPER		ULTRA	BASS	
	NECK	BRIDGE	NECK & BRIDGE	NECK	BRIDGE
PART #	701500B	701600C	702600A	701300A	701400
USED ON THESE MODELS	1271	1273 1275	1291	1261 1262	1261 1262
COIL PART #	701510C	701610D	702610A	701310A	701410
WIRE GAUGE	43	40	43	43	43
# OF TURNS	10,000	5,000	10,000	19,000	13,500
COLOR OF LEAD WAS IN / OUT	RED BLACK	YELLOW BLACK	RED BLACK	RED BLACK	RED BLACK
COLOR OF LEAD NOW IN / OUT	RED BLACK	YELLOW BLACK	RED BLACK	RED BLACK	RED BLACK

NECK

BRIDGE

MODEL	PREACHER		VIPER		3 PICKUP VIPER		
PART #	700100B	700200B	701500B	701600B	701500B	702700B	701600C
USED ON THESE MODELS	1253 1281 1283 1285 1251 1252	1253 1281 1283 1285 1251 1252	1271	1271	1271	1273	1273 1275
COIL PART #	700110C	700210C	701510C	701610C	701510C	702710B	701610D
WIRE GAUGE	43	43	43	43	43	43	40
# OF TURNS	10,000	10,000	10,000	10,000	10,000	5,000	5,000
COLOR OF LEAD WAS IN / OUT	RED BLUE	BLACK YELLOW	RED BLACK	RED BLACK	RED BLACK	YELLOW BLACK	YELLOW BLACK
COLOR OF LEAD NOW IN / OUT	RED BLUE	RED BLACK	RED BLACK	RED BLACK	RED BLACK	YELLOW BLACK	YELLOW BLACK

NECK

MIDDLE

BRIDGE

• = SAME PICKUP   o = SAME PICKUP

OVATION

Preacher

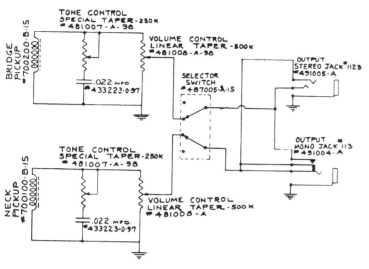

Ovation Preamp

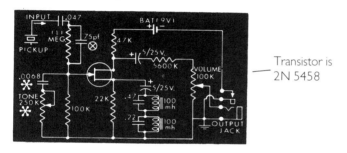

Transistor is
2N 5458

Used only on 12-string guitar preamps.
* Used only on preamps with tone control.

Viper

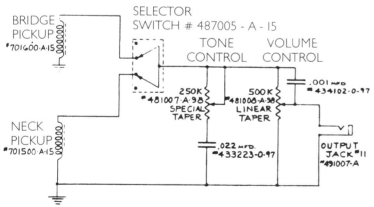

Peavey T-60

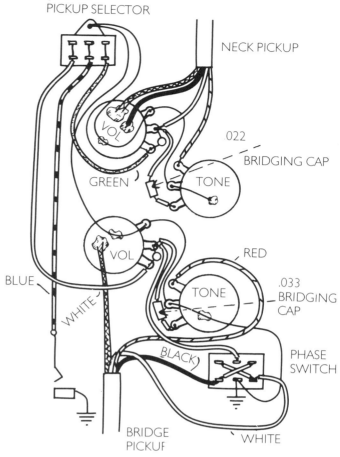

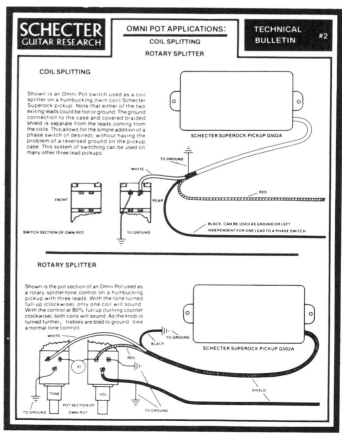

SCHEMATICS

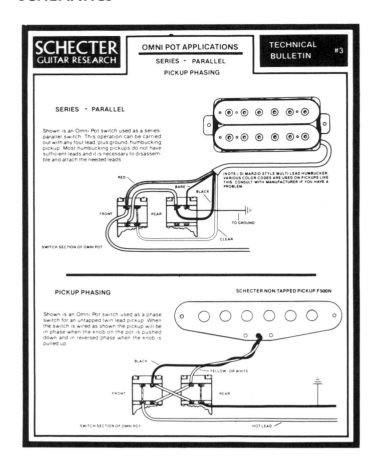

SCHECTER GUITAR RESEARCH
OMNI POT APPLICATIONS
SERIES - PARALLEL
PICKUP PHASING
TECHNICAL BULLETIN #3

SERIES - PARALLEL

Shown is an Omni Pot switch used as a series-parallel switch. This operation can be carried out with any four lead, plus ground, humbucking pickup. Most humbucking pickups do not have sufficient leads and it is necessary to disassemble and attach the needed leads.

(NOTE) DI MARZIO STYLE MULTI-LEAD HUMBUCKER. VARIOUS COLOR CODES ARE USED ON PICKUPS LIKE THIS, CONSULT WITH MANUFACTURER IF YOU HAVE A PROBLEM.

RED
BARE
BLACK
FRONT
REAR
TO GROUND
CLEAR
SWITCH SECTION OF OMNI POT

PICKUP PHASING

SCHECTER NON-TAPPED PICKUP F500N

Shown is an Omni Pot switch used as a phase switch for an untapped twin lead pickup. When the switch is wired as shown the pickup will be in phase when the knob on the pot is pushed down and in reversed phase when the knob is pulled up.

BLACK
YELLOW OR WHITE
FRONT
REAR
SWITCH SECTION OF OMNI POT
HOT LEAD

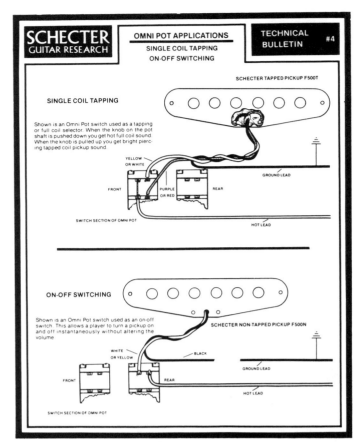

SCHECTER GUITAR RESEARCH
OMNI POT APPLICATIONS
SINGLE COIL TAPPING
ON-OFF SWITCHING
TECHNICAL BULLETIN #4

SCHECTER TAPPED PICKUP F500T

SINGLE COIL TAPPING

Shown is an Omni Pot switch used as a tapping or full coil selector. When the knob on the pot shaft is pushed down you get hot full coil sound. When the knob is pulled up you get bright piercing tapped coil pickup sound.

YELLOW OR WHITE
FRONT
PURPLE OR RED
REAR
GROUND LEAD
SWITCH SECTION OF OMNI POT
HOT LEAD

ON-OFF SWITCHING

Shown is an Omni Pot switch used as an on-off switch. This allows a player to turn a pickup on and off instantaneously without altering the volume.

SCHECTER NON-TAPPED PICKUP F500N

WHITE OR YELLOW
FRONT
BLACK
REAR
GROUND LEAD
HOT LEAD
SWITCH SECTION OF OMNI POT

Schecter Tapped Strat Style Assembly

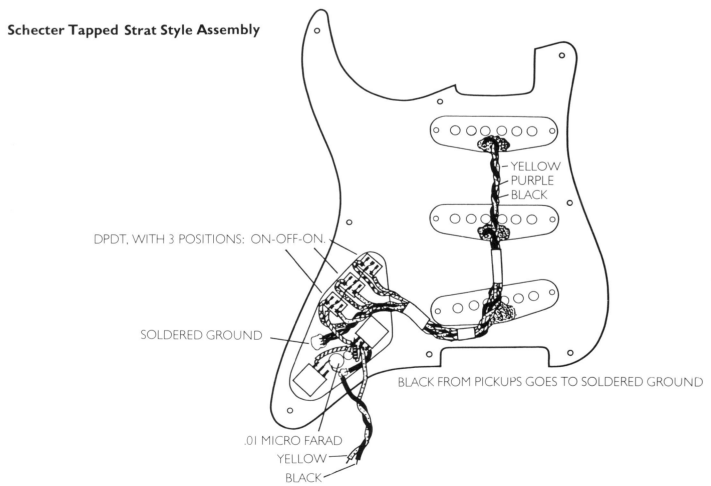

YELLOW
PURPLE
BLACK

DPDT, WITH 3 POSITIONS: ON-OFF-ON.

SOLDERED GROUND

BLACK FROM PICKUPS GOES TO SOLDERED GROUND

.01 MICRO FARAD
YELLOW
BLACK

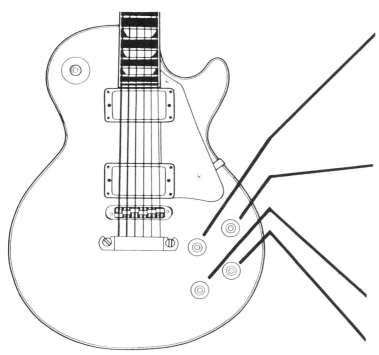

Functions of Superock Assembly

Lead Volume

Pulling out this pot does two things. First, it puts the lead pickup out of phase in relation to the front pickup. It also will select which coil remains on when the lead pickup is in single coil mode. The coil closest to the bridge is on when the pot is in, and the coil closest to the neck is on when the pot is out.

Rhythm Volume

Pulling this pot out does three things. First, the two humbucking pickups are connected in series, as opposed to parallel when pushed in. Second, the selector switch is by-passed (i.e. regardless of how the switch is set, both pickups will be on and in series). Third, the rhythm pickup volume becomes a master volume for both pickups.

Rhythm Tone

When this pot is pulled out, the rhythm pickup is in single coil mode.

Lead Tone

When this pot is pulled out, the lead pickup is in single coil mode.

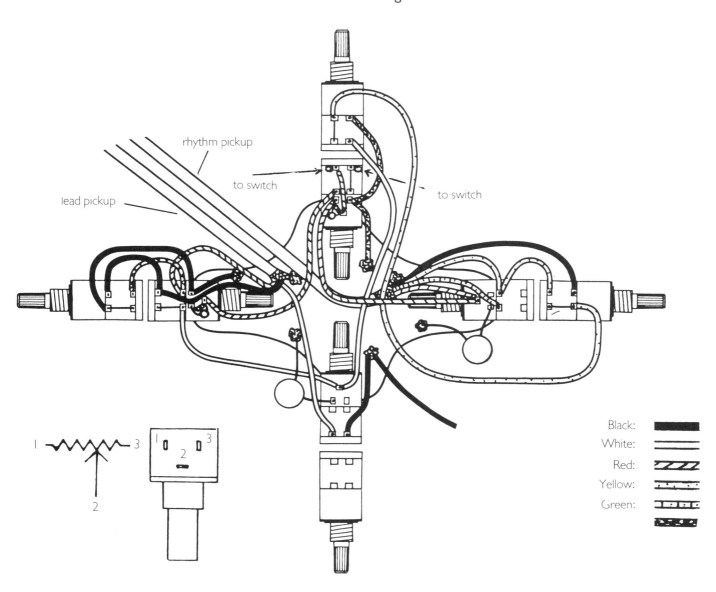

Black:
White:
Red:
Yellow:
Green:

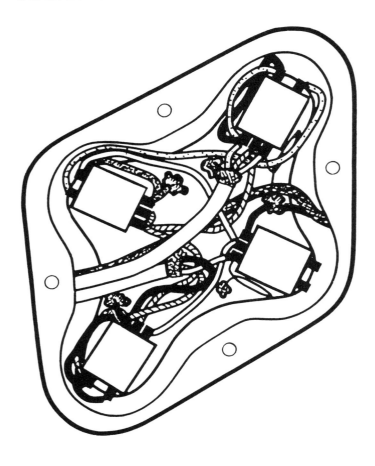

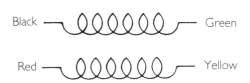

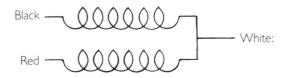

F520T TAPPED SINGLE COIL PICKUP
For Telecaster* Style Guitars (Lead Position)

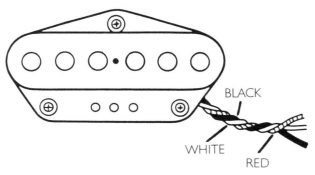

Thank you for selecting a Schecter pickup

The F520T is a tapped single coil guitar pickup. This pickup offers two sounds: the bright sound of the tapped mode and the hot sound of the full coil mode. The F520T is rugged and dependable while still being sensitive to delicate string vibrations through the use of oversize cylindrical magnets. The pickup is solidly constructed so it will be non-microphonic. The F520T uses 500K pots for volume and tone controls, with a .020 to .027mf tone capacitor.

To install an F520T you will need the following tools:
1. Soldering iron or gun (75W or 150W)
2. Solder
3. Small Phillips screwdriver
4. Small blade screwdriver
5. Wire strippers
6. Diagonal cutters
7. Small pliers

In your package you will find:
1. F520T Pickup
2. 3 pickup mounting bolts
3. 3 lengths of rubber shock absorbing spacers
4. Instructions for installation

STANDARD WIRING

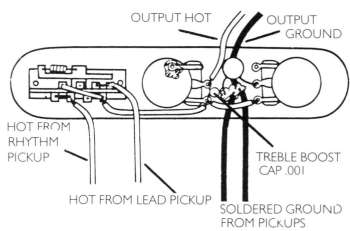

NOTE: WIRING SHOWN IS CORRECT FOR CONTROLS MOUNTED ON A CONDUCTIVE GROUNDING PLATE. IF ONE IS NOT USED, A GROUND WIRE MUST BE USED TO CONNECT THE PICKUP'S GROUND WITH THE GROUND POINTS OF THE POTS AND OUTPUT JACK.

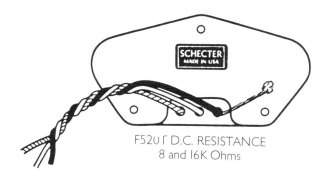

F520T D.C. RESISTANCE
8 and 16K Ohms

Installing an F520T in a Telecaster* style guitar

The installation of an F520T into a Tele style guitar will require the addition of a switch to select either tapped or non-tapped modes. This can consist of either a DPDT switch or an Omni Pot. Both of these are shown here . Omni Pot use has the advantage that no new holes have to be drilled in the pickguard or control plate. An Omni Pot is a SCHECTER creation that combines a pot and a switch. See SCHECTER Technical Bulletin #1 for Omni Pot operation.

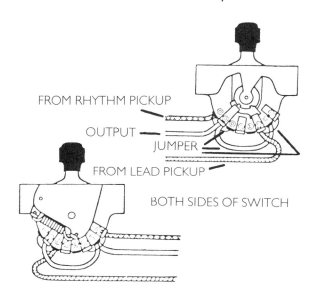

FROM RHYTHM PICKUP

OUTPUT

JUMPER

FROM LEAD PICKUP

BOTH SIDES OF SWITCH

If one or two tapped pickups are to be used, it is suggested that you use a SCHECTER Omni Pot(s). SCHECTER uses this arrangement on their own instruments and it is highly recommended since it gives easy access to all tones possible. See SCHECTER information sheet on the F420 Assembly.

1. Remove strings.
2. Remove screws attaching the pickguard and control plate and lift it up and turn it over.
3. Disconnect the old pickup.
   A. Unsolder lead (white or yellow) from switch.
   B. Unsolder ground from back of pot.
   C. Unscrew 3 pickup mounting screws and remove pickup.
4. Install F520T using rubber spacers instead of coil springs.
5. Install an Omni Pot or DPDT switch.
6. Solder wire from pickup to tap selector and then solder ground wire to ground point on back of pot (or to metal grounding plate if one is used).

7. Solder lead wire from tap selector to pickup selector switch.
8. Replace pickguard and strings.
9. Enjoy your new SCHECTER F520T Pickup.

Omni/DPDT Switches

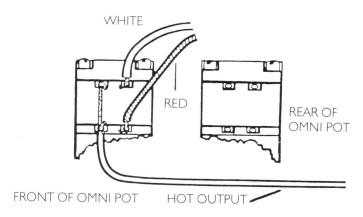

WHITE

RED

REAR OF OMNI POT

FRONT OF OMNI POT   HOT OUTPUT

SCHECTER SUGGESTS USING AN OMNI POT AS A TAP SELECTOR ON A TELECASTER* STYLE GUITAR. SOME PERSONS, THOUGH, PREFER TO DRILL A HOLE FOR A DPDT SWITCH BETWEEN THE VOLUME AND TONE POTS IF ONLY ONE TAPPED PICKUP IS USED. USE THE DRAWING OF THE TELE CONTROL PLATE AS A GUIDE TO HOOKING UP THE LEADS FROM YOUR SWITCH.

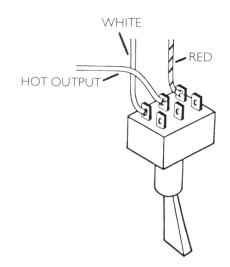

WHITE

RED

HOT OUTPUT

ONE DPDT SWITCH AS TAP SELECTOR

Glossary

A

A.C. – An alternating current with a steadily changing polarity.

ACOUSTIC PICKUP – A pickup designed for use on acoustic instruments such as a fiddle, mandolin, banjo, or Spanish guitar. It creates a more natural sound.

ACTIVE CONTROLS – Volume and tone controls which incorporate amplifier elements so the output can be boosted.

AGING PICKUPS – Restructuring the magnetic field of a new pickup so that it resembles the magnetic field of an old pickup. This process can create an old or vintage sound.

AIR COIL – A coil of wire with a hollow space in the center. Normal coils in pickups have an iron or magnetic load in the center, air coils do not.

ALCOHOL SPRAY – A term given to several solvent sprays which are used in pickup winding. The solvent is sprayed on the coil as it is wound. This softens the insulation and causes it to fuse together. When it dries, it leaves a very solid coil free from microphonics.

ALNICO – A type of magnet material which stands for ALuminum, NIckel, and CObalt.

ALTERNATING CURRENT – Electrical current which reverses its polarity during every cycle. Household current in the U.S.A. is 60 cycle a.c. (alternating current) which means that the positive and negative poles change place sixty times a second.

AMP (AMPLIFIER) – An electric circuit which causes a boost in the signal it receives. For example, if a five watt signal is fed into an electronic device and the output is twenty watts, this electronic device can then be termed an amplifier.

ANTENNA – A long wire which is used to detect electromagnetic waves passing through the air.

ANTI-HUM – A humbucking pickup or hum cancelling shielding. Refer to those headings for definition.

ANTI-PHASE – British term for out-of-phase. Refer to out-of-phase for definition.

AUDIO JACK – A female output that receives a male plug. The standard guitar size jack accepts a one-quarter inch diameter shaft.

B

BACKGROUND NOISE – Unwanted hissing or humming sound that accompanies a signal.

BALANCED OUTPUTS – Outputs of equal strength.

BANDPASS – A filter that boosts or decreases a selected bandwidth.

BANDWIDTH – A selected width of a wide range of frequencies. For example, if you have a wide frequency range of 10 Hz to 10,000Hz and you select the portion of 400Hz to 600Hz, you then have a bandwidth of 200Hz.

BAR MAGNET – A magnet of a rectangular shape as opposed to a magnet of cylindrical shape.

BASE PLATE – A plate under a pickup that is sometimes made of magnetically conductive metal. This plate can add output to a pickup by reshaping the lines of magnetic flux, but it can also create an increase in hum.

BELDON – A name brand of one of the most commonly used wires.

BLACK BOX – A symbolic term used to denote an unknown electronic device.

BOBBIN – The form around which the copper wire of a pickup is wound.

BRAIDED SHIELD – Fine wire which is woven into a tube-like structure. This woven tube surrounds and protects any wires that pass through the center of it. Braided shields can be obtained by themselves (empty) or with wires inside.

BRIDGE MOUNTED PICKUP – A pickup which is mounted in a bridge and it is generally in or under the bridge saddle. This mounting can provide great sensitivity to the strings.

C

CABLING LOSSES – When an electrical signal has to travel a long distance through a cable, the strength of the signal is reduced. Cabling losses are a result of resistance and capacitance losses. High impedance signals can not be sent on cables exceeding twenty feet in length without experiencing serious cable losses.

CANCELLING HUM – A means used to eliminate interference noises that are not part of a signal. The most common method of cancelling hum is to use two pickup coils that are linked out-of-phase. Refer to shielding and ground.

CANNON JACK – A low impedance jack that is comprised of a multitude of connection pins.

CARBON PATH – The most common material used for the resistance path inside a pot. It is formed out

GLOSSARY

of compressed carbon.

CAPACITANCE EFFECT – A trapping of high frequencies which occurs when there is close proximity of two or more current carrying wires.

CAPACITANCE LOSS – The failure of the high frequencies to reach their destination due to capacitance effect.

CAPACITOR – A device which can store an electrical charge.

CAST MAGNET – A magnet that is made from molten metal.

CERAMIC MAGNET – A magnet made from a powdered mixture of fine metal particles suspended in a clay base. This mixture is solidified by baking until it fuses together.

CHOKE – A coil generally with an iron load, that is used to regulate frequency response.

COIL – A winding of many turnings of fine wire.

COIL LOAD – When referring to pickups, a coil load is analogous to a coil core. See Core.

CONDUCTOR – Any material that carries an electrical flow.

CONTACT PICKUP – A pickup that directly senses the vibration from an instrument body.

CORE – The material that is often placed in the center of a pickup's coil. The most common cores are composed of soft iron or magnets. Cores cause a significant increase in a coil's output, but a massive core can reduce clarity of tones.

COVER – The metal cover that is often fitted over a pickup. This cover aids shielding, but it can also reduce output; therefore, it should be thin and contain no material that could disrupt a pickup's sensitivity.

CURRENT – An electrical flow.

D

D.C. – A steady current without a change of polarity, a direct current.

DE-SOLDER – To remove excess solder when forming connections or removing solder when disassembling connections.

DIRECT CURRENT RESISTANCE (d.c. resistance) – The resistance to direct current. A d.c. resistance can be thought of as a gate on a river which can be closed (high resistance) or opened (no resistance).

DIRTY SOUND – Sound which is not clear; it is produced by high induction pickups which in turn distort sound. Some people prefer this distortion, it's a matter of taste.

DISTORTION – The result of a pickup sending excess voltage into an amplifier. See Dirty Sound.

DISTORTION PICKUP – A pickup that has such a high output level that it causes an amplifier to distort. A distortion pickup does not produce a distorted output.

DOG EAR – The name given to a specific Gibson model of single coil pickups. They have triangular mounting brackets on either side of the coil assembly.

DOUBLE COIL – A pickup composed of two coils.

DOUBLE POTTING – A term used to designate a pickup that has its coils solidified by saturation, and has its internal assembly encapsulated in resin.

DOUBLE SOUND – A pickup that can produce two distinctive sounds. This can be the result of a tapped winding on a single coil pickup or a series-parallel switch on a humbucker.

DUAL COIL – A two coil pickup, usually a humbucker.

DUAL SOUND – A DiMarzio trademarked name for a series/parallel linked humbucker.

DUMMY POLE PIECES – To give the illusion of functional pole pieces. Inexpensive pickups have painted spots or plastic projection which serve no useful purpose.

E

EDDY CURRENTS – Secondary magnetic currents that move against the main current of magnetic flow. This reduces magnetic efficiency.

ENCAPSULATION – Encasing a pickup within a solid material such as epoxy resin. Encapsulation helps counteract microphonics and other pickup problems.

F

FARADAY, MICHAEL – He invented the dynamo and he is associated with the law of induced electromotive force.

FEEDBACK – A device amplifying its own signal. The most common feedback is a screeching sound which occurs when a microphone picks up its output from a speaker and recycles it. Pickups can feedback in a similar way.

FILTER – A circuit which can boost or cut a particular portion of a signal, usually bass or trebles.

FLUX PATH – The path of magnetic lines of force. If the flux path intersects the vibrating strings, a pickup will be more sensitive to string motion.

FREQUENCY RESPONSE – The volume level of all the frequencies (notes) produced by an electronic device. A flat frequency response has notes of all the same volume.

G

GAIN – The amount of boost provided by an amplifier circuit.

GAUGE – A measurement of magnetic force which can be measured with a gauss meter.

GRAIN ORIENTATION – The direction of metallic crystals making up a metal, within that metal.

GROUND – An electrical interconnection. Generally grounds are connected to the negative terminal of a power source.

H

HERTZ (Hz) – Unit of measuring frequency. One hertz equals one cycle per second.

HIGH PASS FILTER – An active control that regulates only high frequencies.

HIGH STRENGTH MAGNETS – Magnets with a higher than normal attraction strength.

HOT RODDING – Modifying manufactured pickups and their circuits so as to increase power output or create new tones.

HUM – Unwanted low frequency noise.

HUMBUCKING PICKUP – A pickup designed to cancel unwanted signals.

I

IC (integrated circuit) – A solid state circuit that is very versatile and composed of transistors, capacitors, diodes, resistors, etc.

IMPEDANCE – The electrical resistance to the flow of an alternating current.

INDUCE – The creating of a positive or negative current in an inductor (coil). A current is induced in a pickup's coil when a steel string is vibrating in the pickup's magnetic field.

INFINITE OHMS – A complete blockage of current flow; in practical usage this means there is no electrical connection.

INSULATION – Material that is used to separate

components in an electric circuit so as to prevent shorting.

INTERFERENCE – An unwanted signal that intrudes into a circuit.

IRON CORE – A load made of iron. See Core.

L

LACQUERED WIRE – Magnet wire with a lacquered insulation. Synthetic plastic coatings are a substitute for lacquered coatings.

LAMINATED CORE – A core that is made from several pieces of grain orientated magnetically conductive metal. A laminated core reduces eddy currents and this reduction improves efficiency and helps create a cleaner defined sound.

LAYERING – The stacking of one layer of coil windings over another layer.

LC NETWORKS – An electronic construction that uses an inductor (L) and a capacitor (C) to create a bandpass device. LC networks are passive not active.

LINES OF FLUX – The invisible force of a magnet. These lines of force are made visible by sprinkling iron filings in the flux path.

LOAD – See Core.

LOW IMPEDANCE – The circuitry used by most solid state electronics.

LOW PASS FILTER – An active control that boosts or decreases the low frequencies.

LUG – A projection for connecting conductors to a pot, jack or similar device. Lugs that resemble hoops are used for attaching wires, whereas lugs that resemble flat pins are used on printed circuit boards.

M

MAGNET – An object having the property of attracting iron or similar metals.

MAGNETIC CONDUCTOR – A material that becomes temporarily magnetic when it is placed in the field of a magnet. Iron is the most common magnetic conductor.

M (MEG) – The abbreviation of megohm. One million ohms.

MID-IMPEDANCE – A term used to describe circuits and components that are between high and low impedance.

GLOSSARY

MIL. SPEC. – Abbreviation for military specifications which require very high quality electronic components.

MULTI-AXIAL – A shielded wire which has several internal leads.

MONO-OUTPUT – One channel or circuit.

MONOPHONIC – Transmitting and reproducing sound via a single channel.

N

NEGATIVE – One of the two electrical poles. Electrical current flows between negative and positive poles. Negative terminals are normally used as an electrical ground connection.

NORTH POLE – One of the two magnetic poles. The other is south.

O

OHM – The measuring unit of electrical resistance.

OHMMETER – A machine with a meter for measuring ohms.

OLD SOUND – The sound of older prized pickups.

OUT-OF-PHASE – The linking of two signals so they are working in opposite directions. That is, when one is positive the other is negative and vice-versa.

OUTPUT IMPEDANCE – Impedance at the output terminals of a guitar as sensed by the device it feeds into.

OUTPUT JACK – The place on an instrument where a cord/cable connects so as to link the instrument and an amplifier.

P

P.A.F. – Patent-Applied-For abbreviation. It is also the earliest Gibson humbucking pickup model.

PARALLEL – An electric circuit that has all the positive points joined together and all the negative points joined together. See Series.

PHASE – The relationship of positive and negative wave forms. See Out of Phase.

PICKUP – A device that picks up the sound of a stringed instrument and then turns it into an electrical signal.

PIEZO – Electric current produced by applying stress to certain crystals.

POLARITY – The relationship of positive and negative electric currents or magnetic poles, to each other.

POLE PIECES – Objects that can control the magnetic flux of a magnet's pole. It is also used for controlling or focusing flux of a magnet's pole.

POSITIVE – One of the two electric poles. Opposite of negative.

POT – Abbreviation for potentiometer. A device that can produce a variable degree of electrical resistance. It can be used as a gate to control the flow of current.

PREAMPLIFIER – Used before a large power amp to help boost the signal.

Q

Q – The efficiency of a coil.

R

RARE EARTH MAGNETS – Magnets made from rare earth elements such as samarium.

RESISTANCE – An obstruction of the free flow of electric current.

RESONANCE – The tendency of a mechanical or electrical device to oscillate at a particular frequency.

ROTARY SWITCH – A switch that turns in a circular motion and is used to provide very complex switching networks.

S

SAWTOOTH WAVE – A sawtooth shaped wave that builds steadily to a peak and then drops sharply, or vice-versa.

SCATTERWOUND – A coil that is wound with a crisscross pattern. This winding produces many air gaps and reduces the capacitance effect of the windings. The opposite of scatter winding is layering.

SERIES – Electrical linking of positive and negative poles. Refer to the photos of humbucking pickups for series linkage.

SHIELDED WIRE – A wire with a conductive shield surrounding one or more insulated inner leads.

SHIELDING – A conductive surface that is grounded. This helps eliminate interference noise and hum.

SIGNAL GENERATOR – A machine used to create

selected frequencies. These frequencies are then used to test the frequency response of pickups and other devices.

SIGNAL-TO-NOISE RATIO – Ratio of desired signal voltage to unwanted noise and hum voltage. A high s/n ratio is very desirable. It is expressed in decibels.

SINGLE COIL – A non humbucking pickup.

SLUGS – A term given to individual cylindrical metal pieces in a pickup.

SOAP BAR – Same as Dog Ear.

SOLDER – A soft tin and lead material that melts at low temperature. It is used to make electrical connections.

SOLID STATE – Electronic devices that are composed of solid materials as opposed to vacuum tubes which are hollow.

SOUTH POLE – The second magnetic orientation. See North pole.

SPLIT PICKUP – A dual coil pickup that has a splitter switch to ground one coil and therefore produces a single coil sound.

SYNCHRON-WOUND – The process of winding two coils at exactly the same time, this helps create balanced coils.

T

TAPER – The rate of resistance change of a pot.

TAPPED COIL – A coil which when wound part way, has a tapping wire attached and then is wound to completion. A tapped pickup has two hot leads of different d.c. resistances and one ground lead.

TENSION – The tautness of wire wrapped on a bobbin.

TONE CONTROL – Control circuits used to vary the proportion of bass and treble.

TONE FILTER – An electronic network that is used to control the tone of a signal. It can be passive or active.

TRANSDUCER – A device that converts one form of energy into another form of energy, e.g., string vibration (kinetic energy) into electrical energy (a pickup's output).

TUBE AMP – An amplifier that uses vacuum tubes.

TURN – The amount of wire it takes to wrap wire once around a pickup bobbin.

V

VARITONE – A Gibson invention which consists of several capacitors and a choke. Basically, it functions as a replacement for the single tone control capacitor.

VIBRATION SENSOR – A transducer that is used to detect vibrations and convert them into an electric ouput.

VINTAGE SOUND – See Old Sound

VOLUME CONTROL – A device to control the output level. In most systems this is done with a pot.

VOM – Abbreviation for **V**olt, **O**hm, **M**eter. Used for measuring volts, ohms, and amperes.

W

WAX SATURATION – Used to permeate air gaps in a pickup.

WINDING MACHINE – A machine that winds magnet wire around coil bobbins.

WIRE FOR COILS – Copper magnet wire is used for making pickup coils.

X Y Z

X – An algebraic term in a formula that stands for any unspecified figure.

Y – An algebraic term which can be used like X if an X is already used in a formula.

Z – The symbol representing impedance.

ZERO OHMS – No resistance to the flow of current.

Index

INDEX

INDEX

Footnotes

1. The P.A.F. patent was filed on June 22, 1955, the patent was granted on July 28, 1959, and the assigned patent number was 2,896,491. The patent number on later non-P.A.F. pickups (2,737,842), is for the tailpiece bridge assembly. This apparently was done to hinder other companies from checking the patent papers. P.A.F.s were first made in 1956, but Gibson didn't have them in a catalog until 1957.

2. The alnico formula (patent #2,295,082) was devised by G.B. Jonas in 1939. He added cobalt to the pre-existing magnet formula ALNI. The power of alnico formula magnets allowed guitar pickups to be made smaller and therefore, more practical.

3. To create more output or higher inductance and where space is a factor, 43 gauge wire is often used.

4. A hot (temperature) pickup will have less output than a cold one due to the fact that resistance increases with temperature.

5. The Fender Starcaster has humbuckers with three adjustable pole pieces per coil.

6. Four slotted plain brass screws hold the coils to the base of all P.A.F.s. Later humbuckers use four nickel plated Phillips head screws.

7. P.A.F. pickups have two black leads coming from each bobbin, and these bobbins are .015 of an inch taller than those used on Gibson Originals. On the top and bottom of each bobbin there is a square hole with a circle around it. The bottom hole is used as an exit for the lead connecting to the beginning of the coil. Until 1963, both leads of each coil were black, after that the lead connecting to the inside wire of each coil was changed to white. All P.A.F.s have dark olive or faded black electrical tape around the coils. This color tape was standard for the '40's and '50's. The P.A.F. square holed bobbin was used until 1967 when it was replaced by a new bobbin that was slightly shorter, had round instead of square holes, and had a T molded into the top. The magnets of P.A.F.s are .125 x .500 x 2.50 of an inch, those in Original humbuckers are .125 x .500 x 2.325.

8. Most electric guitars and basses have an additional ground connection. This consists of a wire, usually bare, that goes from a soldered ground connection in the control compartment to a connection underneath or onto the bridge. Usually the connection to the bridge is simply having the bridge clam clamped on top of the end of the wire. This is commonly referred to as a string ground. When a player touches an instrument with this type of ground, hum will be reduced. Since single coil pickups are not humbucking, guitars with these pickups need the string ground to have quiet operation.

9. The IN and the OUT wires could be reversed. This change would not affect which direction is ON and which is OFF.

10. Pickup covers that are open on top can allow a pickup to sense strings easier while still providing some shielding. The importance of open top and slotted top covers is questioned by some guitar experts because it is believed that hum primarily enters a pickup through the top and bottom of a coil.

11. Another possible shielding procedure involves conductive paint shielding. See that heading in the index.

12. A loose cover can produce feedback if it creates vibrating sound chambers.

13. Another type of feedback is acoustic feedback of hollow body guitars. This feedback is the result of the guitar body vibrating and causing the strings to vibrate over a pickup. This problem is often counteracted by filling a guitar with sponge-like material.

14. The first pickup hot rodded by many people was the Gibson large humbucker because switching the magnet in this pickup is very easy. Distortion/high output pickups were inspired by these hot rodded Gibson humbuckers.

15. The polarity of a P.A.F. type humbucker can be reversed by turning the magnet around.

Photo Credits

Audio Technica Fig. 5

Barcus Berry Fig. 9
10
11
12
13
18
19
20
186

Bartolini Fig. 45
Beldon Fig. 178
B.C. Rich Fig. 199

Carlsen/Brosnac Fig. 3
Cook Fig. 51
Centralab Fig. 222

DiMarzio Fig. 14
52
54
56
57
181
159
160
240

Duncan Fig. 58

Fender Fig. 61
64
67
68

Frap Fig. 15
Fre-Ax Fig. 236

Gibson Fig. 73
79
81
82
83

G.R.D. Fig. 84
235

Judge Fig. 161

Lawrence Fig. 182

Micro Switch Fig. 158

Nady Fig. 170

Ovation Fig. 16
17
234

Power Pots Fig. 165
237
238

Rowe Fig. 1

Schecter Fig. 100
101
108
109
110
114
115
116
117
118
121
150
151
152
154
174
175
191
206
208
217
221
241
242
243

Shergold Fig. 102
Stars Fig. 239
String Vision Fig. 103

Velvet Hammer Fig. 104

The Author

Photo by Alan Hunter of Sandpoint, Idaho.

The Author with a few of the guitars he has built; from left to right: (1) A 24 fret solid body with a stereo humbucker made with four Duncan coils, a Lawrence L500LTS, Bartolini active controls (with stereo volume, treble, midrange, and bass), and two six-position pickup selectors; (2) A 24 fret acoustic electric hollow body with Schecter Z+ pickup and Omni Pots, and a Barcus Berry Hot Dot; (3) A 21 fret solid body with a custom DiMarzio PAF, and a tapped humbucker; (4) A 24 fret stereo 12 string acoustic electric with a Barcus Berry Hot Dot, a super thin humbucker, and a Schecter Omni Pot; (5) An acoustic guitar with a Bartolini mini Beast II.